In Glass

a history of the
Military Provost Staff Corps
by

Robert Boyes

Military Provost Staff Corps Association
Berechurch Hall Camp
Colchester, Essex.

Military Provost Staff Corps Association
Berechurch Hall Camp
Colchester Essex.

Copyright © 1988 Robert Boyes

ISBN 0 9513467 0 9

Printed and bound in Great Britain by
Anchor Brendon Ltd, Tiptree, Essex

Contents

Foreword v
Introduction vii

Part 1 – Before the Corps 1
Chapter 1 – Hang, Curse and Flog 3
Chapter 2 – Clenshaw and Some Colleagues 9
Chapter 3 – The Prisoners 19
Chapter 4 – The Tide Turns: Monkswell Reports 26

Part 2 – The Corps Is Formed. 1901–1919 37
Chapter 5 – Father Of The Corps 39
Chapter 6 – The Corps Is Formed 44
Chapter 7 – The Governor's Story 51
Chapter 8 – The First World War 54
Chapter 9 – Military Prisons in the Field – Rooke's Funnies 64

Part 3 – Between the Wars 69
Chapter 10 – Between the Wars 71
Chapter 11 – Between the Wars: Personal Views 79
Chapter 12 – Mission to Mespot 86

Part 4 – The Second World War 91
Chapter 13 – Wally Watson Remembers. 2 93
Chapter 14 – The Dempsey Report 99
Chapter 15 – From the Outside: Mill Town Temporaries 105
Chapter 16 – The Other Temporaries 117
Chapter 17 – Murderers of Poor Sammy Clayton 123
Chapter 18 – With the First Army in Africa 130
Chapter 19 – Ginger Gordon 135
Chapter 20 – Across the Straits and up the Leg 141

Part 5 – Post War Blues	147
Chapter 21 – Woodbines and Players	149
Chapter 22 – Austria – The Lienz Mutiny	153
Chapter 23 – Number Three and Before	157
Chapter 24 – Trouble at Northallerton	164
Chapter 25 – The Glasshouse Goes	169
Chapter 26 – The Mallet	173
Part 6 – The Big Wide World	183
Chapter 27 – Egypt and Beyond	185
Chapter 28 – In the Canal Zone	195
Chapter 29 – Cyprus	206
Chapter 30 – Corradino and Windmill Hill	209
Chapter 31 – Kure	215
Chapter 32 – Stonecutters	219
Chapter 33 – Ipoh, Kinrara, Tanglin	226
Chapter 34 – Last of the Thirties	233
Chapter 35 – Odd Job in Aden	237
Chapter 36 – Aden – Another Odd Job	245
Part 7 – Colchester	251
Chapter 37 – As it Was	253
Chapter 38 – Camp 186	260
Chapter 39 – The Goldfish Bowl and Others Matters	266
Chapter 40 – Horror Stories	275
Chapter 41 – The Pyjama Game	280
Chapter 42 – Not a Horror Story	283
Chapter 43 – The Customer, Some curiosities of the Period	289
Chapter 44 – Fetch Astiz!	291
Chapter 45 – Minute Memories	297
Chapter 46 – The Sixties and After	302
Chapter 47 – The Very Last Word	314

iv

Foreword

by Lt General Sir Norman Arthur KCB
Colonel Commandant, Military Provost Staff Corps

The MPSC have guarded and run British military detention centres since 1901. Their "clients" have often been vicious men, thieves or looters. More often, however, they were only men who had stepped outside the close bounds of military discipline in ways which, though unacceptable in any army, would usually not merit imprisonment under civil law. Often they were absentees and deserters, men who have refused to obey orders, reneged on their duty, offered serious insubordination to a superior, or committed some other military offence. It is for this reason that, even in peace-time, military offenders are rarely sent to join criminals in a civil prison. In a detention or, as it is known today, a corrective training centre, they are both corrected and trained, rather than imprisoned. The correction is firm, the training hard, but the objective nevertheless is to return a better man to the ranks of his regiment, or if further service is not possible, a more balanced and reasonable character to civilian life. These aims are usually achieved successfully and proof of this lies in the numbers who go on to successful Army careers or, as civilians, never again cross the path of the law.

This story is mainly of the small Corps and of the officers and men, who make the system work, but it cannot be told without frequent mention of the men in their charge.

The story, till now has been unsung. It is not a glamorous tale but an earthy one, a tale of times, not all of them so long ago, when men behaved more roughly towards one another, but often in understood, indeed entirely expected, manner. Sometimes brutality shows in the tale, sometimes compassion. It is the story of a hard regime for hard men but humour runs consistently through it, just as it usually does where the words and doings of British soldiers are recounted.

Soldiers reflect the attitudes of the nation they defend, even though, being somewhat conservative, they may not reflect changes in them as rapidly as does society as a whole. The military administering of detainees has therefore developed to suit our times and provides now a system which is markedly enlightened and well ordered. Parliament watches over it, through an Independent Board of Visitors. Today's Centre, at Colchester, comprises modern almost enviable, but nevertheless secure, accommodation.

The duties of the Military Provost Staff Corps don't end at the camp boundaries however. The Corps today is trained and ready to advise on setting up prisoner-of-war camps in Europe, or wherever necessary, in the event of war and, through its command elements, to help cope with local Home Defence tasks. Trained Soldiers, all with a wealth of experience between them, its officers and men are blessed with the humour, down-to-earth good sense and robust capability of their forebears.

Introduction
Danny, Paddy Nolan and Others

Danny and I made lance corporal on the same day. It was the time of the Berlin Airlift and we were both employed in a unit supplying RAF Wunstorf for onward flight to the beleagured city. The unit did the job and did it well but the military state of Danny, myself and the forty odd others would have driven an infantry RSM into apoplexy.

Danny was from the coalfields of Fife, but he wasn't the sinewy, small man so often seen on the coalfields. He was big boned and, at nineteen, was already beginning to spread. He liked his food and – possibly too much – he liked the local beer, which we fetched by the barrel weekly from the local brewery. This he chased with Steinhäger, available – fatally – at two shillings and sixpence BAFVS per bottle. After a night of this mix he would weave over to his bed singing. It was not only that he liked singing but the near-English tones of "Mother McCrae" assured the Sten gun-carrying Yugoslav guards that this was no German prowler, but a British soldier about his lawful occasions and that the safety catch could be returned to a – comparatively – safer position.

It was probably the Steinhäger that did for Danny. He spoke no German but was sure that the German in a local dance was ex SS and wanted to go outside with him. The German's jaw was quite badly damaged and Danny was court martialled.

Three months later, I went with the Tilly along the scarred and almost deserted Autobahn to Bielefeld. The German who was driving knew the way to Number Three and we parked near the main gate – near enough, at any rate, to see Danny when he came out but far enough away to stay out of trouble. We could see slit-eyed windows in the upper stories over the wall and there were ominous yells of command, quite unlike the sounds we heard back in the unit.

The gate finally opened and a tall soldier came out, field service marching order scrubbed white, brasses gleaming, toecaps flashing like black mirrors. He had his kit bag over one shoulder and his rifle over the other. A small man in a peaked cap had come out with him and he said something quietly to Danny, who looked around, then marched . . . marched over to the Tilly. I got out, first to check that it really was Danny then to give him a hand with his kit. The grin on his big red face was indeed Danny's, but the grin went when he looked me over in an uncomfortable drill sergeant-like fashion.

"Man, Bob", he said "Ye're a bag of shit".

This upset me. I was wearing the battle dress I had had specially tailored by the little Latvian tailor, who could work miracles for a few fags. The lapels had been tastefully narrowed and covered, the back was box-pleated and the trouser cuffs flared. Now here was Danny, my mate, telling me that I looked like bagged manure.

I climbed into the back of the Tilly. Danny had already put his kitbag in there and was taking off his webbing. He looked with disgust at the cargospace and made jocklike noises, then draped the pristine straps, and pouches, like an old maid with an antimacassar, over the bag.

Jock, in fact, was a changed man. On the run down to the Autobahn, we passed two of the men in peaked caps, smart as paint and, I am convinced, striking sparks from the pavement with their metal heel plates. Danny growled "Bastards" but not loud enough for it to be heard outside the Tilly, then he settled into his seat and said nothing.

It was when we were back in the unit that the real change showed. I had expected him to allow his webbing to sink back into the greasy, dusty state we all favoured, or at least to pass it over to the German cleaner for the occasional going over, but no, Danny bought a special tin of number 103 blanco, a shade not favoured by us at it showed dirt all too clearly. With it, he lavished care on his straps, pouches, valise and haversack. He was easily the smartest man in the unit, had soon been given his tape and within a few months was a full corporal. This led to some muttering amongst the regulars, but even they admitted that Danny deserved it. Soon, he signed on and I met him some years later as a warrant officer, sweating on a quartermaster's commission.

I myself became a regular and a Schoolie, marginally smarter in dress, but still singularly unsmart in the ways of the Army. In my first sergeants' mess, when the talk around the bar had exhausted memories of Alamein and Caen, a trio attempted to outdo each other with horror stories of their days in the Glasshouse and I found to my surprise that almost a quarter of the mess membership had spent a spell in one or the other of the detention barracks then scattered throughout the world. Paddy Nolan, one of the last of that once common type, the permanent sergeant: a man with no ambition to go further but with an encyclopedic knowledge of the Service, could make the claim of a pre-war spell in the Aldershot Glasshouse "De daddy av dem all".

Why am I writing all this? In this book I want to look at the Dannies and Paddies of history. I want to look at the systems and the men, who made Danny and Paddy into what they were in their very different ways: military successes. Paddy insisted that the Glasshouse was the best cadre course a soldier could have and he may well have been right.

Many people will certainly disagree, particularly those National Servicemen, who found ordinary military service a chain around the ankle, without the added ball of detention. I had letters from many such as I prepared this book – one was written by an eminent poet; another by a successful writer, with whom I spent a pleasant lunch break. No, the system had certainly not worked for them.

I wonder if it worked for Edgar Wallace? He was an inmate of Aldershot Military Prison for some months as a young medic. A story I have not been able to check is that the prison chaplain arranged for him to have writing materials in his cell. Did this start something?

I am convinced that the system works now for the majority of those young soldiers who have, like Danny, done something stupid, usually in the same befuddled state which caused Danny's downfall. The letters and reports from commanding officers prove this and even more convincing are the letters regularly received from old – usually satisfied – customers. It doesn't work every time, but it works for most.

In this book, I hope to show how the system has developed from the repressive regimes of Victorian times, to the modern idea of retraining and rehabilitation. I am not in the business of whitewashing and there are episodes that are distasteful and regrettable. These will not be ignored and should not be ignored, but I contend that these were isolated incidents and the resultant repercussions when published in the Press helped to push reform further and faster.

If you bought this book to read a treatise on penology I am afraid you are about to be disappointed. I am not a criminologist, sociologist or psychologist. I am not even a historian, though my interest in Army history spans thirty odd years. What I hope you will find in the book is a great deal about people in the special environment of a variety of penal institutions.

Much of my material came from serving or retired members of the Military Provost Staff Corps; some also from previous "customers" (one particularly useful piece of information came from a retired officer of the Corps, who could speak with authority on one outpost, as he had been a soldier under sentence there before the Second World War!)

These are not the only people who have made the book possible. Beyond the grave, I must thank Captain S. J. Griffin who started to write a history of the MPSC in 1934 and Major Wally Watson, who wrote down his recollections in the fifties. More recently and very much this side of the grave, Major Bill Humphries, Lieutenant Don Yates, Sergeant Major David Hood, Warrant Officer 2 (ORQMS) Alan Licence produced much excellent material. My own team was Staff Sergeant Vick Leppard, who did sterling work, aided by the ladies of the Manuals Section of the MOD Library, and Squadron Leader John Lawrence, my old friend and former colleague, who goes at any research like a terrier. I would also like to say a personal thankyou to John Harding of the Historical Branch, MOD, who was infinitely helpful, infinitely patient and to Paul Vickers of the Prince Consort's Library, who scoured the country for my requests and never let me down.

PART ONE

Before The Corps

1
Hang, Curse and Flog

"Farrier Simpson took the cat as ordered; at least I believe so – I did not see him but I felt an astounding sensation between the shoulders, which went to my toenails in one direction, my fingernails in another and stung me to the heart, as if a knife had gone through my body. The sergeant major called "One!"

The sergeant major in this case counted up to one hundred lashes, laid by the reluctant Farrier Simpson on the back of his friend, Alexander Somerville. Somerville was lucky: he had been ordered one hundred and fifty lashes but was cut down from the triangle at this point.

The lash ruled in the British Army until the 1850s but, by this date, it was rarely applied outside the military prison. Somerville's account was describing events in the 1830s, his regiment being the Scots Greys. I quote it, because it is the only account of a flogging known to me, which tells the story from the receiving end.

In Wellington's Peninsular army, twenty five strokes was the minimum award and the maximum, reserved for bad cases of desertion, robbery with violence, or striking an officer, was 1200 lashes, a sentence that would kill or permanently disable. This was the sentence awarded only nine times during the six years of the campaign. Alternative punishments were the Provost gallows or the firing squad.

Wellington's was a mobile army and there was no place in it for imprisonment, but imprisonment does begin to appear as a sentence towards the latter end of the campaign. On following this up, I found that this was not imprisonment in some fortress in Portugal or Spain, but transportation to New South Wales, there to serve in the guarding corps of the convict settlements. If the sentence was imprisonment with hard labour, then the transportation was as a convict, rather than a guard.

But the lash remained the main keeper of discipline in the

field and in barracks. In some barracks at home, the regiment would provide a rudimentary kind of cell system: the black hole and the dry hole. In the black hole the defaulter sat, without any kind of furniture, in a cell without windows and without any other source of light. In the dry hole the habitual drunk was left to dry out in his own vomit. Some hard men, who were proud of their ability to take fifty lashes without a sound, preferred to "go to the halberds" rather than the black hole: one suspects that they preferred their bit of theatre in front of the audience of the full regiment to the anonymity of the dark cell.

Civilian revulsion at the use of the lash was growing and there are also many accounts in which officers, who have witnessed a flogging, resolve that they will never resort to the lash, when they themselves achieve a command. Sir George Bell, who later commanded the 34th, wrote:

"I have seen men suffer 500 and even 700 lashes before being taken down, the blood running into their shoes and their backs flayed like raw, red chopped sausages. . . . I made up my mind that, if ever I had the chance of commanding a regiment, I would act on another principle. That time did come. I did command a gallant corps for eleven years, and I abolished the lash".

Surprisingly, at least two of the rank and file writers from the Peninsular War, are totally in favour of flogging. Private Wheeler speaks up for it, as does Quartermaster Sergeant Anton of the 42nd Highlanders. His remarks are, I think, worth quoting:

"Philanthropists, who decry the lash ought to consider in what manner the good men – the deserving, exemplary soldiers – are to be protected; if no coercive measures are to be restored to in purpose to prevent ruthless ruffians from insulting with impunity the temperate, the well-inclined, and the orderly-disposed, the good must be left to the mercy of the worthless. . . . In civil society, the mechanic, the labourer, yea even the pauper, can remove from his dwelling or place of abode if he finds himself annoyed by a troublesome neighbour; but the good soldier cannot remove without this despicable demon of discord accompanying him, and yet we are told that the lash is not to be used. The good soldier thanks you not for such philanthropy; the incorrigible laughs at your humanity, despises your clemency, and meditates only how he may gratify his naturally vicious propensities".

A retired member of the Corps, ex Staff Sergeant Dennis Carr, when putting in order the affairs of a dead relation, found a copy of The Times. It had obviously been kept for the main news item: the official despatch from the field of Waterloo, but the Parliamentry page was also not without interest. Members are debating the issue of corporal punishment in the two services, as a recent court martial has brought the subject into the public eye again: the commander of a famous cavalry regiment has been cashiered and the leading speaker states that the colonel had ordered 62 members of the regiment to be flogged within the previous year, a total number of 14,100 lashes. The speaker compares this to the more enlightened treatment of Continental armies, including our Russian allies. He asks if no alternative to flogging can be found. The debate ends inconclusively.

The Napoleonic Wars ended with Waterloo and, apart from the army of occupation and the garrisons overseas, the army came home. The normal British routine of disbandment and penny-pinching followed, but the fact remained that the Army was once again on the British peoples' doorstep at a time when, for once, the British were proud of the Army's achievements and when the nation was turning away from the brutishness of the Eighteenth Century. The lash was still there; branding (the tattooing with a pattern of needles and gunpowder of the letters BC on the chest of a bad character) was still in the Mutiny Act and stayed there until 1870, but the general mood was towards less brutality.

The trouble was that the Army still recruited indiscriminately. Men still only enlisted because they had no alternative "having got bastard children or for drink" in the words of Wellington, so the bad bargains still joined. Also, then as now, the young men who wanted to see more than the village street and the blunt end of a plough horse. These last would drink their pay, then do something silly. Though humanity was in the air, something had to be done with the military offender and the obvious solution was to commit him to the local gaol.

We are Twentieth Century people, conditioned to the idea that something like the Prison Service is a nationally organised thing, one of the organisations for which we pay taxes. This is an idea that would be foreign (and I use the word by choice) to the normal Briton of the beginning of the last century. Central government, they felt, was all right for the French and the Prussians, but for England, the Tudor ideas of local administration had proved themselves over the centuries, so were obviously the right thing. So local gaols were just that, locally administered by the justices, occasionally helped (or hampered!) by the parson and paid for by the rates.

Then as now, the English showed their reluctance to pay rates and they positively hated the "temporary" infliction of income tax, that had been introduced in the recently ended war. But gaols had to be kept, so rates had to be levied – the important thing was to ensure that the rate stayed as low as possible, so gaoling had to be done on the cheap. Purpose built gaols came expensive, so the obvious solution was to take over some existing building and spend a minimal amount on the conversion. Shepton Mallet was a good example of this procedure. In his book "Heritage of a Prison", Francis Disney tells the early story of "The Mallet", when a property called Cornhill House and an acre around it are purchased from a nearby parson to make a House of Correction to contain rogues, vagabonds, prostitutes and idle apprentices.

The warders and guardians were not a charge on the rates, because they received no pay. Sometimes they paid for the privilege of taking the job. They then had to use the resources at their disposal to make a living. Prisoners were lumped together in common rooms in the most basic conditions imaginable. The food when supplied was swill, but the prisoner with money could send out for what he wished and the turnkey took his cut. The prison population was hired out as field labour and the services of female prisoners were available if you could pay the turnkey. Prisoners were employed as clerks and relief warders.

A former inmate of such a gaol wrote "If you went in bright, you came out tarnished" and it was exactly this that worried many commanding officers. Some of the bad bargains probably felt quite at home in the local gaol and welcomed the rest from guards and sleeping out, but how about the ploughboy, probably from a family whose main nightmares had been the workhouse and prison?

Reformers were beginning to criticise the local gaol system and the Government found itself compelled to start taking a hand in the control of the local gaol. They appointed visitors and laid down that gaolers in future would be paid. The justices were required to visit the gaols quarterly and to report on their state. Many justices complained of overcrowding and, when possible, for example in the garrison towns, blamed the numbers of soldiers confined for the situation. They also complained that soldiers imprisoned were responsible for "unruly and riotous behaviour".

In 1836, a Committee of Investigation was appointed and recommended that separate places of confinement should be established for the soldiery, the stated reason being that "a soldier, though under punishment, should not lose sight of the profession against whose rules he has offended, nor should he be placed in contact with other men, whose notions of crime are not very strict and have none whatever of the nature of military offence".

The findings of the committee were noted, but no action was taken and the situation in the local gaols stayed as it had been. Then, in 1844, a Royal Commission was set up chaired by Lieutenant General Earl Cathcart to examine the possibility of establishing prisons in which only military offenders would be confined subject "to the discipline best suited to their military habits" and whether drill, breaking stones or other hard labour, might not be substituted for their confinement in civil gaols. The commission was also to report on diet, clothing and bedding for the prisoners.

The committee took its job very seriously and called for evidence and advice on all the military elite of the period, including the Duke of Wellington, who was opposed to the idea of imprisonment for soldiers. The final findings were "That assuming *in limine*, the concession to public opinion of the general disuse, though not total abolition, of corporal punishment . . . the Commission considered that they had no alternative but a choice between civil and military prisons and would not hesitate to prefer the latter." They further ruled that there would be two types of punishment provided: solitary confinement and imprisonment with hard labour. The Commission then had to outline a command structure and a system of inspection.

The time now came to put the findings of the Commission to work and to commence the task of building prisons and a prison service. In the world outside the Army, much had been happening and the central government, reluctantly, was finding itself becoming more and more involved with penal institutions. By 1844, there were two convict prisons and a juvenile prison at Parkhurst. Two inspectors had been appointed with Captain Joshua Jebb RE as the first Surveyor General and the first Chairman of the Directors of Convict Prisons. He was a natural choice for the first Inspector General of Military Prisons.

By 1850, there were military prisons at home in Chatham (a conversion of Fort Clarence), Southsea Castle at Portsmouth and a section of the huge Ordnance Stores at Weedon had been converted. Cells at Devonport were closed off and a hospital attached to the barracks at Greenlaw, near Edinburgh became the prison for the Army in Scotland. There were four prisons in Ireland, all converted from Provost cells (Dublin, Cork, Limerick, Athlone). Abroad, the distribution is an interesting comment on the overseas tasks of the Army: Gibraltar; Quebec; Halifax, Nova Scotia; Barbados; Bermuda; Mauritius; Vido for the Ionian Islands (!) and St. Elmo on Malta.

Jebb was particularly proud of the one prison, which was purpose built in these early times and I suspect that most of the planning was his own. This was the prison at Gosport and it will be often mentioned in later chapters. I have his description and his plans for it before me as I write. It consists of three stories, each of 24 single cells each cell measuring 11 feet by 7 feet. Outside, there are shot yards and stone breaking yards. There is a chapel, with an adjacent schoolroom and the heating for all the interior is from a central furnace. The pattern of life in Gosport and the other military prisons will be the matter of my next chapters. I think that you will find them more interesting than the dry bones I have had to rattle in this!

2
Clenshaw and some Colleagues

I have two documents which I have used for this chapter: the letter book of the Inspector of Military Prisons and an account, written on paper that has now yellowed, in ink that has long gone rusty, by Chief Warder Clenshaw. The letter book is a ponderous, leather bound volume, each entry meticulously written out in clerical copperplate. Each page has a file number and the subject title of that file. Many have simply a name, then what follows down the page is the history in summary of the named warder.

Clenshaw's account was written when he was eighty, obviously at the request of Captain Griffin, who first started to research the history of the Corps in 1934. It is in a bold hand, every word legible and it has a great deal to tell us of the military prison service before the formation of the Corps. I make no apology for quoting word for word.

"*After serving ten years with the colours, I was appointed Assistant Warder in the Military Prison, Taunton, Somerset and reported for duty on the 9th October 1883.*

The military prisons at that time were under the Home Office and all appointments were under Civil Service conditions.

The accommodation, as far as I can remember, was about 150. The other military prisons existing at that time were Brixton, Aldershot, Chester, Gosport, Lancaster and possibly another. There were two in Ireland: Dublin and Cork; two in Scotland at Stirling and Glencorse, I think the former taking the place of the latter. Abroad, there were ten, as far as I can recall.

At this time, all the prisons at home were under the charge of a Governor and the remainder, I believe, under a Chief Warder.

The staff at Taunton numbered twelve, including the Chief Warder, seven of whom were taken over from the civil side when the place became a military prison, but several of them had previously served in the Army.

All came on duty at 6am. Summer and Winter alike. Prisoners were unlocked, clothes taken in, water served out for washing,

9

slops collected, oakum tasks weighed out and fresh tasks weighed in. Closetting, cleaning and scouring of cells and corridors, everything had to be spick and span. Those employed outside their cells had to be under close supervision all the time. The oakum task was for four ounces an hour for all the working hours. If employed at anything else, fatigues etc. time of course was deducted from the task.

At 7.45 am breakfast was served and the officers returned at 8.40. I might add at this point you had to be there to the minute or be reported for being late, which led to a half sheet and a certain fine.

Exercise now commenced, half the men at a time in the prison yard, ¾ hour each batch; First stage men to shot drill in another part of the yard out of sight of the others. At 11am there was a chapel service about 10 minutes, after that labour until 12 when dinner was served.

At all times when the men were in their cells, warders had to watch them through the spy holes to see they were picking their oakum and not idling. Afternoon was a repetition of the morning, hour after hour being passed in their cells, though occasionally some would be taken from their cells to prepare dry earth for the closets. At 5.45, suppers were served and officers went off duty. At 7.45, the bell rang for bed. Then two officers went to each cell and the prisoners shook out each article of clothing, made all into a neat bundle, including boots and socks. The bundles were placed outside the cell door and collected, also the man's mattress if not entitled to it by stage. Every cell was then double-locked and masterkeyed and a bar of iron was put across the door.

Of the staff, the Warder Clerk and the Cook Baker (all bread was made in the prison), were the only ones excused from night duty. Four were on duty every night, two being on nightwatch and two sleeping in the prison, one at the gate, the other in the infirmary, so you may guess at the number of hours we spent in the prison.

Warders were reported for the most trivial things. Only one warder had a clear day on Sunday and two had to attend for church and exercise only, which was greatly appreciated, I can assure you.

At this time, oakum picking was the only labour. There were four stages of prisoner, the stage being shown by a coloured badge worn on the collar of the jacket. The first 28 days were passed in shot drill twice a day: one and a half hours in the morning and the same in the afternoon, with a stand at ease at intervals. The remainder of the day was for oakum picking.

About the year 85, a laundry was erected and the prison washing need no longer be sent out. In the following year, I think it was, flax dressing was started and carried on in a big shed until the prison closed in 89. It was disagreeable work. The big shed had formerly housed the treadmill.

An amnesty for Queen Victoria's Jubilee released many men and we never recovered the numbers.

Now the Governor of Taunton Military Prison had been Deputy Governor of Dartmoor and he was a heartless bullying tyrant. The system prevailing in those days was bad enough, but he made it worse by his treatment of staff and of prisoners. Punishments for the latter were both numerous and severe: two or three days bread and water and a loss of stage for the most trifling offence. He had at this time many rough customers to deal with, serving sentences from six months to two years. Some of them kicked up rough at the treatment they received and started to break up their cells, singing and shouting and otherwise violent. It usually ended with figure of eight handcuffs, Board of Visitors and 25 lashes with the cat, sometimes 14 days in the dark cells in addition. There was one man at this time, who was sentenced to leg irons for attempted escape, but I don't remember for how long.

I remember two men being flogged five separate times and several others two or three times. There is no doubt that the enforcement of the terrible Silent System affected the nerves of many.

I remember one noted character, a fairly well educated man called Spencer Lynes. You couldn't tame him. He was flogged five times in his two years. Often when he recognised the Governor's footstep, he would shout "Ah, Captain Bell, fast going to hell". Once, when he was being released from the triangle after twenty five strokes, he spat in the face of the Medical Officer, who was standing by and shouted "You flogged me on Number Two Diet, you grim looking bugger", then a stream of defiant and filthy words at the Governor and Visiting Officer, who had to be there when a flogging took place. As a last sally, he yelled "You might tame lions, but you won't tame Lynes".

We had another notorious man, a little fellow belonging to the Rifle Brigade. Once, in the dark cells, he heard workmen hammering on the roof of the boilerhouse nearby and shouted "I say, chummy, is that my coffin you're making? Much longer in here and I'm bloody sure I'll need it". On another occasion, he was being brought out to receive fifteen lashes and shouted "I faced the bayonets in Afghanistan, so I'm bloody sure I can face the cat". However, although he was frequently punished afterwards, he never went so far as to merit another flogging.

Taunton was closed in June 1889 and I was transferred to Aldershot. The only labour there was oakum picking, but there were great numbers of short sentences, so we always had many on shot drill. Men under 10 stones worked 12 or 14 pound shot; the rest worked 16 pounds.

About the year '92 bed making was introduced and was still carried on when I left in '99.

In March '95, the Chief Warder died and the Clerk Warder carried on until the appointment of Captain R A Henderson in '96.

About the year '98, drill was introduced and there was talk and rumours about a new system for military prisons. In the meantime, new forms of labour were taken on: cornsacks, haversacks, halters etc. Bootmaking was also tried, but proved a failure. A warder was sent to Wormwood Scrubs for a course in mat making, but I do not know if it was ever introduced.

In '99, on the eve of the South African War, I was offered Clerk Warder in Cairo with a view to promotion. I reached there in mid-October and found the system there similar to that at home. Colonel Garsia made an official visit in 1900 or 1901 and soon the system began to change. The men brought in their full kit and wore their own clothes, but it must have taken some time to bring the system into full working order, for no gymnasium had been built up to the time of my leaving in '02.

In that year, I was offered Chief Warder of Ceylon but could not go as my family was medically unfit. I asked for a similar chance at home, but there was no vacancy, so I returned home to Aldershot, where Major Henderson was still Governor.

It was about this time that Colonel Garsia died and Major Henderson became the Inspector. How long he reigned, I do not know – about six years, then he had to retire and I heard later that it was one of the new Corps he had been set on forming that was the cause of it.

I then went to Glasgow as Chief Warder under the new system in the Branch Prison. I remained in Glasgow about three years. In that time, Colonel Henderson visited and also Lord Roberts. Whilst I was there, I had a sergeant in the new Corps sent to me from Stirling. He was useless and had to be sent back to his unit.

In '05, I went to Gibraltar, where I found everything under the new system in full working order, under the Governor, Captain R Morris, a very nice man, who could understand the whole working of the present order of things. There was only myself and the Clerk Warder belonging to the old staff. The rest were all sergeants from the new Corps and sergeants from local units. Shortly afterwards, the Clerk Warder was sent home and an Orderly Room Sergeant sent in his place.

There is no doubt in my mind that the introduction of the new system caused a lot of slackness and led to a number of escapes, a thing almost unheard of in the old days".

That then, was the life of Chief Warder Clenshaw. I shall not comment on it but much of what he says will be fleshed out later in other chapters.

Clenshaw, of course, had his page in the letter book. There is something tantalising in the bare bones of the letter summaries. After reading the headings and seeing a life summed up as a series of letters between prisoners and "Head Office" one feels a longing to sit down at a table with, say, A. R. Prior from page 816 and say to him "Mr Prior, did you really tamper with the tell-tale clock? Why were you dismissed, when the GOC himself thought the case not proved?" It's too late, I'm afraid – Prior is long dead. In some ways, the pages of the letter book are the ghosts of these warders long dead.

What kind of people were they? Well, most of them were old soldiers, though some also had come from the county prison services, Alfred Davies, for example, had worked for the prison service of Radnor. When he retires in 1894, his pension from the military prison service is £26.8.4d, but he is also due £3.2.3d per year from Radnor County Council: he is still trying to get it in 1906!

As you will expect, there is a tight hierarchy in the service – you have already read how Clenshaw had to change prisons for promotion. Most of the letter book entries start with an appointment as Night Watchman, though some start immediately as Assistant Warder – there are two mentions of an entrance examination, so I think that we can assume that the starting point was fixed by this. On promotion to fully fledged Warder, there were some possible "side steps". Clenshaw, you will recall, made Warder Clerk, which would give him an extra shilling a day. There are many who try for this, but also many with repeated entries of "not suitable for Warder Clerk".

When education classes are introduced in 1896, the post of Warder Schoolmaster, also at one shilling a day, becomes much sought after and often goes to the Warder Clerk. To qualify, an examination was set by the Inspector of Army Schools. Alexander MacLeod attempts this and is told that he will be accepted when his arithmetic improves. The Schoolmaster was also the librarian, the library being stocked from a list approved by the Chaplain.

The Chaplain's Warder made only 3d per day, but had the added perk of being excused weekend duties. Other "sidesteps" were Hospital Warder and Warder Cook. In one case only is a warder designated Artisan Warder, when James Greenstead is transferred in that rank from Pentonville to Brixton.

Let me quote to you a few of the human stories from the letter book pages. Edwin Faulls is on page 254. Faulls has served as a soldier and his parchment certificate of discharge is returned to him with the news that he will be appointed Assistant Warder in Bermuda 1892. He takes up the post in 1893 and in 1894 has satisfactorily completed his probation. He is to be paid £61 per year. Faulls is doing well, then in 1895, Assistant Warder Lee accuses him of undue intimacy with Lee's wife. Both are put on ten days suspension without pay for "wrangling in the prison". The matter seems to settle, then, in 1897, the Chief Warder receives an anonymous letter criticising the behaviour of Faulls and Assistant Warder Gleeson. There is no further action on this, but it is worth noting that the Chief Warder saw fit to send this letter to the Inspector.

Faulls tries for Warder Clerk and is recommended, but London send out a man senior to him for the post. Faulls applies for a posting to Halifax, Nova Scotia. This is approved and he goes to Canada as a Warder Cook. By this time he is earning £78 per year, but this is soon reduced to £70 for spoiling food. The GOC Halifax considers that this is too severe a punishment and alters it to a fine. In 1903, the Chief Warder complains to London that Faulls is unfit to continue either as a cook or a disciplinarian. He is placed on three months probation, but comes through it well. In 1905, he requests permission to marry and is posted to Gosport, where his first move is to apply for the position of Warder Cook. Did he marry? Did he become Warder Cook (despite the adverse report that the Inspector's office send to Gosport on the subject)? We do not know, because this ends Faull's page in the letter book. We are instructed to turn to volume seven and no one knows where volume seven now is!

Some of the stories are complete. Many have the sum of the warder's pension as the last line (£15.6.1 per year for an Assistant Warder). Some are dismissed and get nothing. Some die.

William Coxhead is serving in Gibraltar, when his page of the letter book opens. He is under a cloud: he has been suspended for using unbecoming language to the Chief Warder. Mrs Coxhead, a Gibraltarian, uses insolent and threatening language and the GOC had ordered that she be removed from her quarter. We next find that Coxhead, as if he hasn't troubles enough, is on the old scale and is not entitled to boots! The strain is telling and the MO reports that unless Coxhead returns to a home station, his health will suffer. The case hangs, then almost a year later, Coxhead is posted to Aldershot, sailing on "The Crocodile".

Aldershot's climate is too much for Mrs Coxhead. Coxhead asks for a posting to a warmer climate or an indulgence passage to Malta for his wife. He also asks for promotion, but the Chief Warder reports that he is too old and too unfit. However, he finally manages a posting to Malta, sailing on the "Assaye" in 1901. By July of that year, the Governor of Malta Military Prison reports his death. There is no pension for Mrs Coxhead. Pensions died with the warder, so Mrs Coxhead asks for the months pay that Coxhead had deposited with the department at the beginning of his service. The bureaucracy wheels turn slowly, but she receives the money three months after Coxhead's death. She is one of the lucky ones: many of the widows received only £1 from the fine fund, a petty cash fund made up from the punishment monies paid by the warders for lateness and other derelictions. This was no Welfare State.

As is to be expected in such closed communities, there was a fair amount of back-biting. The thing that amazes me is how much of it reaches "head office". James Brown at Wynberg accuses the Chief Warder of stealing coal. William Sutherland, the Warder Cook at Stirling is reported to have condoned another warder stealing meat. A. Barrell has been drunk when on leave. Despite the fact that the Gosport police send a commendation to the Governor on Barrell's behalf – he had assisted them with a violent prisoner – Barrell is asked to resign.

We learn something of warder's dress from the letter book, but my assistant Vic Leppard found valuable material in the Manuals Section at the MOD Library. Clothing Regulations show the issue of clothing as follows:-

At Home stations

Warders of all Ranks

One greatcoat	Every three years
Three pair of cloth trousers)	Biennially
One frock coat) In materials	Annually
One forage cap and oilskin cover	Every two years

The cost of making up the frock coat and trousers will have to be defrayed by the warder.

Barbados, Bermuda and Mauritius

Chief Warders

One great coat	Every four years
One frock coat	Every three years
One pair cloth trousers	Every three years
One forage cap	Every two years
One white cap cover	Every two years
One shell jacket	Every two years
One jean frock	Annually
Three pair drab jean trousers	Annually

Warders and Assistant Warders

One great coat	Every four years
One frock coat	Every four years
One pair cloth trousers	Every three years
One forage cap	Every three years
One white cap cover	Every two years
Three drab jean suits	Annually

Gibraltar and Malta
Chief Warders

One great coat	Every four years
One frock coat	Every four years
One pair cloth trousers	Every two years
One shell jacket	Annually
One forage cap	Annually
One white cap cover	Every two years
Two pair jean trousers	Every two years
One jean frock	Annually

Warders and Assistant Warders

One great coat	Every four years
One frock coat	Every four years
One pair cloth trousers	Every two years
Two jean suits	Annually
One forage cap and one white cap cover	Every two years

North American Stations
Warders of all Ranks

One great coat	Every two years
One frock coat	Annually
Three pair cloth trousers	Every two years
One forage cap and cover	Every two years
One winter cap	Every three years
One pair winter gloves	Annually

At stations where the duties of Warders are performed by the military, soldiers so employed are to wear their military clothing.

Cooks and servants at Military Prisons at home stations will be furnished with the undermentioned clothing.

Cooks

One great coat	Every three years
Three pairs of trousers	Biennially
One blue jacket	Annually
One waistcoat with sleeves	Annually
One forage cap	Biennially

Servants

One great coat	Every three years
Three pairs of trousers	Biennially
One frock coat	Annually
One forage cap	Biennially

Clothing that has been in wear the prescribed period (except great coats) becomes the property of the Warder when the next issue is made.

These changed slightly as the years went by and in later lists we find a footnote that carpet slippers should be provided for warders on the night watch!

In the letter book, a storm blows up, when the head office orders that all warders overseas are to wear khaki drill. Ceylon objects, as the white issue uniform is considered more suitable, but I feel that Halifax Nova Scotia had a more justified complaint against KD: the prison reports from there often refer to escapes over the ice and the need to house in the wells against the extreme cold!

When the fresh air of Garsia's reforms is felt in the prisons, some – many – warders react as Clenshaw reacted, fearing an unfamiliar system and resenting the young upstarts arriving fresh from active service and rearing to go. Other warders – I suspect the younger and ambitious ones – took courses in drill. Some of the warder clerks appear in 1902 as ORQMS. Photographs in the MPSC Museum show groups where the heavy blue serge of the old service mixes with the khaki. For Clenshaw and other dinosaurs it can not have been a happy time.

3
The Prisoners

I find it remarkable that, apart from the problem prisoner and something about routine, Clenshaw has very little to say about the inmates of the various establishments where he served.

In the letter books and also in the prison reports, there is a wealth of detail regarding the prisoners and I would like to examine them in this chapter. I must draw a start line somewhere, so I shall start in 1894; not an arbitrary decision, the prisoners of 1894 were very much like the prisoners, who had been incarcerated in the military prisons from their introduction, but in 1894, changes were in the air.

Then as now, the young soldier was the most usual inmate, half of those committed having served less than two years. Some were not even regular soldiers, but militia men who had failed to attend for drills. Many had not completed training and others had been absent for so long that they had forgotten most of what they had learned with the regiment.

In 1894, 5603 offenders were committed to the seven home prisons or to the nine at stations overseas. In the meticulous fashion of the Victorians, statistics are minutely recorded, one table even breaking down the prison population by religion and country of origin. Thus, we find that only 542 Scots and 747 Irishmen were in the prisons in 1894. My surprise is not due to any preconceived idea of Irish/Scottish behaviour, but to the fact that so many Irishmen and Scots were serving in the Army in the period. An additional table shows that only 206 of the five thousand odd could not read and that only 215 could not write, though elsewhere in the reports, it is stressed that the criteria for judging literacy were not high.

The crimes that put them into prison, were desertion and absence, violence, insubordination and drunkness on duty in the large majority of cases, but fraudulent enlistment also comes quite high in the table. In his 1898 report, Garsia, about whom I shall have much to say later, gives an example of one prisoner, who made something of a profession of fradulent enlistment. The soldier first enlisted at fifteen into the Gordon Highlanders and was claimed by his parents as being under age. He then joined the KRRC (now 2RGJ) and deserted when on leave to join the 18th Hussars, transferring from them to the 8th Hussars, from whom he deserted. He joined a militia regiment, headquartered at Dalston and – yes – he deserted from them to enlist in the 3rd Hussars. The 3rd Hussars recognised him as a deserter and sent him back to the 8th. He decided not to stay with them and deserted for the Manchester Militia. His next move was to the 14th Hussars, where he was caught in possession of stolen property and imprisoned. After prison, he was discharged and enlisted into the 6th Inniskilling Dragoons. The Artillery's Garrison Battery in Dublin then took his fancy but he was recognised before attestation and sent back to the 3rd Hussars, where he was tried and received two years hard labour. His name was Smith and he used his own name every time he enlisted, claiming that in the 14th Hussars, for example, there had been 14 Smiths. Garsia goes on to say that something should now be done to control the whole business of fradulent enlistment. He is aware that public opinion is against branding, but suggests "the system of measurement and description that is effective in the detection of habitual criminals", the measurements to be kept in a central office. I have tried to discover whether any such action was taken, but can find only a sketchy description of tattoos and scars.

So Smith was awarded two years hard labour and, one assumes, subsequent discharge. I would like to warp history now and sentence Smith in 1894. I do this because Smith is a good name, because Garsia has outlined his history and, as you will see later, 1894 is a significant date. If we follow Smith through the system, we may get an inkling of what his life in prison was like. He would arrive at the gate, wearing his uniform, but the escort would take this back with them to the regiment, leaving Smith only a pair of socks and braces. The kit returned to the regiment would be sold and the proceeds credited to public funds.

Smith would be given a compulsory bath, in the grey cold water shared by all the others who were admitted with him, then he would be searched and issued with a grey cloth jacket, grey waistcoat and trousers. An infantry Glengarry, with the ribbons removed, was worn on the head. If Smith had been sentenced abroad in a warm weather station, his uniform would have been blue jean and a straw hat would have replaced the Glengarry. In Halifax, Nova Scotia, he would have been loaned a used greatcoat, a fur hat, knee boots and a jersey. Smith would be shown to his cell in the way described by Clenshaw.

He would be a Stage One prisoner and would stay as such for at least his first twenty eight days. After being seen by the Medical Officer and being weighed, he would be put to work.

The idea of Stage One work was for it to be nasty and negative. Clenshaw mentions shot drill, carried on in the shot yard. This was a process of taking round shot from a pyramidical heap at one end of the yard and carrying it to the other end, where it was piled in a pyramidical heap, from which etc and so on for the time laid down. All this done to a word of command. When not engaged on shot drill, he would be returned to his cell, which was without a mattress until he reached Stage Two. In the cell, he was given his task of oakum.

The raw material for oakum picking was old rope, no longer usable and supplied by the dockyards. This tar-stiffened length had to be opened into its individual strands then each separated fibre opened and softened. It was done without tools, but old lags sometimes managed to smuggle in an old nail, which eased the process. The nail had to be craftily hidden, because its use could result in a loss of stage or worse. The finished product of the picking was returned to the dockyards for use in caulking wooden vessels.

Cell work could also be operating one of Mr Underhay's patent cranks, which were available, price £8.10s each and were designed to "grind air". The crank was a simple arrangement: a handle for turning, the turning pressure being capable of alteration, and a dial to record number of revolutions. The prisoner was tasked with a set number of revolutions per hour at a set pressure.

Later, Smith would be employed, possibly in the stone-breaking yard. The task here was to receive a load of rough stone from the sappers and knap them down to a size, which allowed them to pass through an iron ring gauge. The produce was then returned to the Royal Engineers for road making.

There are complaints in the 1894 report that soft stone is being sent and that this eases the punishment.

Kindling wood chopping for the garrison begins to feature about 1896. As I read of this, I thought that a softer option was being introduced, then came across two Chief Warder's comments, both expressing satisfaction with the standard of wood being sent for this fatigue: in one case, the oak of the hulks now being dismantled, and in the other, the wood of gun carriages, from which the rivets and ironwork must first be removed, suggest that the idea of easing the load has not arisen.

In Malta Military Prison, the population increases when the Fleet is in. The sailors "often the lowest type of stoker", are put to military discipline and the Admiral is appalled at the easy life they are living, much easier, he insists, than their life aboard ship. His complaint is sent to Sir Edward Du Cane, Inspector of Military Prisons, who replies with a counterblast. The Admiral in his turn demands that the naval visitors be allowed to visit the prison. Sir Edward an extremely powerful figure in the Nineteenth Century prison world, requests HRH to intervene. The Commander in Chief must have used strong language, for the correspondence ceases.

Back to Smith. When he leaves the first stage, he will still be required to pick his task of oakum, to keep his hands busy in the long periods of being locked up, but will also be employed on industrial work, the earnings for which constitute a fair part of the prison funds. The work varies from prison to prison, very much depending on what contracts the Chief Warder or Governor can rustle up around the prison area. As we have already seen in Clenshaw's account, the prison laundry is being introduced, washing not only the prison clothing, but also the garrison's hospital linen. Brixton makes the grey prison clothes and also the blue jeans for all the overseas military prisons; Dublin has a contract with Messrs Goodbody to produce sacks and bags; Gosport and Aldershot both make the palliasse covers and the new three "biscuit" coir beds, but the Medical Officer at Aldershot warns of the dangers of breathing in too much coir dust. Kendal prison weave Belgian halter heads for Harker & Co at one shilling per dozen. In Halifax, Nova Scotia, the inmates are busy quarrying and building a new sea wall, then putting down a new floor in the coal shed. In Kandy, they work entirely under the Royal Engineers making roads and clearing jungle. In Mauritius, they strip coconuts and clean shell. In Bermuda, much work is done on the chipping of coral, but the glare from this, according to the Medical Officer, has grave dangers for the warders' eyes and he recommends that tinted goggles be issued. The effect on the prisoners' eyes is not recorded but there is no issue of tinted goggles for them!

Smith's routine would be the same as that outlined by Clenshaw, but before Smith left prison, he would be seeing some changes, the result of enlightened thinking within the Inspectorate of Military Prisons and a Committee, headed by Lord Monkswell, that was convened in the year that Smith started his sentence. Squad drill is introduced and also physical training to replace walking exercise. Shot drill is discontinued as a form of hard labour, but is still used as a prison punishment. Smith, in 1896, would be allowed to borrow a library book a week, though the choice would be limited by a centrally approved list and the personal taste of the Chaplain. His cell light would be left on an hour longer to allow him to read and he would be allowed to take part in elementary schooling, given that he was likely to benefit from it. This last ruling replaced a previous regulation, which stated that prisoners could continue their education, if they were already enrolled in classes within their regiment and if their commanding officer had given his written approval to their carrying on.

Smith's diet was monotonous but he did not starve. As a man undergoing sentence for more than 42 days, his daily food would be:-

Breakfast 10 ounces of bread, one pint of cocoa.

Dinner 5 ounces of bread, 5 ounces of meat (always boiled and served in its own liquor, with onion and a slight thickening of flour.

Supper 9 ounces of bread and one pint of porridge. Regulations laid down that scales and weights were always available and that any prisoner had the right to weigh his ration. The same regulation points out that any prisoner who makes a habit of complaining is to be punished. On Mondays and Fridays, the meat was beef, on Thursdays mutton. On Tuesdays and Saturdays, the meat was boiled in mixed vegetables and the resulting soup was served out at the scale of one pint per man, with the addition of two ounces of cheese. On Sundays, they had the added treat of a suet pudding.

Diet was also a part of the schedule of punishments for prison offences. Number One Punishment Diet, which could be given for three consecutive days was literally bread and water: one pound of bread and unlimited water. If this were ordered for longer than three days, then it was alternated with the same number of days of normal prison diet. Number Two Punishment diet was more complete as a meal Number Three consisted of:

Breakfast 8 ounces of bread

Dinner one and a half pints of stirabout, containing three ounces of oatmeal three ounces of Indian meal, salt, potatoes eight ounces, bread 8 ounces.

Supper bread eight ounces. An interesting point is that this self same diet is quoted in the Rules for the Military Detention Barracks and Military Prisons published in 1937, but has now been regarded as the Number Two Scale diet. The bread issue, incidentally, was strictly "health food shop" in quality: fully wholemeal with barm from the local brewery used as yeast. A remarkable fact, shown statistically in all the reports, is that the large proportion of prisoners gained weight during their stay in prison. This may have been flab developing in the long periods of being locked in cells.

Diet, of course, was not the only punishment for prison offences. The most feared was flogging and it still appears on the Prison Regulations of 1897. The number of strokes to be given could not exceed 25 and the punishment book entry had to state whether the birch or the cat had been used. Three visitors had to be present, in addition to the Governor and Medical Officer. The warder administering the flogging received threepence.

The offences attracting a flogging included mutiny, attacking a prison officer; repeated assault on a fellow prisoner "insulting behaviour" (a somewhat vague one this, but no more so than "any other act of gross misconduct or insubordination requiring to be suppressed by extraordinary means"!"

Figure of eight handcuffs were kept in the prison, but the regulations stress that no prisoner was to be put in irons as a punishment, merely as a means of restraint and quite stringent procedures were laid down to ensure that this happened.

Back to the much enlisted Smith. Sometime, Smith will be

released and we have assumed that he is to be discharged. Will he enlist again, wooed by the bounty? We shall never know, but we do know that, on the day the gate opens for him, he will be allowed to keep his boots, socks and braces and will be issued with plain clothes as follows:

One cap, one jacket, one waistcoat, one pair of trousers and one neckerchief. He will be given a warrant for a journey to the place of his enlistment (quite a problem one suspects for Smith to decide!) and he will be given the address of the Discharged Prisoners Aid Society in Charing Cross. The prison reports, annually regret the small number of men, who take advantage of this charity. One source of resettlement training was a society for the instruction of discharged prisoners in the skills required for the service with the Merchant Navy, but this again is not popular with the Smiths and other discharged prisoners.

One thing is certain: Smith will have seen changes in the prison system during the time that he is an inmate. They are small changes, but the beginning of a time of reform that is to change much of the system.

4
The Tide Turns: Monkswell Reports

I knew that I had to face the eighty odd pages of the Monkswell Report, because I had an inkling that it was going to be important. Frankly, I didn't relish the idea, but set aside one week for it. By the end of the week, it was occupying my normal working time but had also replaced a novel as my bedtime reading. The reason for this will, I hope, become obvious during the course of the chapter.

You will not want to spend a week on it, so I am going to do the kind of thing that makes the real historian curl his toes in horror: I am going to try to recreate the committee room as it may have been during the Spring of 1895.

I see it as one of the better rooms of the Old War Office, reached by a sweep of staircase and long corridors. Its floor will be parquet and its ceilings high. There will be a long table, covered in green baize.

Lord Monkswell will sit in the centre position. He is the Permanent Under Secretary of State for War and would not have been chairing this committee, but Lord Sandhurst, who was originally appointed to it in 1894, has been called away to govern Bombay.

HT de la Bere will be at one end of the table. He is Deputy Accountant General and will have very little to say, merely keeping an eye on the purse strings.

The real inquisitors will be the other members and the committee has been carefully chosen: Surgeon Major General HF Paterson is Principal Medical Officer in Aldershot and Colonel H Kingscote is the Assistant Adjutant General, both concerned with people, in particular with soldiers, including soldiers in prison.

At the end of the table is a civilian. I see him as a grey, austere figure, with something of the hangman about him. He is H Wakeford Esquire, sometime Comptroller General of Convicts in Western Australia, now Director of Convict Prisons and Inspector of Military Prisons at Home.

No real surprises on the committee, then. One would, possibly, have expected a cleric, this being a Victorian committee on penal subjects, but the padres will appear later as witnesses.

It is here, among the list of witnesses, that the surprises come. In rigid, caste-ridden Victorian Britain, witnesses are to be called, not only from if you like, the officer class. Two of the witnesses will be provost sergeants . . . two of the witnesses will be former prisoners!

The terms of reference are not revolutionary:

To consider the regulations affecting the discipline and diet of soldiers confined in military prisons, and to report whether, having regard to the introduction of short service into the Army and the gradual change which is taking place with regard to length of sentences and the enforcement of discipline generally, any changes are desireable.

Diet is dispensed with as soon as the proceedings open: a previous committee in 1893 has examined prison diet and found it to be adequate. Monkswell gets straight down to business and spells out what the committee is really there to examine: whether a soldier returns from prison to his regiment as a better, fitter man. He also – he has been well briefed by someone! – wishes the committee to examine barrack cells and provost prisons. These last are a particular abomination of Garsia and this is, I feel, the place to examine them.

Barrack cells were regimental guardrooms, as we know them today, but subject less to regulation. The provost prisons were garrison affairs, staffed from the garrison troops and "licensed" to hold men for 42 days, though this could vary. In the provost prison, the soldier had his hair cropped and he spent his time on pack drill, shot-drill and garrison fatigues. They were worked on the "give them hell" principle.

The committee is set to ask fairly simple questions, which seem merely to scratch the surface of the problem:

Should drill and gymnastics replace shot drill and the crank?

Should the use of the lash be allowed in provost prisons?

Should the prisoner be allowed library books throughout his time in prison? If so, should he be allowed a choice of books?

Should remission of sentence be introduced?

As I have said, not world shattering. . . . it is the answers from the witnesses that are important.

Let's wheel them in.

First witness: Colonel Parr, Assistant Adjutant General

He has been a battalion commander and has also commanded a prison in Natal. His feet are well on the ground.

In Natal, he tells the committee, he started a scheme whereby well-behaved prisoners were allowed two hours reading every evening. He also introduced a school for illiterates, where they had worked hard and done well. He feels that books and instruction should be allowed in provost and regimental cells: the supervision could be done by regimental schoolmasters – "not hard worked men" in his opinion.

Drill and gymnastics? Certainly! Parr also thinks that, as military prisons could provide best facilities, prisoners should be sent there rather than kept in provost prisons. He doubts, however, that warders would do the job well.

As to flogging, Parr thinks that it should be introduced into provost prisons.

I do not intend to assess witnesses on some kind of ten point scale to determine whether they are dinosaurs or reformers. If I were to do so, Parr would be a difficult man to assess.

The chaplains would not be difficult: they are both very clearly on the side of reform. Not surprising you say, but believe me, in the letter book there are padres who would be the last men to reform anything!

Both the Protestant and the Roman Catholic chaplains are widely experienced in prison service. Both are very strongly for the idea of books being issued as soon as possible during a man's sentence. Reverend Alexander, the Roman Catholic, says that "without books, they sit and brood". He also insists that they are to be the right books, things that a soldier will want to read. He tells us that "in Aldershot, the books are mainly of an unreadable nature". Reverend Bush, Church of England, extends the argument by saying that two hours should be allowed every night for reading and that books should certainly be available to all, whatever the length of sentence, if they are to be in prison over Sunday. The long time locked up over Sunday, says Bush, is inhumane unless there is something to occupy the mind.

Both speak out clearly for compulsory education. As to flogging they are not completely against it, but both agree it should be limited. Alexander says "I think that flogging is good sometimes, but I have seen disastrous results from it. I saw a man in Brixton flogged five times in two years, but it had no effect on him".

One of the Governors is military, the other a civilian. Both are restrained in their attitudes to reform, but the military governor is the more forward thinking. Of the doctors, similarly the military witness Brigade Surgeon W F Ruttledge is the reformer and the compassionate one, with Mr J H Parker Wilson FRCS, showing himself extremely fond of statistics, but with little real knowledge of his imprisoned patients. Ruttledge – over six years at the Aldershot Military Prison and with thirty years before that in India and regimental work, feels that flogging should be kept on the rule book, but that it should be limited to six lashes "I once saw fifty men flogged in one day and it was the first six strokes only that told". Parker Wilson is for flogging and for maintenance of shot drill, provided that it is supervised, but his main preoccupation at the session is to stress the importance of having a gentleman as head of the prison "NCOs in such situations are no use; soldiers must be ruled by somebody else" Surgeon Major General Paterson asks, shrewdly "You think it is undesireable that an uneducated warder should be head of an institution like the Brixton Military Prison, with a highly trained Medical Officer theoretically subject to his orders? Parker Wilson agrees.

Before leaving Parker Wilson, I cannot resist a direct quote: Question: Do you see any advantage in the replacement of hard labour with drill and gymnastics?

Answer: I think that the present prison labour is good enough. When you come to gymnastics, you open a very big question. The manipulation of gymnastics would be very much against a proper carrying out of discipline. You might have dozens of them jumping about ladders and running up ropes, and if you have one troublesome man amongst them you would soon have them going on like a load of monkeys.

Sergeant Dewar is next, who has been the provost sergeant at Chelsea for three years. The Bible, he says, is the only book available in the regimental cells and he considers that other books would be an advantage, as "they never look at the Bible". He is against shot-drill, regarding it as degrading, and would keep it only for offences committed in custody.

The physical condition of men on release, he says, is worse than on entry. He is convinced that drill and gymnastics would cure this . . . On Sunday, the prisoners go to church twice and during the rest of the day, they are in their cells. He is strongly against the introduction of flogging for offences in provost prisons or regimental cells.

Thomas Cresswell has been the Garrison Provost Sergeant of Woolwich for six years, controlling provost cells licensed for 56 days. Woolwich provost prison at the time is operated in the total silence rule and the main forms of hard labour are shot-drill and stone breaking. Each prisoner does three hours of each on all days except Sunday. The Commission ask Cresswell his opinion on the substitution of drill and gymnastics for the hard labour and he is strongly against it: he thinks that it would make prison too pleasant a place, but he suggests that the last half of a sentence could be occupied with soldierly exercise. In his prison there would also be a difficulty of finding a suitable place for gymnastics and drill, as one yard is occupied by the stone breaking area and the other is reserved for shot-drill. On being asked about the physical shape of soldiers leaving his prison, he says "I have not noticed". Cresswell is asked if any serious disciplinary problems arise in his prison, such as refusing to work or striking non-commissioned officers. He admits that a few, not many, cases of this kind have arisen. There had only been one case of a prisoner striking a NCO and the man had been tried by court martial and sent to military prison. The Commission then suggests that the right to flog would act as a deterrent in such a case and Cresswell agrees that it is possible. The last question is answered in traditional dead-pan NCO fashion. Question: Do you think if the lights were put out an hour later, that the prisoners would have long enough to sleep? Answer: Yes, but there are no lights, Question: Still, if there were lights, they could read. Answer: Yes.

Next come the two ex-prisoners. Corporal Robinson, Scots Guards, has served 42 days in the garrison prison at Wellington Barracks for fraudulent enlistment. He is asked about the routine there. He recalls a timetable as follows:-

6am Reveille, clean cell and shot-drill until 8a.m.

7am – 8am Pack drill. Marching order, carrying full kit.

8am – 9am Breakfast

9am – 10am Pack Drill

10am – 11am Shot-drill
11am – 12 Pack drill
12 – 1pm Fatigues
1pm – 2pm Dinner

The after dinner routine was a repetition of the morning and went on until 6pm, when he was allowed free time in the cell until being ordered to bed at 8pm. On being asked whether he had been allowed to read in his free two hours, he answers "Yes, but there was no light in the cell". He has already stated that there was reading matter available; a Bible and a prayer book.

Robinson is then asked what he thinks would be the effect of allowing prisoners to read and he considers that it would *make prison less feared, though he is not sure whether this is an entirely good thing.*

His views on education in prison are more positive and he thinks that some kind of elementary education would have real value.

The Commission then asks him about his condition on leaving prison and he says that he has never been the same man since, having permanent back pains, which he attributes to the shot-drill. Outside he had worked as a blacksmith and a stoker, but none of the work he had done had been so hard as the shot-drill. The pace on shot-drill is too short, he says, and the time too quick.

"Many a court martial is caused by the men shouting over you. I had the worst man you ever came across to drill me. If a man is doing wrong then check him, but don't stand barking over him all the time".

Should shot-drill be abolished, he is asked, would it make prison more attractive. There is a depth of feeling in his reply that prison would never be a pleasant place. *When asked about prison clothing, he confirms that the loss of uniform is a degrading thing.* He finishes his evidence by saying that, before joining the Army, he did seven days work as a stoker at the gas works, but that the shot-drill exhausted him far more.

Private Cormack of the Scots Guards is the next witness. He is twenty years old and has just completed a 56 day sentence in Aldershot for desertion. He needed only a book on Sundays, he says, as there was no time on other evenings, as the task of oakum had to be picked: he was required to pick two pounds a day. After this and two hours shot-drill, he then did fatigues in the laundry. The shot-drill was the part that he hated most. At Aldershot, it appeared, each man was given a slate and a pencil and allowed to do what he wished with it and he confirms that he would have welcomed instruction on arithmetic, though he has no idea where the time would have come from, as the time between six and eight was the only time to ensure that the task of oakum was completed. He is sure that pack drill would have more value than shot-drill. Cormack had worked on the docks before joining the Army and Aldershot had been harder than the docks.

It is really for the next evidence that I have inflicted the Monkswell Committee upon you. If you had skipped the rest, it is important that you read the evidence of Colonel Thomas Kelly-Kenny, Chief Staff Officer, Aldershot.

When I had read his evidence, I wanted to know more about him. Irritatingly, his name was somewhere in the back of my memory, so I searched my shelves for a book on the Boer War and there he was, by this time a Lieutenant General and having trouble with Kitchener. Nothing about him as a person. When I am in this kind of difficulty, I turn to one of my "leg men", either Squadron Leader John Lawrence or Staff Sergeant Vic Leppard. The indefatigable Vic came up in two days with the obituary of General Sir Thomas Kelly-Kenny in The Times of 28th December 1914, and it told much that I hadn't even guessed. I knew that he had commanded his battalion and that he had seen active service. I also knew that he had been Assistant Adjutant General before coming to Aldershot. I was more interested to learn that, in the time that Garsia was fighting to establish the Corps: from 1901, Kelly-Kenny was Adjutant General – in the position best placed to influence the innovation. When you read his evidence, you will see how important this is.

His evidence summarises as follows:-

He would allow schoolbooks from the day they went in.

He would encourage the reading of travel books, history and military history from the 14th day of imprisonment.

He supports the idea of educational instruction, not in cells, but with prisoners in association.

He would like to see workshops, where trades were taught, rather than mere shops for repairing boots and clothes.

Prisons should be reduced in number, but made bigger, to

concentrate effort and resources. The time in barrack and provost cells should be reduced to allow prisoners the opportunity of being able to use the military prison facilities.

He is against the introduction of flogging to the provost cells.

He wishes to see drill and gymnastics introduced, but thinks that the old warders would not be capable of them: "That all warders should be non-commissioned officers in the Army and not merely old soldiers".

Arms drill should be taught, even if old weapons are used.

This last statement sends the traditionalists on the Commission into a dither. How would you control prisoners with weapons in their hands? Kelly-Kenny points out that hammers are already issued for stone breaking and that a hammer is a weapon.

Education, he thinks, should be compulsory.

He would never sentence soldiers to long periods in a military prison. If they deserved a long sentence, he would put them to a civil prison, then discharge them.

The Commission returns to the revolutionary idea that the Colonel has put forward: that serving NCOs should be employed as warders.

Question: You say that warders should come from the NCOs of the Army, do you mean any special class of NCO?

Answer: No, but only good NCOs should be selected and put forward by Commanding Officers.

Question: Do you think that it would be an advantage if they had some special previous training, such as men of the Medical Staff Corps receive? The Colonel agrees that this would indeed be an advantage.

The rest of his evidence supports his idea of centralised prisons, but he does say in conclusion that he is against the barbaric idea of shaving a man's head, thus marking him as an ex-prisoner when he is released.

This is the voice of the reformer and he has obviously raised his voice previously to the Adjutant General – he almost says as much at one stage of his evidence. I submit that all the reforms that lead finally to the formation of the Corps can be attributed to Kelly-Kenny's backing of Garsia. After all, Garsia could only speak with the voice of a retired Lieutenant Colonel; to have at his back an officer as powerful as the Adjutant General at the very time when he had crystallised in his mind exactly what was needed to reform the system, must have been a vitally important thing for Garsia.

The recommendations of the Committee are as follows:

The appointment of a person, who holds, or has held commissioned rank, as Governor.

A closer look at the provost prisons and an attempt to make conditions there, and in the regimental cells less onerous. Inmates of provost cells would be drilled and given gymnastic training. Lighting would be improved, hair cropping cease.

A syllabus of drill and gymnastics to be initiated in military prisons, all of which would be equipped with gymnasia. The drill would be without weapons.

The crank to be used for prison punishment only and shot-drill to be limited.

Book lists to be compiled and the opportunity given for prisoners to select a book of their own choice. Lights Out to be extended until 9pm.

Compulsory education for all who would benefit from it.

But what about the Kelly-Kenny evidence? you will ask. No mention here of forming the Corps.

You may have forgotten Mr Wakeford, sometime Comptroller of Convicts in Western Australia, the grey man sitting at the end of the table. He is the representative of the dinosaurs. Throughout the hearing, his questions have favoured the status quo, the "Give them hell" school of penal administration. At the end of the hearing, he insists that a memorandum be added, dissociating him from most of the reforms and it is his attitude that waters down the proposals. To back him, a four page memorandum is received from the south of France and it bears the name of Sir Edmund du Cane KCB.

Not a name to be ignored in Victorian Prison Britain! In fact, the biggest name in that area, but before I speak shortly about him, I should point out that he had been invited originally to join the enquiry, but had refused.

I would have liked to write a chapter on Sir Edmund, but it would have taken us away from the main stream of the subject, so I must content myself with a paragraph and hope that anyone interested in more will contact me.

Edmund du Cane was born in Colchester in 1830, son of a major in the 20th Hussars. He attended the Royal Military Academy, Woolwich and was commissioned into the Royal

Engineers in 1848. Shortly after this he went to Western Australia to supervise convict labour and to act as magistrate. It cannot be a complete coincidence that Wakeford had a similar career! After some Sapper work on the Plymouth and Dover defences, du Cane, in 1863 – at the age, therefore of thirty three, became Director of Convict Prisons and Inspector of Military Prisons. It was his hand that was to shape the English prison system for the rest of the century. . . . and Wakeford was his prophet! When one realises this, it is surprising that any reforms at all resulted from the Committee.

The reforms were not widely sweeping, but they were the foot in the door. The implementation of the "implied" reforms was to be the last work of a man who must have had considerable influence in the background of the Committee. I refer to Lieutenant Colonel Michael Clare Garsia, whom I can fairly label The Father of the Corps.

PART TWO

The Corps Is Formed.
1901–1919

5
Father of the Corps

Lieutenant Colonel Michael Clare Garsia CB died at his home in Queensbury Place, Brompton, on the 20th of April 1903 in his sixty fifth year. He had been awarded the Companionship of the Bath two years before, a fitting reward, but the greatest reward for him must have been to know that, by his efforts, the military penal system had been freed of the shackles of Victorian thinking and was ready for the new century of which he saw so little.

Who was he? Colonel Jim Robinson and I have used a fair piece of our leisure time over the past year attempting to find an answer. We know what he did, we know that it was his thinking that created the Corps and we know that he would have looked at the Military Corrective Training Centre with complete approval, but we wanted to know about the man himself.

Finding the answers has been like reading a detective story with vital pages missing, but we can now put together something of the story, although some gaps are still there.

We do know that he was born in November 1838 and that he was first gazetted to a militia regiment in Kent; The West Kent Light Infantry, so we can assume that he was living in the county at that time. We can also assume that he was either a younger son or that his family was of limited means, because his first regular regiment was the West Indian Regiment. This was the time before Cardwell's reforms and commissions were still purchased, the smarter the regiment, the more expensive the commission and the West India Regiment was by no means smart.

In the days when commissions were bought and sold, there were two ways of promotion open to the officer with no money: a bloody war and dead men's boots, or promotion for bravery in the field. Garsia had his chance in one of those little obscure wars that are so much a feature of Victorian military history. A combined naval and military force was sent to the Gambia on the West African coast in February 1861, I suspect on some kind of anti-slavery expedition. He was officially there as assistant engineer (an intriguing line which I have attempted to follow up without success) and was present at the destruction of many stockaded villages. At the action outside Saba, he had a horse shot from under him and was wounded in both legs. This earned him a mention in despatches and the next step up the promotion ladder. It was a promotion in two ways: he was given a lieutenancy in a regiment numbered in the Line, in fact in the 56th Regiment of Foot, which later became the Essex Regiment and is now a part of The Royal Anglian Regiment. He served with them for ten years, six of them as adjutant, then, in the year that Cardwell abolished the purchase system, became captain and company commander in the 30th of Foot, now a part of the Queen's Lancashire Regiment.

In 1868, the 56th of Foot was serving in County Waterford and it was in this Irish county that Garsia met Margaret Anderson, of Grace Dieu. They married in the same year and a son, Clare James Garsia, was born in 1869. Clare James was later to be commissioned into the King's Shropshire Light Infantry and served in the Boer War as Station Staff Officer and later Assistant Provost Marshal.

Garsia himself joined the Prisons Department on retirement in 1878. This was a fairly common step for retired officers: there is a standing complaint amongst Victorian prison reformers that too many ex-officers are governors of the civil prisons and too many of the warders are retired old soldiers.

Garsia is mentioned only once in the literature of civil prisons of the period, when he is described as Governor of Millbank. Millbank Prison, which stood on the Tate Gallery site, was something of a showpiece prison and Garsia is noted as one of the few governors, who had established a training system for his warders.

By 1895, he was Commissioner of Civil Prisons and Inspector of Military Prisons.

It was the time when the heavy hand of Sir Edmund du Cane was being lifted from the reins of the prison system, civil and military. Captain W J Stopford CB had been appointed Inspector General of Military Prisons, so Garsia, was technically his subordinate. As many of the reforms of the system were carried out in the period when Stopford was Inspector

General (the reforms resulting from the Monkswell Commission, for example, were already being implemented in the same year as the commission had sat: hardly typical Civil Service – or military – speed of reaction!), could we assume that Stopford also was a reformer with "fire in his belly"? The answer, we think, is in the last paragraph of Stopford's 1897 report, when he acknowledges the "valuable assistance of Colonel Garsia, who in my absence has carried on the duties of Inspector General".

Garsia took over the post officially in 1898. The Monkswell reforms had already alleviated the situation in military prisons, bringing them nearer to the aims, which Garsia expresses in his first report as Inspector General.

"Military prisons are, in fact, schools of discipline and military training, and the treatment of the prisoners, as I have shown, is, in no way, degrading. Useful work, however hard, must and does elevate the worker, whilst drill, so carried out as to be a punishment, can only disgust the soldier with his legitimate duties. The soldier is sent to prison as a punishment for serious offences against military discipline, and he is now punished by loss of liberty, by being subjected to a stricter discipline, and by being compelled to work. By industry he earns the privilege of being allowed to do drill and military exercises, and of receiving school instruction. Without the foregoing conditions, imprisonment could have no deterrent effect, and might even be preferred by the idle soldier to the hard work of summer manoeuvres. I claim for the system I am, with your Lordship's approval, endeavouring to carry out, (1) that it does not err on the side of severity, (2) that the penal element is reduced to a minimum, and (3) that, in a military sense, it is distinctly reformatory; and I cannot doubt that the result must be to return the young soldier to the colours in every sense improved and better fitted to resume his place in the ranks."

In the same report Garsia recommends that all future military prisoners report in their undress uniforms and carrying their kit. Maintenance of uniform and kit will become an essential part of the prisoner's training and governors are expected to take military parades and to inspect their charges as soldiers. Gymnasia are to be built, rather than relying on the Indian Club and dumb-bell exercises. The first of these gymnasia is to be at Aldershot.

Garsia in the same report suggests, in very low key, that, as there is no limit to service abroad for prison officers, however hard the station, selected NCOs should be employed at all overseas stations to give relief and he ties his suggestion with the most potent of Government persuaders: that this should save money.

I feel that at this stage, Garsia is very much aware of the weakness in the link of the reform chain: it is futile to introduce drill and gymnastics to the organisations when the only instructors are old and time-served with no real idea of the advances in military training that have been taking place in the rest of the Army.

Having inserted the thin end of the wedge, he hammers it farther home in his report of 1899. He argues, first, that, in light of new developments in the prison regime, it is becoming increasingly difficult to find warders capable of handling the new situation. "They are, in fact, civil servants with no military status or rank, although placed in command of soldiers only temporarily withdrawn from the Colours. It has consequently become necessary that the staff should consist of *good non-commissioned officers and of men possessed of military zeal, the military spirit, and thoroughly efficient as drill and disciplinary instructors, themselves capable of soldierly qualities and soldierly bearing*. I have accordingly recommended that in future the staff of the military prisons shall be a distinctly military body, in fact a special corps of warrant officers and non-commissioned officers serving on their army engagements; that their rank shall be actual military rank not lower than that of a sergeant; and that they shall wear a military uniform, which shall serve to distinguish them as members of an honourable service in which they are entrusted with very important, difficult and responsible duties".

In 1900, he confirms that the idea has been approved and is sure that "when the conditions of service are known to the non-commissioned officers of the army, we shall have no lack of good candidates. I believe that a large number of good non-commissioned officers who are not fit to return to South Africa, but who are perfectly fit for home service, could now be obtained".

In the same report, he pushes training a little nearer to the objectives which he must have discussed with Colonel Kelly-Kenny, whom you will recall, spoke up in the Monkswell hearing for a specialist corps but also for weapon training. Garsia writes:

"I have also recommended that each military prison should be supplied with a field gun and a machine gun. These need only be sufficiently serviceable for training purposes. I propose also to arrange for the instruction of every military offender in digging shelter trenches, also in first aid and ambulance drill."

Garsia was backed in his efforts by the Governor of Aldershot Major R A Henderson, mentioned by Clenshaw, who was to succeed to the office of Inspector General and continue Garsia's work. The 1902 report is, however, signed by Major E J Clayton, one of the Inspectors of Prisons, who obviously filled the gap. It was written, of course, in 1903 and ends with a tribute:

"I cannot close this report without placing on record my deep sense of severe loss which the Military Prison Service has sustained by the death of Lieutenant Colonel Garsia. His skill and energy were always ungrudgingly devoted to the public service and were exercised without stint in the heavy and important work of reorganising the Military Prison system in which he engaged until his death. In him, the State has lost a capable and zealous public servant."

Garsia's obituary appeared in the Times, bare bones of a life, whose real memorial is an advanced and enlightened corrective training system. As you will see in future chapters, his precepts were forgotten at times, but they run as a strand throughout the history of the Corps.

6
The Corps is Formed

Garsia – and Kelly-Kenny – must have felt some satisfaction when they read Army Order 241, made in the first year of the reign of Edward VII, for one of their main aims: the creation of a Corps of serving soldiers specifically trained for the running of the new military penal institutions had been approved. I print the full text of the Order here:-

Military Prison Staff Corps
Edward R. (A.o.241.) December 1901

Whereas We deem it expedient that a corps of our Regular Forces shall be formed to discharge the subordinate duties in Our military prisons;

Our Will And Pleasure is that such corps, to be designated the "Military Prison Staff Corps," shall be formed accordingly, and that the title of the corps shall be inserted in the schedule attached to the Warrant of Our late Royal Mother, dated the 28th January, 1899.

1. The daily rate of pay of warrant and non-commissioned officers of the Military Prison Staff Corps shall be as follows:-

   #### Warrant Officer
   Sergeant-Major ... ... 5s. 0d.
   #### Non-Commissioned Officers
   Quarter-master sergeant ... ... 4s. 0d.
   Staff-sergeant ... ... 3s. 9d.
   Sergeant ... ... 3s. 2d.
   Lance-corporal ... ... 2s. 1d.

2. Additional pay at the rate of £12 a year shall be granted to a warrant officer, and £6 a year to a non-commissioned officer, when employed in a military prison abroad.
3. A warrant officer who performs the duties of clerk and school-master in a military prison shall receive extra duty pay at the rate of 6d. a day.

4. A soldier serving with the Military Prison Staff Corps on probation shall receive pay at the same rate as a soldier of corresponding rank in that corps.
5. Except as provided in Article 689 of the Pay Warrant, a warrant or non-commissioned officer of the Military Prison Staff Corps shall be discharged on attaining the age of 50 years.

Given at Our Court at Sandringham, this 26th day of November, 1901, in the 1st year of Our Reign.
By His Majesty's Command,
St. JOHN BRODRICK

With the order, came the Secretary of State's instruction, which was an analysis of the kind of NCO wanted in the new corps. Read carefully, they are an extremely shrewd set of criteria and could just as easily be used today.

The candidates for the Military Prison Staff Corps were to be assessed as of "Very good" character by their Commanding Officer and to be sober and temperate. One entry for drunkness during the previous six years, or more than two entries since enlistment, would automatically disqualify.

Tact and good temper were to be classed as essential qualifications and commanding officers were only to recommend men who had shown zeal and intelligence in their regimental duties.

The candidate was to be a good disciplinarian and an efficient drill instructor. Skill in a trade would be a strong additional qualification and candidates were made aware that instruction in a trade would form part of the engagement criteria.

Transfer was open to corporals but they would only be considered if they had already passed the second class certificate of education.

All candidates were to be "of active habit" and their medical officer had to certify them fit. They had to be at least 5'7" without boots and under 35 years of age.

As members of a Corps, the basic colouring of their uniform was dark blue, but with a facing of red, which showed mainly on the cuff. S/Sgt Vic Leppard, in his searches in the Manuals Section of the MOD Library found the following list in the

45

Clothing Regulations for 1904, which we assume to have been laid down originally on the Corps' formation:-

Boots, ankle, pair (of a design, incidentally, that the Old and Bold would readily recognise as ammunition boots). These were to be replaced every six months.

Cap, forage, with oilskin cover and chin strap, to be replaced every eighteen months.

The next items intrigued us and I have tried without success to explain them: frock and trousers, tartan. The frock, of course, was the longer tunic . . . but tartan?

Abroad, frocks and trousers, khaki drill, replaced the tartan and a helmet, white drill was worn with them. A great coat was replaceable every four years in most stations but was expected to last only two years in Halifax Nova Scotia. An interesting change from the scale of the old warder is the omission of gloves and fur hat on the Halifax station.

The carpet slippers for night duty, however, carried over from the old order of things and the cook still received two canvas suits, an apron and a linen cap annually, the cap to be bought locally.

We have seen, through the jaundiced eye of Clenshaw that the old order saw the new Corps as a threat, and I suspect that the occasional attempt to sabotage the system happened but is nowhere recorded – obviously. What we have, are two accounts, both a trifle bald, by members of the new Corps: RSM C W Bailey MBE and RQMS W G Ellerby, both of whom play down the old undercurrents but obviously felt them quite strongly.

Bailey returned with his battalion from South Africa in 1902 and read a circular letter asking for transfers to the MPSC. "At the time we were discussing the letter in the Mess, a sergeant major from the Military Prison in Colchester came in and I asked him what the advantages were in transferring, then I put in my application to the CO. After an interview, he allowed me to apply."

Bailey's probationary period of three weeks was served at Gosport, then one of the most important of the military prisons, handling prisoners shipped from abroad. At Gosport, he found that there were only four serving sergeants on the staff, the remainder being civilian warders "wearing the rank corresponding" (this is a reference to one of Garsia's transitional measures, whereby he equated the civil grades to military rank to give more authority during drill and gymnastics. The move was praised by Chief Warders in the prison reports and the order resulted in a flurry of letters in the letter book about saluting, wearing swords and other military minutiae, but I feel that the idea was not generally successful: perhaps Garsia did not intend it to be!)

"The situation was not all that rosy", writes Bailey "as the civilians thought that we were out to oust them". His main complaint at this stage is that promotion for the MPSC was within prisons, depending on length of time served in one specific place, rather than on an overall Corps list.

In this description of Gosport, one feels a certain disenchantment, but in 1904, he is posted to Aldershot, where he feels happier because "Training was carried out by the soldiers and not interfered with by the civilians" He gives a good idea of this training routine: "Company drill, musketry, bridging, gymnastics, signalling, in fact everything a soldier needed. In addition there were lectures of all kinds, whatever the Commandant, Major Haines, ordered and which he had a great interest in. All the training took place in the morning from 9.15am to 12.15pm, then the squads would be marched to the workshop for their tasks".

Family illness caused a change in station and Bailey came to Colchester, where he found the routine similar to that at Aldershot. In 1908, he was posted to Gibraltar and it was here that he served with an all MPSC staff for the first time.

He returned to Colchester in time for mobilisation for the First World War and I will mention his experience during this time in a later chapter.

Ellerby's account is less clear than Bailey's and was, I suspect, written in old age. He joined the MPSC in 1902 and also did his probation at Gosport where "discipline was very severe and, truth to tell, the old warders did not like the introduction of time-serving NCOs and let me tell you, there was no love lost between the old timers and the newcomers".

He goes on to describe the prison routine at Gosport and one has the feeling that Garsia had never existed: the crank and shot drill were still in use and oakum was still picked, the stone yard was still in use. Ellerby, in fact, describes a duty in the stone yard, where each man sat in a small cubicle with a hammer and wearing wire goggles. On this particular day, a prisoner deliberately took off the first joint of his index finger between the hammer and the stone, in the hope of being invalided. He was sent to hospital, was court martialled on return, then was compelled to continue his sentence, without discharge. Ellerby's next posting was Aldershot, where he confirms Bailey's experience of the excellence of training, mentioning also that a miniature range was much in use. He did duty there as Sergeant Cook, a carry-over from the old warder days (though one must also remember that regimental cooks were the norm outside prisons). Wynberg in South Africa was his next move and he proudly records that, when he was there, he painted a copy of a Hill Sifkin (landscapes) target 100 feet by 20 feet on one of the buildings for use in weapon training.

His final paragraph echoes Garsia:

"It is human nature and human character to kick at times. When he steps through the gate, he is treated as a man, not as in the old days, when he was told to face the wall and woe betide him if he looked round.* Of course, when he is sent to these places, he is not going on furlough and he is losing many of the privileges he has outside. There is no canteen and no leave in town. He must be given time to see what a fool he has been and 99 cases out of a 100, you never see the same man back".

Two voices from the early days, then, and both appearing to conclude that the new system was working. The prison reports from 1902 onwards confirm this, the main cry from the Governors being that they want more members of the MPSC to replace the old warders. Many Governors also report that they are sending members of the new Corps to the branch prisons – successors to the old provost cells – to increase their efficiency and to bring them into line with current thinking.

The next major step was to introduce some new name for that part of the military penal system concerned with reform and retraining, rather than with retribution. This had been one of the subjects for discussion on the Buller Committee of 1899, of which Garsia had been a leading member. Garsia, supported by Buller, had pushed the idea of the introduction of the term "discipline company" or something similar, with

---

* A reference to the old prison system, where the prisoner was compelled to turn his face to the wall if he met anyone approaching in a prison corridor.

the aim of removing the smear of having been in prison from the soldier returning to duty. The committee could not agree on this and it took considerable pressure by Henderson and Major C O Johnstone, Governor of York Military Prison, before the idea became accepted. Henderson writes "The proposal met with some opposition. I remember being told by a very high official that it was all damned rot, but it went through when I became Inspector General".

In fact, it went through in 1906, when Army Order 114 amended the Army Act and again I quote the complete order, because, as you see, the other change involved is a renaming of the corps from Military Prison Staff Corps to its present name.

A.O. 114 (1906)
Army Act Amendments

1. The attention of all concerned is called to the amendments to the Army Act contained in the Army (Annual) Act, 1906.
2. These amendments will take effect from the dates on which the Army Act is continued in force in the various commands and stations as laid down in the Army (Annual) Act, 1906, and the Army Act, Rules of Procedure, and King's Regulations will be construed to have been amended accordingly.
3. Consequent on the introduction of detention as a punishment, the following changes in nomenclature will take place:-

Present nomenclature	Future nomenclature
Inspector of Military Prisons.	Inspector of Military Prisons and Detention Barracks.
Governor, Dover or Curragh Prison.	Governor, Military Prison, Dover or Curragh.
Governors of Central and District Prisons.	Commandants, Detention Barracks.
Military Prison Staff Corps	**Military Provost Staff Corps.**
Dover Central Prison	Dover Military Prison.
Curragh Central Prison	Curragh Military Prison.
All other central and district prisons	Detention barracks.

Branch prisons	Branch detention barracks.
Barrack cells	Barrack detention rooms.
Guard room prisoners' rooms, and guard-room cells	Guard detention rooms.
Prisoner	Soldier in arrest.
Prisoner at large	Soldier in open arrest.
A soldier arraigned before a court-martial	The accused.
A soldier after being sentenced by a court-martial or by a commanding officer	**Soldier under sentence.**

7
The Governor's Story

Colonel RD Turton was, like Henderson and Johnstone, another of the enlightened governors, who made Garsia's system work. He had a wide infantry experience, including a period with the mounted infantry in Egypt, prior to becoming Governor at Corradino Military Prison in Malta. What he saw of the old system there convinced him that Garsia's reforms were overdue. Griffin – the initiator of the research for a history of the MPSC – served as one of his sergeant majors and he writes in his notes "He will always be remembered for his generous treatment of his staff and the tactful, patient way he handled the soldier under sentence".

After Malta, Turton was transferred to the Military Prison at Dublin in the year of Garsia's death. I will let him tell his own story from that point.

"By this time, the new system was getting into its stride: soldiers were arriving in marching order with their kit and their rifles and military training was the objective.

I found that there was little space for military training at Arbour Hill Military Prison, but just outside there was an old military cemetery, unused for fifty years. It was in a terrible state with tombstones fallen down and cows wandering through it. I got permission from the Commander in Chief to take over the wilderness, level it, place all the tombstones against the wall and it made an excellent parade ground. I mention this because there was an interesting sequel. During the Easter Rebellion of 1916, many of the rebels were imprisoned in Kilmainham Detention Barracks, formerly a civil prison. Some of the rebels were sentenced to death and their bodies were buried in the drill ground I had constructed thirteen years before. When I was at HQ in that year, the AAG said that a rather awkward situation had arisen; that the clergy were objecting to the executed rebels being buried in unconsecrated ground and that moving them to Glasnevin Cemetery would probably result in disorder. I was able to

51

assure him that the ground was indeed consecrated, which relieved him very much.

In 1913, I took over from Colonel Haines as Governor of Aldershot. The reformed system had now been in full swing for eleven years and the results were startling. In 1912, there were 12,000 soldiers committed, whereas there had been over 20,000 a few years before. In the old days, the same men came back frequently, but between 1910 and 1914, you rarely saw the same man again. Every man took the greatest interest in his training and many commanding officers told me that their men had come back to their regiments far better trained than when they went away."

I will interrupt Turton's account at this point, because his 1914-1918 experience fits more appropriately into a later chapter. Turton's narrative continues in 1919.

"In 1919, Lord Rawlinson was C in C Aldershot. He often visited the barracks, quite unannounced and took the greatest interest in the methods of instruction and the routine. When he was appointed C in C India in early 1921, he found on his inspections that the military prisons and detention barrack were far behind the times, so he asked the War Office to send out an experienced Commandant as Director. I was selected and went out to India late 1921.

When I got there, Lord Rawlinson said that I was to have a complete free hand and that he hoped that I would put up as good a show as I had at Aldershot.

I found that things were rather prehistoric, to say the least. The staff was composed of conductors and sub-conductors, assisted by lance corporals and acting lance corporals, who were attached. Most of them had never seen a detention barrack and certainly knew nothing of the system. I found Headquarters most helpful. It was agreed that a sergeant major and a small staff of MPSC should be sent out from England to help me. They also agreed that selected NCO's would replace the conductors and sub-conductors. Everything would be carried out as in England.

Sergeant Major Taylor and his small staff shortly arrived and, thanks to their hard work, we had in about 12 months a staff of NCOs attached to each DB in India, that would compare favourably with the staff of any DB in England.

The result was much the same as when the system was started in England. The soldiers committed took a real interest in their training. Few came back again and detention barrack offences were practically unknown. Several commanding officers wrote to me to say that their men returning were so well trained, that they had shortly been appointed lance corporals: a very different thing from the old days, when the returning man had been looked on by his commanding officer as a pariah.

When Lord Rawlinson inspected our detention barracks and military prison in Poona two years later, he was so pleased that he gave me 10,000 rupees to install electric lights in the mess rooms, which had previously been in darkness from sunset to sunrise. The GOC Poona was much annoyed at this, as he had been attempting for a long time to get funds for electric light in some of his infantry barracks!"

Colonel Turton left India on retirement in 1925 and was decorated with the CMG for his success there.

8
The First World War

S.F. Griffin, the member of the Corps who first started to collect material for a Corps history, was a sergeant when mobilisation was proclaimed. He was stationed at the Aldershot Glasshouse and he wrote this piece for the first issue of the Corps Journal.

"Detention Barracks Aldershot August 1914."

The somewhat electrical calm was rudely broken by the order to mobilise. At 6.30 pm on August 4th, a member of the Staff was hurriedly sent to Headquarters, to return very shortly with special instructions.

Our Commandant was soon a busy man, and for two days what was to happen was a subject of conjecture. However, we were soon to be enlightened. Fresh faces rolled in and within a couple of days the veil of mystery was lifted.

How we envied them their luck!

We were also amused at their efforts to master the intricacies of the French language, and by common consent, or some other common denominator, everyone appeared keen to become lip perfect with a phrase that had something to do with a walk with mademoiselle.

Blue patrols gave way to Service dress, and at this we thought that we were getting to the Hun.

The infection for Active Service got into the loyal minds of the inmates, and to their credit let it be recorded that the needs of their country were paramount in their minds and wholesale volunteering took place.

Homes had to be broken up and families moved. Oh! . . . the tears, the anguish and the fortitude displayed. The wives, brave souls, suffered the parting with equanimity. One perspicous (sic) case was however particularly distressing. The wife, a pathetically sensitive lady, on wishing her husband goodbye, predicted that they would never meet again. Her words turned out to be all too prophetic. As a contrast to the story of affection, the following is amusing. A not so loving little lady

– aggressive is perhaps the word – was so elated at the removal of her hubby, that in the joy she destroyed the whole of her front room window, by hurling her household goods through it, much to the amusement of the "gunner" reservists who were being paraded in close proximity to the quarter.

Virtue Villa became less virtuous. It became the den of all the latest rumours, and not a little secret elation, coupled with something that cheers.

How we roved round to find places at which to feed! The proprietrix of the Farnboro' Road Shop thought that the war had reached her establishment when at a very early hour one morning twelve stalwart members played a tattoo on the windows. Madam poking her head from the upper storey, in broad Irish enquired our wants: "Tay, is it yers afther. If yers not off it's wharter ye'll be gettin' – and none too clean at that."

We called her "mother", told her that there was a war on, and that we were hungry would she oblige? She did.

Real Sergeant-Major's tea, with eggs and bacon. Her feminine vanity did not appear to be of great moment, for she carried out our commissions with her dressing gown on. Peeping from her collar was a very tousled curl, which she was pleased to term her "Merry Widow back piece."

She had many drawbacks, lack of cleanliness being one of them. If ever a lady believed in the proverb that all persons must eat a peck of dirt, she did. However, we got fond of Biddy as she became known and thought kindly of her for a long time afterwards.

In a short time the equipping of the overseas staff had been carried out, and the sounds of the revolver practice on the range struck a queer note.

Together with the other troops this party left us for the field towards the late middle of the month.

War at the moment had not been significant. Then quickly to its first results.

The German waiters at the Queen's Hotel were suddenly rounded up and sent into the DB. When a member of the Staff was sent out to inform the wife of the head waiter that her husband was in confinement, she collapsed. She was an English woman, and her husband had been resident in England for twenty-two years. This little episode made us think.

Next came the German sausage maker of Liptons Ltd. A real jolly faced Fritz, with an enormous girth. We felt sorry for him because he was arrested on his wedding night.

Then we had a real bad devil of an Austrian. He was arrested at Alton, and had made a desperate effort to make a good getaway.

Following we had the boy German waiters taken from the hotels in the district. We were sorry for them at the time, but no doubt as events proceeded they thanked their lucky stars at not being able to "get back" and be offered as fodder.

Soon we were to receive the seamen from Koenig Louise. These poor devils were broken up twice, and were in a sad way when we brought them in. Their boatswain died very soon after their arrival, in the Connaught Hospital. Although we were not feeling particularly chivalrous at the time his mortal remains were not interred without due respect for a gallant enemy.

Frith Hill Prison Camp soon opened, all prisoners of war transferred there. What a scene there was at the D.B. gates as they left. There was a crowd of married women of regiments already in the Field, to give them a terrific "booing" off.

Whilst at the D.B. they were located in the gymnasium. They kept fit with a little voluntary PT. The seamen played "Black Koenig" (?) for hours on end. The fascination of the game never became apparent to the onlooker.

Towards the end of the month, a first reinforcement party was ordered. This meant more fresh faces for duty. Gallant old boys returned from pension and assumed their places as though they had never been away. The then serving members of the Staff had a particularly trying time, because the old boys were not "au fait" with the drill methods then existing. They soon picked it up, however.

The gatekeeper complained of extra work, and asked for clerical assistance. It was supplied in a partial way.

Before the month ended we saw the first lot of wounded arrive at the Connaught.

On retrospect, in this one month there appeared crowded a life-time of normal events."

The practice of using detention barracks for internment was not general (though there had been cases in the Boer War). Two related sidelights emerged during my research.

On the 4th August 1914, the APM, Malta, is ordered to shut down Corradino Detention Barracks and to return servicemen under sentence to their units. The MPSC staff are ordered to report to the civil prison. The order is cancelled on the 18th August and Corradino is reserved for all who are ordered Field Punishment for 14 days or more and for hard labour sentences. The reason why a detention barracks should be closed at the beginning of a war eluded me until later reference is made to German, Austrian and Turkish internees and prisoners of war (including a Prince of Prussia). I can only assume that the original plan was to use Corradino as an internment camp and that alternative arrangements were made. Later, in the year, the APM is ordered by the island's Governor to use part of Corradino to house any POWs sentenced to Field Punishment. The first customer is an Austrian, Ranich, awarded 3 days No 1 and 70 days No 2, for breaking into a store.

In Hong Kong, the APM is engaged – almost obsessed – by the possibility that the many Germans and Austrians in the colony are engaging in espionage. There is a novel to be written about this period in Hong Kong (or a farce) but this is not the place for it. However, the APM decides that the only safe location for an internment camp is Stonecutters Island, and this is the first reference that I have found to this old favoured outpost of the MPSC. The idea, incidentally is dropped after a short time.

Meanwhile, back in the main stream, Aldershot was the mobilisation centre for the Corps. Colonel Turton was appointed Inspector of Detention Barracks and Colonel P Umfreville, Commandant of Colchester DB, became Inspector of Military Prisons in France.

The South African War had shown that many soldiers had found that the easy way to avoid the rigours of campaigning on the veld, was to strike a NCO and be shipped to either Gosport or Malta (the Bird Cage of Cape Town, Wynberg and the temporaries at Pietmarzburg and elsewhere appear to have been used for short DB sentences only). To seal this gap, a Committee had assembled in 1907 under Major General GF Browne CB, Director of Personal Services "To consider the compilation of a code of rules suitable to Military Prisons in any country in which operations against the enemy may be conducted" Colonel Henderson, Inspector of Military Prisons and Detention Barracks and Umfreville, from Colchester, were members of the Committee.

It was decided that the new rules for military prisons and detention barracks were too enlightened for active service situations and that conditions in imprisonment should always be worse than conditions in the field, so severe in fact, that a short period of imprisonment would be enough of a shock to allow for an early return of the delinquent to the front.

Governor's powers were to be limited by the Army Act but would include field punishment. The Provost Marshal was to be given the powers of a Governor for those undergoing field punishment outside military prisons – I shall have more to say about field punishment later. The Committee also resolved that the system of Visitors was not relevant to an active service situation: the Governor would always be of field rank and would be given the powers of a Visitor.

Prisoners would be employed on "work of a useful character" – loading and unloading stores at ports and railheads, digging entrenchments, stone breaking and sanitary duties are quoted as examples. Should these not be available, shot drill, for a maximum of 3 hours per day, would be substituted. In the 1913 Rules for Military Prisons in the Field (the same rules, incidentally, later to be modified by Wally Watson: in 1940:), a hard day's work is scientifically defined as equivalent to 450 foot tons "and this amount should be demanded of any prisoner, particularly as his comrades in the field are probably doing at least as much". A long table follows, showing, for example, that marching a mile with a sixty pound pack equals 25.93 foot tons.

The prisons were to be located at centres in the theatre of war, such as railheads and advanced depots where the prisoner's labour could be best used.

The Committee ruled that the stage system would not be used and that all prisoners would be treated alike. It would, however, be possible to earn remission.

Diet was under no circumstances to be better than that of troops in the field and all extras and luxuries were to be excluded, including jam, cheese, tobacco, rum, pepper, tea and coffee. No variety was to be allowed and the diet was to consist "largely of the ordinary field rations – tinned beef and biscuits".

The scale was laid down as:

¾ lb of beef or mutton
24 oz bread or biscuit
4 oz potato
2 oz rice or oatmeal in form of stirabout
1 oz suet or lard or dripping to spread on biscuit
½ oz of lime juice could be served daily or ½ lb of fresh vegetables twice a week, but only when these were available to troops in the field. Punishment diets were allowed to the Governor as "only by restricted diet can the worst offenders be brought into subjection".

These then were ground rules which Umfreville took with him to France. When he got there, he found that accommodation was scarce, so he established his first two prisons on ships, one moored in the port at Havre, one on the river in Rouen. By the 25th January, 1915, both ships were full, with 700 locked up at Rouen and 500 at Havre. Before the end of the war, there were to be five military prisons in the rear areas.

Major Wally Watson, now deceased but formerly of the Corps, joined the MPSC in 1919 and his writings are the only-flimsy-account that we have of the period – and he is writing at second hand. The prisoners and staff worked a twelve hour day, loading supplies and ammunition. The staff were armed with pistols and had to prove that they had attempted to prevent an escape by showing empty cases. Escapes were few, though some are shown in the absentee circulars distributed by the APM. Wally was told of one escape, where a prisoner rode to freedom on the axle of a railway wagon.

No reports appear to have been issued by the military prisons during the war, so my information is slender indeed. What we did find were the APM, reports, but they visited the military prison only rarely and the reports are skeletal, telling only of good organisation, full cells and a shortage of staff.

One bald report during the week ending 1st July 1916 reads "A further 22 men of the NCC were transferred to the military prison, Rouen to undergo 10 years penal servitude". These were members of the Non Combatant Corps, conscientious objectors, who were subject to fierce sentences throughout the war. The entry caused me to examine the notion of conscientious objectors introduced into the rigid military discipline of a military prison and I read with interest the book "Conscience and Politics" by John Rae. It appears that most conscientious objectors served sentences in military prisons or detention barracks, rather than civil prisons, in the early years of the war. If they were serving in France, then they were also subjected to field punishment. At home, the Governor of Wandsworth, which had been taken over as a detention barracks in 1915, was dismissed when questions were asked in the House about the treatment of conscientious objectors detained under his command. The Governor Lieutenant Brooke, later wrote to the Daily Express justifying his conduct and the letter is quoted by Rae. I reproduce a part of it here:

"No doubt some of the men were treated with some roughness. There was no other way of treating them and they were not physically injured. Some of the early batches when nothing could be done with them, were taken singly and run across the yard to special rooms – airy enough but from which they could see nothing. They were fed on bread and water and some of them presently came round . . . I had them placed in special rooms, nude, with their full army kit on the floor for them to put on as soon as they were so minded. There were no blankets or substitutes for clothing left in the rooms which were quite bare. Several of the men held out naked for several hours but they gradually accepted the inevitable. Forty of the conscientious objectors who passed through my hands are now quite willing soldiers."

As I have already stated, there were finally five military prisons in the field, but references to them eluded me. There are two mentions in recently published books: In Judge Babington's "For the Sake of Example" to a mutiny in a military prison at Blargies, near Rouen; and in "The Monocled Mutineer" by Allison and Fairley. On researching both, I found that neither was a military prison, both being Field Punishment Centres. It is about field punishment that I must now write.

Flogging disappeared as a punishment in 1881 and some alternative punishment had to be devised. The Army Act of 1881 laid down that Field Punishment No 1 and No 2 would be the substitute. They were regimental punishments, together with pack drill and confinement to regimental cells. Field Punishment No 1 involved being fettered hand and foot to a fixed object for a stipulated number of hours per day. Field Punishment No 2 involved fettering but there appear to have been variations, one of which: the tying to a wheel with arms outstretched – led to uproar, as the position too much resembled crucifixion. If fetters were not available, rope could be used but had to be thick enough not to leave a permanent mark.

Robert Graves in "Goodbye to all That" describes his batman being tied to the company limber wheel when the battalion was out of the line and supposedly in rest. One can imagine the bitterness of coming from the hell of the trenches to find that rest consisted of pack drill mixed with two hours per day fettered to a wheel.

Very early in the war, the APM of the Lines of Communication is arranging Field Punishment Centres in the fortress of Boulogne, then in cages near key areas. He is already complaining of running out of handcuffs before the end of 1914 and is asking for permission to purchase handcuffs locally (local purchase of handcuffs must have been something of a problem). Soon, it was laid down that soldiers put to the Centres should head the draft lists when sentence was completed.

Inevitably, field punishment led to resentment and to disorder. At Blargies fettering was one of the main reasons for a mutiny in the FPC, for which six of the ringleaders were sentenced to death. One of the leaders was actually executed, the rest given fierce prison sentences.

There is a short entry in an APM's report in 1915 stating that patients at No 9 Stationary Hospital at Havre had attempted to free their comrades, who were tied for punishment. Many commanders objected to the punishment, as obviously did many civilians, yet it was only removed from the Army Act in 1923.

At first, the FPC's were staffed by military policemen, but in time there were so many soldiers for punishment in the FPC's and so many calls to the CMP elsewhere, the APMs were recruiting "warders" from other units.

These appear to have served a probationary period, then received extra pay.

Before I leave the subject, I would like to offer this last gem from an APM's letter book:

"It has been decided that sentence of Field Punishment

awarded to Coloured Troops, e.g. British West Indies Regiment, Bermuda Contingent, RGA, "Cape Boys" and Kaffir Labour Units etc.; who are serving on the Lines of Communication will for the present be carried out regimentally.

On no account is Field Punishment awarded to white troops to be carried out in the presence of Coloured Troops."

They may have been tied up like cattle, but my God, Sir, they were British!

By 1915, with the cream of the Old Regular Army wiped out and no conscription, the manpower situation was so desperate, that a Suspension of Sentence Act was passed. This meant that a man, after sentence continued at the front, but with the knowledge that another blot on his copybook would put him away, possibly for as long as ten years, irrespective of whether the war had finished or not. This same eagerness to return soldiers to the front was foremost in Turton's mind as Director of Detention Barracks. He writes:

"The offences committed were not really serious, but being committed on active service the sentences were very heavy and after some months I found we had many thousands of soldiers in detention barracks with sentences of 18 months and 2 years.

I pointed out to the War Office that these men ought to be in France and finally I got permission to send a Draft every week to the 3rd Echelon from Aldershot.

Every Monday we received drafts of trained and fit men from other detention barracks and every Friday we sent a draft of 150 or more from Aldershot to France.

Untrained soldiers were put through a course of musketry, taken to the bombing school to throw live bombs and were throughly trained in bayonet fighting and signalling. Altogether we sent direct to France about 40,000 soldiers, and many more thousands returned to their units thoroughly trained, fit and ready for transfer overseas."

It is obvious that the prison accommodation designed for the small regular army was not enough to hold the great numbers required for a world war and Turton had to look for new buildings. His taking over of Kilmainham in Dublin has already been mentioned also a part of Wandsworth was requisitioned – later the whole prison was to become a detention barracks. Similarly, a part of Wakefield Prison was taken over, then all of it, then the whole gaol is returned to the

Home Office in November 1916. Stafford Gaol had one wing requisitioned and some former MPSC member of its staff told Wally Watson that the grounds were so extensive that it was possible to hold a route march without leaving them. Barlinnie, near Glasgow, set apart D Block as a DB. Interestingly enough, Barlinnie was also one of the first civil prisons requisitioned in the Second World War. Hereford Gaol joined the list as did Brecon and Chelmsford. The Criminal Lunatic Asylum attached to Parkhurst Prison became a branch detention barracks and just as incongruous was the requisition of St Paul's School, West Hartlepool and St David's Convent in Mold.

Many of these had only a short life as DB's but some only closed in 1919.

Much a sign of the times, 1920 sees an Army Order setting "the ground floor of the East and West wings of the military prison at Bonner Wall, Cologne Germany, as a military prison and the 2nd, 3rd and 4th floors as a detention barracks. Colonel Jim Robinson has the documents, including his billetting requisition, for S/Sgt Oliver, who was posted to the MPDB for BAOR, when it really was on the Rhine.

As you see, my findings for the history of 1914 to 1918 are pathetically slim and I am still waiting to find more, or to have someone come forward who knows more . . . too late for this edition, but willingly accepted for the next.

9

Military Prisons in the Field
Rooke's Funnies

No war is funny and the First World War certainly wasn't. Military prisons in the field were also not the kind of places where people were rolling about in laughter. Having said that, we all know that there is some humour in most situations. Colonel A S Rooke OBE, Deputy Director of Military Prisons in France and Belgium contributed these lines to the 1935 Journal. If the reader does not find them particularly funny, at least he will find an insight into the life in a military prison of the time, as seen from the – almost – outside.

Military Prisons in the Field. 1914–1918
Colonel A S Rooke, O.B.E. (Late Deputy Director)

"It may not be amiss to give a short account of the military prisons in the Field before starting on my personal recollections. We started with one Military Prison, and as the troops in France increased so did the prisons, and at the end of the War we had ten prisons scattered over France, as far apart as Marseilles and Dunkirk.

I was astonished with the efficiency and economy with which they were run under the very able guidance of Brig-General P Umfreville, C.M.G, C.B.E., ably abetted by the various Governors and their staff. I am afraid that G.H.Q. never fully recognised this, or understood the difficulties in which we were placed. Gen. Umfreville was untiring in his work and supervision, in fact, I may say that from the beginning to the end of the War, he hardly had any rest at all, and I personally found him the finest officer I ever served under and my truest friend, and nobody regrets his early death more than I do.

On mixing with the men as I naturally did a very great deal, I have always found that you could usually soften the heart or get under the skin, as it were, of an English, Scotch,

Welsh or Irish prisoner, but a certain Colonial element understood nothing but a heavy jolt to the chin. As an instance in point, one of these great hulking fellows, when he came in first, got very fresh and started abusing our staff, and three or four of our men got rough handling him a little. He shouted out "Here, you leave me alone. I'll fight any one of you singly." His eye fell on the smallest of the four. He said, "Here, I'll take that man on." Unfortunately for him he had picked on an ex-middle-weight champion of the Army. They squared up; in less than twenty seconds the man was lying down and out with a beautiful point to the chin. When he was brought around, he said "Where am I?" They explained where he was and he said: "What hit me?" They told him it was a miscalculation and all he said was: "Mother always said I was the damnedest fool she ever came across."

Another case in point was a Glasgow tough who came in with thirty-five civil convictions for assault and battery and kicking men nearly to death when they were on the ground. I discovered that this poor fellow had a good many good points and got as friendly with him as I could under the circumstances. I explained to him what a brutal thing it was to kick a man when he was down, etc. In the room in which he was serving his time there was another notorious bully and he tried it on with our friend. The end was a foregone conclusion and the bully got more than he bargained for. That same evening they were up before me for fighting and quarrelling and I said to my friend "Are you guilty?" He said "Yes, Sir, but I took my boots off before I tackled him." This just shows that there is some good in the most depraved.

One Sunday, visiting unexpectedly at one of the Military Prisons, I dropped into the dining room of the staff, and much to my surprise saw on the table a most magnificent York ham which weighed at least twenty-five pounds, if an ounce. Knowing that they never got this in their rations I enquired from the Quartermaster-Sergeant where they got it. He looked long and hard at me, and said, "Well, to tell you the truth, Sir, the Sergeant-Major of the Detail Issue Store and I are very great friends, and as a matter of fact, he's coming to dine here himself in ten minutes."

Another amusing incident – the General inspecting another prison said to the Governor "Have there been any visitors here lately?" "Yes," he said, "Some posh General drove up last week. He didn't seem such a fool as most of them, and seemed to know all about it." The General called for the visitors book and much to his surprise he saw General Sir Nevil MacReady's signatures, then Adjutant-General of the B.E.F. This officer had started the Military Prisons and forgotten more about them than the Governor was ever likely to know. General Umfreville's face was a study.

We occasionally got in men of the R.A.M.C. and their services were utilised when possible in the prison dispensaries, when they had any. I looked in one day to ask the dispenser, an R.A.M.C. man, if he could tell me the effects of a certain drug. He answered he couldn't but would consult his colleagues when he returned from the camp – both prisoners.

Visiting a certain prison one day without letting the Governor or any of his staff know when I was coming, I asked where the Governor was. They told me he was out visiting the various working parties, so taking one of the staff with me, I did the same and eventually met the Governor on the railway siding. I found him gazing with joy on a very nice cottage piano. I asked him where he got it and he said he had taken if off a truck passing through on its way to the front, and if I would excuse him he would go and fetch a working party to convey it to the prison about a mile away. I continued my rounds and returned in about half an hour when I found the Governor white with fury. He said in unprintable language that he had never come across such a terrible lot of thieves in his life, that he hadn't been gone more than five minutes and on his return found the piano missing. I noticed that the piano was by "Collard and Collard".

For labour purposes the B.E.F. had to employ thousands of Chinese as labourers and as they increased a special prison had to be opened for them. As a well-known American writer says:
"For ways that are dark,
And tricks that are vain,
The heathen Chinese is peculiar,
Which same I am free to maintain".

Three of these Chinese gentlemen clubbed together and kept a French woman. It came to their knowledge that she had ten one-thousand franc notes hidden in her room. They wanted this, so it was decided to murder her and share the proceeds equally. They tossed up who should do it, one man to remain on watch while the other two did the job. The two ruffians stabbed her all over, and to make quite sure cut her head off neatly. The Chinese usually speak of each other as "this honourable person." The man who was on watch demanded his share from the other two who refused to give him more than two thousand francs, as they said that was enough for that honourable person. Finding his protests in vain he got back quickly to the camp and gave away the other two who were arrested with the notes on their arrival. These two were shot next morning and the Chinaman who had turned King's evidence got two years' rigorous imprisonment but the Court Martial who sentenced him forgot to take his money away and he joined us with two thousand francs. He thus earned the envy and respect of all the other Chinese prisoners. He was an intelligent fellow and was made the prison cook. When these prisoners came in and were searched, they were usually found to be in possession of every known coinage in the world.

A Labour Corps officer strolling near the Chinese camp saw a big dump where refuse was thrown away. He poked this with his stick, being of an inquisitive turn of mind, and found something hard. He dug it out and found it was a brand new Singers' Sewing Machine. He called for a working party and thirty-five other Singers' Sewing Machines were found. The point then arose, how did the Chinese get rid of these sewing machines? On enquiry it transpired that they employed a French traveller who disposed of them in France on a fifty-fifty basis. These Chinese were employed in this particular place, unloading ships, hence the mystery of the disappearance of the Singers' Sewing Machines.

Another prisoner who came in, feigned madness, and he started rolling over and over the length of the compound. He never stopped for ten days except to feed, so I got hold of an interpreter who explained to him that he could roll day and night for the two years he was with us. After ten or twelve days of this exercise, finding it was no use, he became perfectly sane.

Just one more. Towards the end of the Autumn of 1918, thousands of German prisoners were being concentrated in camps round Abbeville. Meeting the O.C. of the camp one day he said that I must come to dinner that night as they had just received the Kaiser's cook and he was preparing a turbot such as the Kaiser loved. I went – it was very good – we were well waited on by German and Austrian prisoners, oh, such splendid waiters, whilst the lovely string band played German tunes and I shall never forget their rendering of the "Blue Danube." As I listened to it the years seemed to slip away and I fancied myself a young man again dancing with the only girl in the world – to me. On the King's health being proposed and drunk, to my great astonishment the whole of the band numbering some forty performers, all shouted out "The King – God Bless Him." On telling my host how amazed I was, he said "Why?" They are all – bandsmen, waiters, etc. – men who lived in England and are longing to get back."

A.S. Rooke, Colonel

PART THREE

Between The Wars

10
Between the Wars

Conscription, by the end of the 1914-18 War, had brought the strength of the British Army to something over three million men – the pre-war army had usually been 240,000. Demobilisation started almost immediately in 1919, but not quickly enough for some, and there were many disturbances, particularly amongst troops in France, who heard of home-based soldiers being demobilised quicker than they. The DBs and military prisons opened for the emergency began to close.

Two old established military prisons also disappeared from the lists, both in 1922. These were in Cork and Dublin and had been much used, together with another at the Curragh, in the time when a large garrison was kept in Ireland. The birth of the Irish Free State saw the withdrawal of that garrison. The disbanding of the great Southern Irish regiments: The Connaught Rangers, The Leinsters, The Royal Munster Fusiliers and The Royal Dublin Fusiliers, all of whom became the basis of the Irish Free State Army, reduced further the size of the British Army.

It was not only these fine regiments that left. It had always been the usage of Britain to trim its Army to the bone at the end of any war in the name of economy. This time, the Geddes Axe hacked its way through the regiments. Ten regiments of cavalry were amalgamated with others and, including the Irish regiments, a total of twenty two battalions was taken out of the lists.

In the 1914 Prison Report, the following MP & DBs were listed:

At home: Aldershot, Colchester, Gosport, York Castle, Cork, Dublin, Stirling.

Abroad: Bermuda, Cairo, Gibraltar, Hong Kong, Jamaica, Kandy (Ceylon), Malta,

Mauritius, Pretoria, Sierra Leone, Singapore, Tientsin, Wynberg.

With the cuts in the army, inevitably there were cuts in

the MP & DB establishments. Colchester, which had only opened, together with York Castle, in 1897, closed in 1924 (York closed in the early 1930s): Gosport, the oldest establishment, closed in 1927 and Stirling, which at one time had served the whole of Scotland and a part of the North of England, closed in 1935. Thus, in 1939 the only MP & DB in the United Kingdom was Aldershot and you will later read how this becomes the base and training centre for wartime development.

The 1937 "Rules for Military Detention Barracks and Military Prisons" lists the following DBs overseas:

China: Hong Kong, Shanghai, Tientsin.

The Citadel, Cairo.

Khartoum – this was a small two man affair with eight cells certified only for a 42 hour stay.

Windmill Camp, Gibraltar.

Up Park Camp, Jamaica.

Corradino, Malta.

Tanglin, Singapore.

You will note that many of the attractive sounding pre-war postings have left the list. Some of these were not as attractive as they sound – Mauritius and Kandy both had fever troubles and much invaliding home. An interesting side-light on Mauritius is thrown in ex RSM Vic Bint's account of his wartime service, which appears elsewhere. On taking over a detention block on Mauritius during the Second World War, he found that the Gate Book had been opened by two MPSC staff in 1919. The last entry was 1920, so it is to be assumed that this was the date when it finally closed as a British Army establishment.

A description of some of the establishments will appear in the appropriate place but I must say how intriguing it has been to build up pictures of all of them during the course of this research. It was a jigsaw, where the pieces have been scattered between the prison reports, the letter book and correspondence with researchers overseas.

I am digressing. What I want to do in this chapter is to examine MPSC life during this time between the wars. I have three main sources: Wally Watson's account; Issues numbered 1 and 2 of the MPSC Journal and, to show how it should have been, the already mentioned 1937 Rules.

My copy of the Rules came from the late Doug Brinkman,

who joined the Corps in 1944. It is well used, the blue covers bent into pocket shape and recording Doug's promotions until he makes Acting RQMS. It stayed as the Bible of the MPSC throughout the Second World War and a whole way of life can be read into its stilted paragraphs.

Its tones are still Victorian and there are many echoes of the pre-Garsia rules. The Commandant is required to:

"Exercise his authority with firmness, good temper and humanity and to enforce similar conduct in his staff. It is his duty to endeavour to instil soldier-like and moral principles into the mind of every soldier under sentence, letting him see that he takes an interest in his welfare, and by his good advice and kindly admonition to endeavour to convince him of his error".

To ensure that this is done, there are nineteen paragraphs of specific instructions. The Medical Officer is given seventeen paragraphs of instruction, containing a comprehensive protection for the soldier under sentence, environmental cover and an administrative umbrella. In the pre-war DB, with its own MO and small numbers of admissions, it must have been an extremely efficient medical system and it was only with the war expansion that it was to become less so. The Chaplain is brought to heel in the first paragraph of his section of the rules. He is ordered *"to be careful not to interfere with the rules and regulations of the detention barrack or prison or the routine of discipline and work"*. He is to keep a journal of points which he wishes to raise with the Commandant and the Commandant will comment on action to be taken in the journal. However, the padre is required to report any "abuse or impropriety which may come to his knowledge". Hanging over from the old Victorian system, the chaplain has the right to examine the catalogue of library books and to ban any he considers unsuitable. What he was not allowed was to communicate with soldiers under sentence, who were not of his persuasion.

The picture of life for the MPSC member is a tough one, but his powers are clearly defined; *without being sworn before any justice, deemed to be a constable and to have such powers during his duty as any constable within his constablewick"*.

They should *"strive to acquire a moral influence over the soldier under sentence put under them and to raise the mind of the soldier to a proper feeling of moral obligation by their own example. This will secure the respect and confidence of soldiers and will make the duties of the staff more satisfactory to themselves"*.

They were required to be in their quarters and available on call, whenever they were off duty and the quarters had to be within reasonable distance from the detention barracks or prison. On duty, they were to ensure that there was no communication between their charges and to take special care that *"no ladders, planks, wheelbarrows, ropes, chains, implements or materials of any kind to facilitate escape"* were left carelessly exposed.

All of them had to be capable of instructing in and supervising industrial work and the lists of types of industrial work appear in an appendix to the Rules. They are exhaustive and I will give only a few examples.

They were divided into classes according to standard of skill required and the more skilful attracted added pay for the MPSC instructor of between £12 and £3 per year, depending on the numbers of SUS taught. Some of these skills were: cooperage, twine making, weaving, basket making, hammock making, nosebag making, mop making. Trades not sufficiently skilled to attract the annual payment were pea sorting, wood chopping, nut shelling, stone breaking, plus a few obscure ones like list slipper making and linoleum picking! Perhaps one of the Old and Bold can enlighten me!

There was also added pay for MPSC members who qualified as physical training instructors, the number of these employed at various DBs being laid down by the rules; there were four at Aldershot and one at most of the others.

All staff sergeants and sergeants "particularly those likely to proceed abroad in the next trooping season" received special instruction in clerical duties with the aim of maintaining the standard of detention barracks abroad.

Half the staff were allowed to go off duty at dinner time on Saturday until 6.30am on the following Monday and staff allowed free at the Commandant's discretion on Bank Holidays. During these times, the soldiers under sentence were given a task of work in their cells. If on night duty, one night in seven was allowed free.

The rules also cover civilian employees, who were required to salute any commissioned officer, whether in uniform or not and could be dismissed for drunkenness. Both civilians and MPSC members are informed that "Sobriety among the staff is so important that the circumstances of the intoxication, and the fact that the member of the staff may not have been prevented from carrying out his duty, will not be taken into consideration".

Similarly, the staff are warned against swearing, knowingly incurring debts which they are unable to repay, the habit of frequenting public houses, keeping bad company, gambling or other disreputable conduct". Failing to comply would result in the civilian being dismissed and the MPSC member being returned to his former corps.

Routine when on duty was exactly and inflexibly laid down, though with slight variations on hot weather stations. It was a day starting with the ringing of a bell at 6.30, when all the staff paraded and were inspected by the sergeant major, then keys were issued. Breakfast was at 8am, apart from the duty patrol. Dinner was at 12.30pm, then duty continued until 4.15pm or 7.30pm, when the Night Watch took over. Failures of punctuality were severely punished and several accounts tell of the gates of Aldershot being closed at 6.29am, with a severe reprimand for the unfortunate still outside.

Life was ruled by the tell-tale clock, which was still in use when Colonel Jim Robinson joined the Corps and about which more will be said later. Incredible though it may seem, these were on Colchester equipment tables until the late seventies.

And the life of the soldier under sentence? He was, of course, admitted in uniform and in full marching order, minus weapons, the mounted services carrying "Marching Order – on the man". He was searched "in a manner with due regard to decency and self-respect", weighed, photographed and measured. It is stipulated that the photograph was to be given to no person not officially authorised to receive it. He was given a bath.

In a detention barracks, his day started at 6am, when he would rise and clean his cell. At 6.35, the roll was called, slops collected and room inspected, then work began and carried on until 8am, when he had breakfast, a meal not greatly different from that served in the Nineteenth Century military prison. He then cleaned and prepared his equipment, was "closetted" and on parade at 9.30am for military training. His military training included drill, with and without arms, weapon training, including miniature cartridge practice, Morse signalling (with gunners also learning semaphore), minor tactics (on the blackboard only!) and lectures on a wide variety of subjects, including camouflage. . . . and crime and punishment! They also learned how to pitch and strike tents and anti-gas drill. Trained soldiers were to use the miniature range at least once a week.

After dinner at 12.20pm, the SUS returned to their rooms and worked until afternoon parade, when some did more military training and others school work, then tea and back to the cell to work and clean equipment. From seven until eight o'clock, when they were locked up for the night, they cleaned equipment and read. Lights out was at 9pm.

A man in military prison followed an almost identical routine, apart from the fact that work replaced military training. Sunday routine in both DB and military prison was based on the same timetable: a 6.30am reveille, some general cleaning of the cells and corridors; a church service (compulsory) and long periods of being locked up.

A stage system was in operation, allowing a man to earn progressively more privileges by good behaviour and industry. There were two stages and the main difference appears to be that a soldier in Stage Two was able to sleep on a mattress every night; could write and receive more letters and "to communicate for periods of twenty minutes daily".

The idea of restricting communication between soldiers under sentence was a hang-over from the old Victorian "silent" system, whereby prisoners were totally insulated from their fellows: in church, they stood in walled pews where only the pulpit was visible; a prisoner meeting anyone in the corridor turned his face to the wall. At one stage, masks were worn to keep the face turned forward. The original idea was to prevent contamination of the less evil by the habitual criminal, but it had the additional and practical advantage of preventing conspiracy. After being sealed up in his own silence, reaching Stage Two and being able to communicate must have seemed like privilege indeed. The snag was that it was for twenty minutes a day only; all conversations were conducted within hearing range of a staff member and the twenty minutes were split into two periods of ten minutes. Should they find a lack of suitable topics of conversation, "the Commandant will arrange that special items of news which may be of interest to the men will be announced to the privileged men when formed up". They are, however, allowed to talk of subjects other than the announced item, provided they are not of an insubordinate nature.

Punishment is exhaustively handled in the Rules, as one would expect and there are eighteen punishable situations stipulated, ranging from singing and whistling, to escape. Item Eighteen expands the list by ensuring that any other offence against good order and discipline will also be punishable. Punishments range from close confinement, through loss of remission to deprivation of library books. Loss of mattress for up to three days is the punishment for idleness and a complete chapter deals with Punishment Diets 1,2 and 3. Ray Rigby, in his sensational sequel to his equally sensational "The Hill", sees PD1 as the means by which the RSM of a Detention Barracks seeks to break down the resistance of two recalcitrant Glaswegian soldiers. Mr Rigby puts them into solitary cells for eighteen days PD1. Mr Rigby may well have spent some time in a Field Punishment Centre or a Detention Barracks and thus gathered his material for his two best sellers, but I doubt that he encountered a case where Punishment Diet No 1 was ordered for such a long period, even within an establishment run by the sadistic RSM Wilson, for PD1 is one pound of bread with water. Even in the hardest Victorian days, it was realised that such a diet over a long sentence would permanently damage the health of the man being punished. In the Rules, it is made clear that, should it be ordered for a period exceeding three days, (the longest time that a Commandant, incidentally, could award), then PD1 had to be alternated with equal periods on a normal DB diet. An award of PD1 for longer than three days could only be ordered by a board of visitors and they were restricted to a maximum of fifteen days, with the alternate and equal stipulation made above. But if as a result of several different awards of PD1 they have completed a total of twenty one days on that diet, including the alternate three days, they must then have seven clear days on the normal DB diet. Homework, Mr Rigby!

Another popular misconception is that prisoners and soldiers under sentence could be chained as a punishment. We have already seen that this did indeed happen in the First World War as part of field punishment, but the outcry after the war ensured that chaining as a form of punishment would never happen again. Handcuffs could only be applied in extreme cases of violence. The type of handcuff was severely restricted and their use reported to the General Officer

Commanding. Similarly the use of body belts and strait waistcoats were severely circumscribed. It is remotely possible that some of these rules were flouted, but I myself have been able to find no evidence of this.

However long he did, sometime the soldier under sentence would leave the detention barracks or military prison, in the first case to return to his unit, one hopes as a better soldier; in the other to be discharged from the service. The soldier returning to his unit was, until 1930, escorted back to that unit. In 1930, it was decided that his dignity would be better preserved by his being discharged at the railway station nearest to the detention barracks. From 1935, he was discharged at the DB gate.

For the soldier being dismissed the service, the rules have little to offer. If he had behaved himself in the military prison, he would be recommended for a gratuity from the Discharged Prisoners Aid Society. If there was no branch of the Society available, "the Commandant may expend a sum not exceeding £1 as subsistence money to keep the man while seeking work, provided that proper precautions are taken to ensure that this money is judiciously spent". Shades of earlier days!

In addition, the discharged man was given his dinner before leaving. His unit was required to supply him with minimal civilian clothing as laid down in Clothing Regulations and he was allowed to keep his regimental shirt, boots, socks and braces. He must have presented an interesting figure on Aldershot station.

I have dealt heavily with the Rules in this chapter. In my next, I shall be looking at the men who were applying these rules, as they saw themselves.

11
Between the Wars: Personal Views

As I write this, I have at my side two copies of the MPSC Journal, dulled red covers and yellowing pages, dated April 1936.

Each of the Journals contains a seniority roll for the Corps, much hacked about and amended, both with the feeling of "dead men's boots" about them. Four sergeant majors are listed, one being Sergeant Major Chiddy, the executioner in Mesopotamia, another – newly moved from QMS in that year – is Sergeant Major Wally Watson, whose personal account of these times will appear later in the chapter.

Their station appears at the side of their names. Most of them are stationed in Aldershot, but others are in China, Malta, Egypt, Singapore, Gibraltar, Jamaica, with another heavy contingent in the 1935 Journal at Stirling. By 1936, these latter have been posted elsewhere. Quite low down the staff sergeants' list comes S Sgt W Lloyd, who later became a figure of considerable importance in the Corps.

The new journal is struggling to attract contributors hoping particularly for news from the out stations. Fortunately for me, some of the foreign stations have obliged, so that we have a slight insight into life outside Aldershot. Aldershot itself, on the evidence of the Journal, would appear to have been a training ground for tennis, darts and shooting. In Stirling, life would seem to have been made up of whist and bowling in their proper seasons and family trips to the beauty spots of Scotland. The only mention of SUS comes in the jokes section issued as a supplement called "The Glasshouse Gazette and numbered PD No.1.

From Singapore comes my only real description of the Singapore DB at Tanglin. According to the report, it was an 1870 barracks with accommodation for 32 SUS, but the average number of SUS inside at any one time appears to have been between six and ten, remarkable when one considers the later military importance of Singapore. The staff consisted of two MPSC and three attached NCOs from the Garrison for Nightwatch and gate duties. The SUSs' routine was drill, PT and school in the morning, then oatcrushing, harness cleaning and cookhouse utensil cleaning in the afternoon.

From Malta, again, jokes and accounts of games against the Fleet make up the main news. The report is labelled as coming from the Island of Yells, Bells and Smells, which gives a notion of the level of humour. There then follows an account of the recreation facilities of the island. It's all poor stuff for the 1987 historian.

Half of the 1935 Journal is given up to Capt SJ Griffin, who is trying to drum up cooperation from members, to help along his history of the Corps. He is hoping that "a mass of data, at present hidden, will come to light". How well I know the feeling!

The 1936 Journal writes of the 9th Annual Reunion, held in London, traditionally on Cup Final Day. A Corps tie is being offered at half a crown (silk finish 4s 6d). The Association funds have now reached £277. Griffin attempts to instil enthusiasm for a Corps History.

Elsewhere in the Journal, the last days of the Stirling DB are recorded, and I think the article is worth recording in full.

Stirling

The closing of the Military Prison and Detention Barrack, Stirling, on the 30th September 1935, ends another chapter in the Corps' history.

It is a chapter that will have many happy memories for all who have been privileged to be stationed there, and many lasting associations have been made during the sojourn of the MPSC in that town.

The building, a very imposing one with its battlements, was originally built as a "Debtors' Prison" about 100 years ago, and stands about half way up Stirling Rock towards the Castle and commands imposing views from the Grampians to Falkirk and from the Forth Bridge to Bannockburn.

It was taken over as a Detention Barrack about 48 years ago, and, although small compared with Aldershot, served at various times all Scotland, Northern Ireland, and latterly Northern England, but as was inevitable it is now only a place of memories.

Over a period of years the Detention Barrack and Staff have become grafted on the social life of Stirling and were associated with several sporting and charitable organisations in the Burgh. This happy fraternisation has been commemorated by the donation to the Bowling Club in Albert Place of a Silver Cup, and to the Guildhall Club of a competitive Shield.

By kind permission of the Provost and Dean of the Guild the farewell supper and concert took place in the Ancient Guildhall on the 10th September 1935, and, although for many an occasion of regret, a very enjoyable evening was spent.

Some eighty persons sat down to supper and afterwards the company settled to enjoy a lengthy and excellent programme under the genial chairmanship of SM Watson. Amongst the guests were Captain JH Gurney, Commandant; Mr Corrie, of the "Stirling Observer", Mr Watt, Albert Place Bowling Club; Baillie Amier, Stirling Burgh Council; and last but not least Mr H Hyde, the oldest Hon. Member of the Mess.

During the evening the Honorary Members of the Mess presented the Staff with mementos in the form of silver "Skean Dhu" brooches and this was reciprocated by the presentation to the Honorary Members of a Corps Badge mounted on a small shield with the badge of the Royal Burgh of Stirling, the "Wolf on the Craig".

Many members of the MPSC who read this in the odd corners of the globe will no doubt re-echo the sentiments expressed by SM Watson when he thanked the guests for the hospitality and good fellowship they had always shown to the Staff in Stirling. Replies on behalf of the Hon. Members were mady by Mr T Corrie and Mr Hyde, whilst Baillie Amier spoke on behalf of the Burgh council."

Watson will have more to say about the Citadel, Cairo later in this chapter, but from the Journal, we learn that the area once the DB square, has been converted to a garden. There is a purpose built cinema and a new treadle carding machine has been installed. There are the inevitable jokes.

Gibraltar reports that the staff have been trying without success to find information on the history of the military prison and later DB on the Rock . . . we are still trying.

From Singapore, there is report of expansion of the

garrison. Changi, ironically, is regarded as their change of air station.

Shanghai reports that it has now become a two year station, much to the satisfaction of the staff. The place has been refurbished and the bamboo fencing has been replaced by something which will keep the DB out of the gaze of the military and the ever curious Chinese.

Unfortunately for my researches, comments on their work are few. Also, unfortunately, the Journal appears to have died a death after 1936 to be revived as a typewritten and duplicated affair after the Second World War.

Major Wally Watson, the sergeant major of 1935, is far more help, having taken time during his retirement to write down his experiences. I feel that these will give as good a picture as possible of the life of the small Corps, in the time before the Second World War forced dangerously rapid expansion.

Wally joined the Corps at Aldershot in 1919:

"Training for the SUS at this time was very stiff and no time was lost during the day. All parades were in full Marching Order (what a change today) and except for drill movements all at the "double". Idle men, goodness help them, "On the hands down, arms bend" until they dropped, all in Marching Order. Musketry, Signals, PT. Gas Training, Assault Course, Bridge Building, Semaphore etc., really a full training course at that time. This was all carried out in the mornings and special squads in the afternoon. In the afternoon industrial work, Bedmaking, Coir Teasing, Mat making, headrope making were the industries carried out. During the dinner hour and during lock up period at night, men on Bedmaking and Matmaking were tasked – Sewing up and tabbing biscuits six per hour, Matmaking four inches per hour. One would observe S Sgt Stiff, the Industrial NCO, going around next morning checking and measuring tasks. Those men who were not capable of such work were employed cleaning rusty tins and the number each man was given had to be seen to be believed. Four dirty meat dishes for an evening or sixteen diet tins, and they HAD to be polished on time i.e. 7.30pm or goodness help the poor unfortunate. Bathbricks, soap and rag were the materials supplied. Very few came back the second time. Rooms were spotless and once a man became used to the routine he never entered his room with his boots on, always removing them at his room door and put down bits of blanket to step on. The Patrol NCO was continually going round and observing each man at work and keeping them at it during lock up hours.

Until I became used to it I could not make out whom these men were talking to in their rooms, and then I realised that they were either talking to their wives' or sweethearts' photographs or to themselves in the mirror. It was amusing for the staff but it must have been Hell for the men locked up from 4.15pm until 6.00 or 6.30 next morning. On Sundays only exercise for one hour, church and locked up for the remainder.

I well remember my first few months at the "Glasshouse". During lock up hours all was silent, but as soon as the staff entered the hall it was one roar until all men were out on parade. It seemed that the staff were competing one against the other as to whom could make the most noise. A whistle would blow and "silence", then on "carry on" the uproar would commence again. We poor probationers could not understand anything that was going on. It was simply a matter of watching and learning by time and using your judgement and the six months were up by the time you fell into the routine.

At this period all meals for the men were drawn from the kitchen in the round prison diet tins with one portion in the bottom and one in the top. These were taken to the landings in trays and one member of the staff supervised the issue whilst one unlocked and the other locked up. Invariably a diet was missing, then a search on that particular landing and an empty tin found. God knows how it was done, but the NCO concerned was on the mat next morning and the Commandant, invariably kept the probationers "reports" in an exercise book, which was destroyed when you were transferred, being selected. Very few were RTU'd as unsuitable. Naturally this kind of disciplinary training produced some excellent soldiers.

Admissions to Aldershot at this time were searched and kit checked in front of the reception room, and immediately they were stripped and bathed and the reception cleaner would be waiting in the bathroom for any man that was awkward or giving trouble and somehow or other the man would find

83

himself tripping over and falling into a bath of cold water – a pure accident.

Office hours was also a sight to see. Men for office would line up in a single file outside the side door, the man ready to go in would be on the mat at the end of the passage with an NCO escort in front of him, and the NCO giving evidence in rear. On the word "quick march" the whole party would cover the passage of about six yards in three paces and slide and land in front of the Commandant strictly to attention. The same record would be taken in getting out of the office.

All this time with a staff of approximately one hundred the "Glasshouse" had no Mess and MPSC attached to the RAMC at the Connaught Hospital for this. However, most evenings and sometimes at noon you would see perhaps six or seven trying to get in the space for three in the "Queens' Jug and Bottle department". The staff's sleeping quarters were the top half of the married quarters, the bottom half being occupied by the lucky old hands with their familes. These single quarters whilst comfortable and no restrictions regarding lights out, were rather crowded, and owing to the long and early hours of duty it was a scramble when the bells went for reveille, quarter and five minutes to go for duty. I remember one Lance Corporal who would stay in bed to the five minutes bell, scramble out, back to bed at breakfast time and then another scramble and instead of shaving he would powder his face and shave at dinner time. As time went by he turned out an excellent Staff Sergeant and I served with him in several other stations.

At this period all men under sentence who were suffering from VD were transferred to Woking and this was one of the plumb duties for the staff, as it was a day out and a nice change."

After a two year tour in Mesopotamia, which is described elsewhere, Wally Watson returned to UK and was posted to Stirling already described in this chapter.

With the trooping season, Wally next went to the Citadel, Cairo:

"Egypt with the DB in the Citadel, Cairo seemed to be the most popular. This establishment was situated in the old Turkish Prison in the Citadel, and had 48 single rooms with other rooms suitable for "association" accommodation, but these were not required. The Citadel DB had been functioning for many years and one of the old Governors was later Asst Commandant of the Cairo City Police, namely Mr Tegg and in World War II another of the earlier Commandants returned to us namely Colonel CJ Newport OBE. The Citadel was situated high above the city and out of the Staff Quarters one could look over the whole of Cairo, also next door was the renowned Mohamed Ali Mosque.

Always on off duty hours it was most interesting to go to the Mosque and see the visitors touring round, visitors from all parts of the world. On the ramparts of the Mosque there was a horseshoe cut out in the stone. This was about three quarters of an inch deep and the guides would relate to the tourists that this was the inprint of the horse of a Mameluke who escaped the slaughter of the Mamelukes in the Citadel some 150 years previously. Actually this was cut out by a member of the MPSC while being taken for exercise everyday whilst awaiting court martial. I happened to be there one day and heard the old story, and could not help laughing. A tourist asked what I was laughing at and I told her the real origin of the Horse Shoe. She thanked me and told me her name – Mary Pickford!

Khartoum was a branch of Cairo. This was only a small place of eight rooms and was staffed by one Staff Sergeant and a local NCO. With Cairo and many other overseas DB's it continued well into the Second World War."

Watson came back to Aldershot in time for the Second World War and my account of the MPSC with the BEF in the chapter owes a considerable amount to his description.

12
Mission to Mespot

Both Wally Watson and an unknown source give details of a MPSC task somewhat off the main track of normal prison and DB duties: a party of twelve MPSC staff was sent to Mesopotamia, to do duty at two military prisons, which, until then had been manned by the Military Police.

Two parties sailed in late 1920 and the journey itself appears to have been a memorable experience for both groups. Wally Watson's group embarked on the "Brandenburg", a confiscated German cargo ship, converted to a trooper. Here, the major hazard was the jury-rigged toilets, which were built on the open deck and offered little comfort in rough seas. The other party used a purpose built troopship: the TS Hardinge, which reached Bombay without event. They then transferred to a smaller vessel for the journey up the Persian Gulf to Basra. They had been running for three days and a shipboard concert was under way, when fire broke out below and all were called to assist. The OC troops was so impressed by the action of the MPSC that he put out a complimentary order of the day and reported their conduct to the GOC, Mesopotamia.

One of the parties took over the military prison at Basra; the other the prison in Baghdad.

Both were mud built structures, housing mainly sepoys and the warders were havildars, naiks and lance naiks from the Indian service. The main road into the compound was soft-topped and became a sliding mess of mud in the wet season. The sepoy prisoners were accommodated in long bungalow huts of mud with reed-thatched roofs and one of their prison tasks was to make the string-sprung charpoys on which they slept.

The sepoys formed the main prison population and there was accommodation for only thirty European prisoners. These were not only from the military force: occasionally, deportees were housed before they were shipped out. One Frenchman is mentioned and a German but also many Turks.

On arrival, the first thing to happen to half the party was the award of the Iraq Medal, for they arrived in Basra on the day when the name Mesopotamia was dropped and the country was renamed Iraq. Only half got the medal, as the other half had not yet disembarked.

The staff accommodation was outside the compound. It, too, was mud built and the walls were three foot thick to keep out the heat. There were earthen floors. Wally Watson speaks of spreading a sheet as a canopy over his bed during the wet season to protect against the melting mud of the upper walls.

On arrival of the MPSC party, there was no building organised as a mess and the favoured site was already occupied by an Indian shop. This, mysteriously, burned down and the Garrison Fire Brigade was unable to save it. Soon afterwards, the mess rose, phoenix-like, from the ashes.

With a maximum of thirty prisoners, the workload was not excessive and various hobbies and pastimes blossomed. Tortoise hunting was not merely a lust for the chase: the shells were transformed into inkstands and picture frames. Kingfishers were hunted for their feathers – this was in the days, remember, when the word conservation meant saving water! Wally Watson took up photography.

But the high spot of the sporting calendar was the periodic wild-dog hunt. Buckshot guns and cartridges were drawn up and the hunting party moved out to one of the neighbouring villages, where there were always surplus dogs, always roving wild.

Staff sergeant Chiddy, who was doing the CQMS for the party, managed to combine business with pleasure. One of his tasks was touring for extra stores and he also checked outside working parties. He had earlier qualified as a mounted infantryman and had the certificate to prove it, so he toured on duty mounted, the horse being a member of the Fire Brigade Pump Towing team in its normal role. When staff Chiddy was about his duties, the fire brigade could not answer its calls!

The staff decided that the precarious state of the mud road and the unregimental appearance of the pounded mud used as a parade ground, did not lend themselves to the Corps image and they resolved to improve them. A tennis court for the mess also appeared desirable. Stone for hard core was not readily available, but a liquorice factory not too far from the camp was beginning to fall down, so prisoners were put to "quarrying" it, then carrying the loose stone and brick back to camp, where they laid an all-weather road and the base of the square. This was completed before the owner of the liquorice factory became aware of the shrinking of his assets. This was a pity, as the next project was to be a church in the British compound (after reading the accounts, I had the feeling that a church was sorely needed!). The sacred edifice was finally built of mud and I feel that the description of its furnishing is best quoted from the original, a masterpiece of understatement and wide-eyed innocence:

"Having completed our church, we required a set of Communion rails. These we found in an old YMCA hut out in the desert, likewise window frames and teak to make a cross". Butter would not melt. . . .

Significantly, little is said in the accounts about the actual work and routine, though the hot weather appears to have limited outdoor work for the British SUS. They all say much about the Indian part of the establishment, which I think rather shook them all at first, though the later description will show that some Corps members adapted rather well.

On first arrival, the MPSC contingent had been issued with a cat o'nine tails, at which they had been vaguely surprised, but found that it was a necessary piece of equipment for the Indian warders and was used with enthusiasm and regularity. The thing that really surprised the MPSC was that no firm admission and release procedure was practised and this they remedied from the beginning. They were amazed that the sepoys often did not know why they had been sent for "rigorous imprisonment": the usual sentence. Often, they did not even know how long their sentence was to last!

On arrival, the sepoy prisoner was dressed in ticken shirt and shorts, white with blue stripes. He was then chained, with a chain passing from one wrist to the opposite ankle. The chain was then hitched to a string at the waist and the sound of rattling chains was the normal background to life throughout the time that the MPSC contingent was in Iraq. Feeding the prisoners was difficult, as, despite the animal-like treatment of chain and flog, the diet appropriate to caste and creed was meticulously followed.

In the main prison compound stood a gallows. It was not there for decorative purposes: two sepoys were executed in the eighteen months of the MPSC tour . . . two MPSC NCOs were the executioners (Ssgts Goodman and Chiddy, the only two executioners in the history of the MPSC. Two were required, as one stood on the platform and fitted the rope: the other sprung the trap from below. By a grotesque error, the first execution went wrong and the condemned man dropped through the trap before the rope had been put around his neck. He then calmly climbed back up the steps to the platform and placed himself ready for the second try, which was successful. For their efforts, the man on the platform was paid £1 and the man below ten shillings.

At the end of eighteen months – incidentally, the hottest months that had been recorded in Iraq to that time, economies at home led to recall of the MPSC and the defence of Iraq became a RAF responsibility.

PART FOUR

The Second World War

13

Wally Watson Remembers

In July 1939, Wally Watson, by this time a WOI, was serving at the Citadel in Cairo. He had applied for a five year extension of his tour, but was ordered home with a posting to Shepton Mallet, which was in the process of being taken over for military use. The posting was changed to Aldershot when mobilisation was ordered. Two military prisons were to be established in the field, commanded by Lieutenant Colonel J McK Gordon (of whom much will be heard in a later chapter). It was arranged that, apart from overall command, Colonel Gordon would be Commandant of No.1 Military Prison, with Wally as RSM and WOII Willy Gee as RQMS. No.2 would be commanded by Major Ross with RSM Parker. The staff would consist primarily of reservists and the account of one of these: Rea, appears later.

Only one man at Aldershot had the experience of a military prison in the field, an ex RQMS Glover, and his experience was in the First World War! The regulations for Military Prisons in the Field were dated 1912!

The party moved over the Channel to Cherbourg, where they were accommodated in a rickety cavalry barracks with wire netting bunks and earthen floors. The barracks was already occupied by two hundred reservists, who were employed unloading equipment and the first job of the MPSC in France was to assist the APM in preventing pilferage.

Finally the staff of No.1 was ordered to Arras, where the prison was to be established and where GHQ was already being set up. The staff block for the prison was in a large house and cooking was done in the courtyard. Colonel Gordon found that GHQ had not decided on the actual role of the military prison, that he himself had been appointed Town Major with Wally as Town RSM, so Gordon decided that he would take the initiative and establish Field Punishment Centres as and where required.

The first FPC was established at Arras, a small one accommodating only 20 men. This was joined by another in Arras, numbered Three, in a factory, but the best was No.2 in Wagnonville: an agricultural college, with a central courtyard adaptable as a drill square. Later, No.4 was set up in a large house in Lens. Customers were not slow in arriving.

This was the time of the Phoney War, and the British Army was occupied digging trenches to compensate for the lack of preparation of the Belgians.

They were working in open country in dirty conditions most of the time, so occasional parties would be brought into Arras for a bath and relaxation. It was this circumstance that finally made Colonel Gordon aware of the fact that his HQ was situated in the middle of the Red Lamp district.

Both Colonel Gordon and Wally were not happy with the old regulations, which bore little relationship to modern circumstances, so Wally was given the task of rewriting them in his spare time. Meanwhile, four old hands of the MPSC arrived to join him and NCOs were attached from BEF units. These were given a training course at the Wagnonville FPC and many of them later joined the Corps.

The 10th of May saw the end of the Phoney War, when the powers of Blitzkrieg were unleashed on Belgium and Holland. The SUS were returned to their units, but the FPCs began to fill up again. Defensive positions were being dug, as civilians loaded their belongings on carts, cars, on prams and started to move West. Wally's "landlord" handed him the house keys and told him to look after it. He comments on the remarkable way that houses still filled with a departed owner's possessions were taken over and made into strongpoints without looting.

A Guards battalion in the Arras area had issued rifles, antitank rifles and some Bren guns to the FPCs and the SUS were formed into squads under the staff. Ammunition was distributed, as were all stocks of cigarettes, sweets etc.

It did not come to a confrontation with the Germans. The fortifications were barely completed, when the whole group was ordered to march West to Bethune, marching 20 kilometers until they came to a lorry park, which the RASC was about to destroy. They requisitioned three trucks and made it as far as St. Omer, having often to stop on the way and dive for cover from low flying German fighters. Just outside St. Omer, Wally saw a figure ahead that he was sure was a

German. He found in fact that it was a RAF sentry who had been told to stay at his post until relieved. He was guarding a RAF stores dump, where all equipment had been smashed, apart from a Nuffield radio, which Wally requisitioned. This later became their news lifeline. In the large house which the RAF had used as billets, the party found a full scale dinner cooking and about 200 loaves of bread, all disposed of very quickly. The RAF sentry was dismissed and the party never saw him again.

On hearing that Boulogne had fallen to the Germans, Colonel Gordon decided that they would aim for Calais. After a number of close shaves, they arrived there. They were ordered to take the SUS to the Citadel and to find themselves a boat. They finally located one that had just unloaded armoured cars. As they boarded, there was an aerial dogfight above them and the British pilot ditched in the sea near their ship. He was to join them on their return to England. The boat docked at Southampton and the party was billeted in a school, where they were fed gargantuan lunches, but told to have no communication with civilians outside. Wally was keen to assure his wife, so he wrote out a telegram on toilet paper, wrote a message "You can have this if you send the telegram" and wrapped both pieces of paper around a half crown. He waited for a young boy to pass the window and tossed the wrapped coin down to him. Amazingly the message was received by Wally's wife.

Finally, the HQ party returned to Aldershot, to find that the other FPC parties were still filtering back. The waste ground around the DB was a carpet of French and Belgians, lying around on groundsheets, covered by greatcoats: "The local girls", writes Wally "were having a great time".

Colonel Gordon was detailed as Commandant to the military prison, which was to be opened in Hull and Wally was posted with him as the RSM there. Hull Military Prison was bombed soon after its opening and staff and SUS were transferred to Northallerton Gaol, of which more will be said later.

A Reservists Eye View

Mr Rea was one of the reservists mentioned by Wally Watson. He had served with the Grenadier Guards, then gone to the reserve. He joined the civil prison service, then was posted to Aldershot when mobilisation was proclaimed.

His first impressions of Aldershot were shattering: the RSM was WOI "Taffy" Lloyd and he seemed set to put his imprint on the new arrivals, for Rea found that he was only one of several prison officers, who had been mustered into the MPSC. Relationships between them and the regulars were strained. One RQMS, formerly of an Irish regiment, a small man eager to compensate for his height, used regularly the expression "I will hang you on the hook" as a warning to the newly joined. He was disconcerted when one of the reservists decided that the expression should be interpreted literally and hung the RQMS by the back of his collar from the Sergeants' mess hat rack.

Relations, then, were not good at first and Rea jumped at the opportunity to volunteer for the FPC group being assembled for the BEF.

He was in the group for Arras, which became No. 3 FPC. Accommodation was in a former Boy Scout hut and was basic. The first job of the party was to make bed frames for themselves, using chicken wire and two by two timber. Cooking was done on a Soyer stove outside in the yard and food was always cold when it arrived at the table. Bathing consisted of standing with one foot in a square petrol can and the other foot in another, then sloshing water over oneself with an aluminium camp bowl. Customers started to arrive and conditions became better. Lice were a problem amongst the SUS and few of the staff had much experience of them. In an attempt to get rid of the vermin, Rea visited the MO in the local French barracks to ask for advice, to be told with a shrug "They come, they go". They finally decided that paraffin was more effective than the French method.

It was the Phoney War, so phoney that the staff could be sent on UK leave, many returning with their tennis gear. . . . until the 10th of May 1940.

Alec Rea's part in the defensive arrangements described by Wally Watson covered a town park. In the park was a statue of Romulus and Remus and a Bren was mounted beneath the suckling mother wolf. Houses were made into strong-points but then, as we have already seen, the order to retreat was given and the group started to move West. The party moved independently of Colonel Gordon's party and their encounters along the way have something of the picaresque novel about them.

The tide of refugees was still in spate and progress was slow – made slower by the regular strafing of the Luftwaffe. At one crossroads, they came across a sight not common on French roads: a fully kilted colour sergeant, who had lost his unit. His battalion, he told them, had been years in India and had trooped home arriving at Waterloo Station on the day of the breakthrough to be told that they were required to entrain immediately for France. He had come back to fetch rations and had had his truck shot from under him. He was, he said, dying for a number nine (the horse-pill-like laxative and universal panacea of the old army). He was given two and took them both, was last seen in the corner of a field with raised kilt.

The FPC party trundled on, then set up their soyer stove in a wood with the ingredients for an all-in stew. The stew was coming on nicely, when a German fighter strafed the wood, the only casualty being the stew pan, which was riddled with holes and released brown juices through large holes. The meal consisted of the soggy and sparse remnants of the pot plus two large tins of golden syrup, which were dished out to staff and SUS at the rate of one teaspoon each.

They continued their journey until they were hailed by a Belfast voice from a ditch at the one side of the road. Rea went over, to meet two characters, whom he christened Dilly and Dally in his mind. They were Pioneers and had been separated from their unit in circumstances which Rea never ascertained, but such that a gallon jar of rum had become detached with them. They were far enough down the jar to be able to talk about themselves, but not to be able to remember the recent past. They had, it seemed, served together in the First World War, had married two sisters and both bought fish and chip shops in Belfast. When the new war started, they had joined on the first day. As they told Rea this, they were working systematically through an enamelled mug each of issue rum and the story began to trail and slur towards the end, until both dropped off to sleep. Rea's party took the rest of the rum and Dilly and Dally's rifles, leaving them a whipround of francs and a white flag.

A French Army bus pushed its way through the refugee streams, empty and heading West. Sergeant Chris Payne, who, like Rea was a Grenadier reservist and who spoke some French, stopped the bus and asked the driver why he was driving Westwards empty when the roads were full of fleeing women and children. The bus driver shrugged and gunned his engine, so Payne pulled his pistol, then herded a flock of refugees aboard.

By this time, the party had no rations and there was of course, nothing to be had in the villages they passed, which, incidentally, seemed evenly balanced between pro-British and pro-German sympathies. At last they reached Calais, where they were given a tin of cold sausage each. Miraculously, the RQMS – in the manner of such men – managed to acquire a bottle of whisky and they dined off sausage from the tin, swilled down by whisky from the bottle: a meal that Alec Rea remembered with joy.

They were allocated a boat and arrived in Dover after being dive bombed twice, then all entrained for Aldershot, where Rea received his posting order to Chorley, a town he remembers with affection.

14

The Dempsey Report

The Second World War was to be the occasion when, for the first time in modern British history, universal conscription was introduced at the very beginning of a war. The National Service Acts cast a very wide and fine meshed net and much that was caught in the net was not worth the catching. As a result, the rooms of Aldershot, designed under the Victorian system as single cells, were housing three SUS in each. Temporary alternatives were being sought and these temporaries will be the subject of subsequent chapters.

Incredibly, in 1941, when Britain had her back to the wall, a committee was convened with the terms of reference:

To enquire and report as to whether the treatment, training, accommodation and feeding of soldiers under sentence in Military Prisons and Detention Barracks is in accordance with modern standards and satisfies the requirements of a war-time army.

The Committee was headed by the commander of an armoured division Major General WC Dempsey DSO MC, who was later to be General Sir Miles Dempsey and to command the Second Army from D Day onwards. His committee had two obvious members: Colonel JA Fraser DSO DCM, the Inspector of Military Prisons and Detention Barracks and Mr. Alex Paterson MC, the Commissioner of Civil Prisons. The two other members were less obvious. Wing Commander EL Ardley from the Air Ministry represented the fact that DBs had a small RAF element. The last member was Major Geoffrey Gilbey MC, who, in the same year as the committee assembled, had opened and was commanding a new departure in military corrective training: The Young Soldiers Training Camp, Northern Command. I shall have more to say about this later.

The Committee called five Commanding Officers as witnesses and had the advice throughout of the Governor of Wandsworth Civil Prison. All members were to visit Aldershot, Fort Darland, Chorley, Sowerby Bridge, Maidstone Civil Prison and Stakehill (which was in the process of opening). It is a pity that wartime paper restrictions would not allow for the verbatim recording of the CO's evidence, nor for an account of the DBs visited.

The report starts with an extremely shrewd analysis of the "customers":

"In quality they vary greatly, and the causes of their default are as diverse. Young men in countless numbers whom in normal times would never have sought to join the Army, or had they been so drawn would never have been accepted for service, are now compelled to be soldiers. The process of their training must often cut very sharply across instinct and experience. The slow-moving must grow brisker, the self-willed must obey without question, and the scruffy must get clean. For the first time in their lives many leave home for strange surroundings, exchanging crowded streets for open spaces. When to these tribulations is added the almost inevitable boredom of camp-life, where dullness is a poor return for safety, it is not surprising that there are many defaulters, and that they should be several types of human material."

They then examine the methods, which have been tried before, producing in a paragraph the summary of this book up to the time of the report, finishing:

Those who in recent years have been charged with the administration and command of Military Prisons and Detention Barracks, have done much to mitigate the ruthless severity of the earliest regime, and have introduced a more human and constructive tone, into the idea underlying them was to much criticism, and the equipment allowed for its expression was not always over-generous.

The basic principles of future policy are then laid down:

"In the mind of the ordinary soldier these places should have a definitely unpleasant association. We cannot afford at this stage to dispense altogether with the preventive value of deterrence.

On the other hand a purely punitive system will not transform a bad soldier into a good one. The young Englishman bored with the repetition of squad-drill and marching, will not grow to love them the more, if the daily dose is trebled.

A programme of training, more accurately described as retraining, requires a period of time. A slummock cannot be made smart, as a brass handle can be polished.

Where the more unpleasant shock of punishment alone is needed this should be inflicted in a short sharp dose, for a man in the course of months can get so used to Hell, as to be hardened rather than re-shaped by it."

In their examinations of the various types of establishment available to handle the problem, the committee echoes all the arguments of the previous century regarding civil prisons but go one step further and suggest that a soldier sentenced for a civil offence should be allowed to choose whether he be confined in a military or civil prison.

An establishment new to my experience is also discussed: a Corps guardroom, staffed by NCOs from the battalions and regiments of the Corps, and used for purely punitive – non training – purpose, pretty much like the provost prisons so disliked by Garsia. The committee recommends that all Corps should have one, with ten to fourteen days as the maximum sentence handled by them.

The MPDBs, of course, are most closely examined and several reforms recommended. Firstly, there are too few officers – three to each DB. The establishment should allow for one company commander for every fifty SUS. There should be a Chief Instructor. Officers should change frequently and some should be young enough to be able to appreciate the young soldier's outlook.

NCOs, on the contrary, should be "of some service", old enough to be able to advise the young offender on the ways of the world. The report states further that there are not enough NCOs and that the establishment should be increased by 25%, some of the increase coming from the RAF.

None of the DBs, says the report, have private rooms where the Chaplain is able to conduct personal interviews. Further, any establishment catering for more then 500 SUS should have a resident Chaplain and Medical Officer. Psychiatrists should be employed in the DBs. Wally Watson and Bill Flecknoe both recall a period immediately after Dempsey, when psychiatrists did visit DBs, but this appears to have fallen quickly by the wayside. The Chaplain and MO recommendations also, I suspect, were not universally applied and I consider that two, at least, of the Glasshouse Horror style of press story could have been avoided if the recommendation had been followed.

One recommendation was introduced and – fortunately – was to become normal practice: the introduction of the post of Welfare Officer. The original idea was for an attached young officer who was to be a kind of combined Education and Entertainments Officer and I intend sometime to research the transition of the post from this rather wet role to the vitally important function of the Welfare Officer today.

Training comes in for a battering from the committee. The DB staffs, they state, are out of touch with current weapons and training methods. DBs are also starved of recent equipment. There are no assault courses at Aldershot and Sowerby Bridge and Chorley's is too small. Three DBs have only two Bren guns on issue and there is none at all in Fort Darland. There is no technical training for the skilled corps or for the RAF. Dempsey suggests that DB training should be the responsibility of the Director of Military Training.

Under the heading of "Individualisation", Dempsey stresses the need for the Commandant and his staff to know all SUS personally and to form regular boards to assess each man's progress. Dempsey also raises a problem not unknown today: the inadequate documentation by units of SUS.

Now to an experimental unit examined carefully by the committee and already mentioned in passing by me. I refer to the Young Soldiers Training Unit of which one of the committee members: Major Geoffrey Gilbey was the first commander.

The committee had visited the unit and was so impressed that Dempsey recommends that each Command should copy Northern Command's lead. The idea so intrigued me that I rooted around for more information and Paul Vickers, of the Prince Consort's Library Aldershot again came up trumps. The two books I recommend to anyone who would like to pursue the matter further are "Out of Step", written by John Trenaman, published in 1952 by Methuen and "Crime and the Service", published in 1954 by Routledge, Keegan and Paul.

The problem was posed by the young soldier, often but not always, a product of Borstal, who made a career of absenting himself and who was a general nuisance in his unit when not absent. He was invariably a bad influence on the other young soldiers and had little military value, but discharge would have played straight into his hands. Confinement to barracks and spells in the guardroom had both proved futile. Sir Ronald Adam, the Adjutant General, decided that a new approach was necessary.

Pontefract Racecourse was set up as a training camp. The establishment was for 240 trainees with 60 staff. The aim was to treat each trainee as an individual, finding the root of his problem, then attempting to put him on the right lines – not dissimilar to modern MCTC practice.

I do not need to say that the system did not work for all. In a latter chapter, the reader will meet some of the YSTU members who have graduated to Sowerby Bridge and are there the source of more trouble than all the rest of the SUS. It would be interesting to discover how many of them later graduated to Northallerton or Shepton Mallet . . . or to Dartmoor.

Following Dempsey's recommendations, three YSTUs were set up. No. 1 originally started at Pontefract, later moved to Wetherby; No. 2 was at Lowestoft and No. 3 at Redhill. Originally, they were intended to serve their own Commands, but, by 1944, it had become the practice to send all the poor material to Wetherby; the doubtfuls to Lowestoft and the potential good soldiers to Redhill. Reading the two references I have given above will reveal a very interesting experiment, which fills me with admiration. Later, you will find that Colonel "Ginger" Gordon initiated a related scheme in Italy.

In the book "Crime in the Services", there is mention of another experiment of the period, again not a MPSC responsibility but one worthy of mention here. It concerns the Labour Battalions.

During the First World War, penal battalions had been set up. I assume on the German pattern (though I have no information on the subject). The Labour Battalions were a last desperate answer for those who had constantly been punished within their units, or by detention without appreciable improvement. They were to be recruited from the 21 to 28 year olds, who were outside the young soldier bracket. The regime was to be similar to the YSTUs, with the stress on knowledge of the delinquents as individuals.

The men were allocated to companies depending, as with the YSTUs, whether they could be considered as redeemable as soldiers. The worst were sent to No. 10 Company located at Braal Castle in Caithness, from which desertion was virtually impossible. This company was unarmed and did almost no military training. The other companies were housed in open camps without a perimeter fence. The experiment was not successful and both YSTUs and Labour Companies closed down in 1945.

What did the Dempsey Committee achieve? Before I answer, let me say without banging the big drum, that I feel rather proud to belong to a country, which at a time when everything seemed to be going against it, it could find time – and inclination – for a Dempsey Committee that could look with humanity at the King's Bad Bargains. Back to my original question. Certainly, the increased number of officers and NCOs made the committee worth while and brought in some first-class material. The introduction of RAF NCOs must also have helped to soften some of the shellbacks of the old regime. The principle of permanent Chaplains and MOs was also excellent, falling down only because of the extreme scarcity of both valuable commodities. Training aids also became more readily available, though still not up to the scales that Dempsey had envisaged.

It all sounds watered down as I write about it, but, looking not just at the war years, I get the impression that much of what Dempsey and his committee recommended laid the pattern for what we are doing: there may have been a delayed fuse, but it went off in time.

15
From the Outside: The Mill Town Temporaries

Bob Firmstone, Bill Bishop, Lew Butler, Alec Rea, all mentioned them somewhere in their accounts. They were names contrasting with Fanara and Gil Gil, even with Shepton Mallet and Colchester. They were the names of Northern Mill towns. My youth was spent in just such a town. As I read the accounts, I suddenly realised that all this book is the view from the inside and here, with the Northern towns, I had the chance to look at how the people at the other side of the wall viewed this intrusion into their tight-knit communities of a regular flow of the Army's baddies . . . and the men who were there to lock them up!

Without a great deal of hope, I wrote to the local newspapers, covering the towns of Sowerby Bridge, Chorley and Stakehill, asking merely for a letter to be placed. The response from all three amazed and delighted me. Two: "The Halifax Evening Courier", covering Sowerby Bridge, and "The Chorley Guardian", published short articles by their local historians. Mr Alex Holt, editor of "The Middleton Guardian", wrote me a long letter full of valuable leads.

That was the start. What I had forgotten was the care with which we read local papers in the North (if you've paid for it, you don't waste it) also how often local papers are sent to friends and relations who have moved away.

The letters flowed in, each one like a key piece in a jigsaw puzzle, adding a little bit more to the picture. Soon I was doing three jigsaw puzzles, called Chorley, Sowerby Bridge and Stakehill. There may be pieces missing, but I can now offer you the pictures.

So, Sowerby Bridge.

At this point, the South of Watford Gap school of readership will be asking where it is – where they all are. The strong Northern element of the Corps will bear with me, I hope, as I explain. Sowerby Bridge is in the Calder Valley, between Halifax and the Lancashire border. In common with most textile towns, it sits alongside the river and the mills, the reason for existence, dominate the town. They are usually many storied and stone built. All too often now, they are sitting idle.

Some humourist in War Office must have selected the two mills that were to become No. 10 MPDB, for their names were Perseverence and Prospect Mills (the same humourist probably selected Fort Jesus in Mombasa!) I know exactly how Perseverence and Prospect look today, thanks to a newspaper block sent to me by 82 year old Reg Tansley. Mr Tansley also sent me detailed information on the mills' history, written in a copperplate hand that belongs in a calligraphy manual.

Although the "outside" view is my main theme in this chapter, I obviously must also say something of the interiors of the mills in those times when they had changed their use. Lew Butler, who went there in 1940 from Carrickfergus, gave me much useful information, but three of my local correspondents gave me more and I am sure that Lew – who gets a fair crack of the whip in this book – will bear with me if I concentrate on these local accounts.

Mr J Dale settled in Sowerby Bridge. He was medically downgraded in 1942 as a sergeant in the Royal Artillery and was posted to No. 10. No. 10 had then been in existence since mid-1940, when the RE had converted the extensive floors by constructing wire and wood "cages", each capable of holding thirty or so men. The cages were furnished with two tier bunks, highly polished night buckets and very little else. There were no velvet cushions.

The lower floor windows had been bricked up and were the administrative area. SUS in the floors above were segregated according to level of training, age and degree of evil. The top floor caused more problems than any other. This was No.3 Company's floor and No.3 Company was made up of the young soldiers from the YSTU which I mention elsewhere.

A member of staff slept on each floor, connected to the administrative area only by a bell. Mr Dean remembers a night when the duty staff of the top floor was attacked by six of the young soldiers and beaten about the head, but had fortunately managed to press the bell before he went down.

All free staff stormed up to the top floor, where all was now quiet, but the ringleader – five times a customer in Borstal – was caught. He was court martialled in Halifax and sentenced to five years in Armley Gaol.

The other two letters "from the inside" were both from ex SUS, who had served in Sowerby Bridge. Mr HVT still lives in nearby Sowerby. He was into the Army young, after having brought himself up and was to sample life in Sowerby Bridge, Barlinnie, Fort Darland and Colchester. Sowerby Bridge was the hardest, he insists, with Colchester a convalescent home after it. Discipline was fierce and he remembers wetting himself on parade rather than move a muscle. There were "gangsters in uniform" amongst the SUS, with a particularly strong element from Glasgow forming a group that stayed well away from all the other SUS and had its own harsh code. Rumour had it that many of the hard men, on being posted abroad, were handcuffed until the ship left port.

The other "consumer" report came from Mr T B, who now lives at Thurnscoe, near Rotherham. I think it is worth while to record it in its entirety:

"My sister who lives in Halifax sent me your letter in the Halifax Local Paper about the detention centre at Sowerby Bridge.

How well I remember it. I was in the Coldstream Guards 1940-1947 and in the years 1942-43 my sister had a Public House in Huddersfield and every time I went on leave I used to go up and help out in the pub.

The trouble was I always used to overstay my leave. Regular as clockwork the Red Caps used to come for me and take me to Sowerby Bridge and hold me until an escort came for me from my own battalion.

The second time my CO the Lieutenant Colonel the Lord Stratheden sent me back to Sowerby to do 28 days detention as the old saying goes "They never return", I didn't and the memory will be with me till the day I die.

There were cages made for six men in each, and you were put inside with the villains from every regiment. I was put in with 2 from Liverpool 2 cockneys and a jock and I can still recall the fights we used to have over 1 cig.

As regards the punishment, you were never still, 3 drills a day with full kit and all your webbing had to be scrubbed white and your brasses polished back and front. Being a

Guardsman that part was easy for me. Then there was PT twice a day. But the worst part was when you were locked up after your tea meal. They used to throw all the dirty pans and mess tins from the cookhouse into the cages and all you had to clean them with were a bucket of sand, cold water and rags, and believe me Major those pans etc had to shine like silver. That was in addition to your own kit and there had to be dead silence. If it was raining they used to throw all the tins outside and when they were rusty they used to give you them back and say you hadn't touched them. In fact some of the younger prisoners used to crack and cry. If you back answered the guard they had a favourite trick of making you run on the spot while you were having your meal, so just try having a plate of stew while you are running on the spot!

The time I was there was in November and the weather was always damp and cold and the problem was how to get warm with only 2 blankets. There was also a outbreak of scabies at the time and nearly everybody had the itch. Luckily I escaped that bit but some of them were in a fair old state.

It was the same on punishment drill. You could always tell the weak from the strong. Some used to stagger and crawl after 20 mins. There was no end to it, it was go, go, go. No Major you can't buck the system choose what you do, so you have just got to obey the rule of law. I might add that it taught me a lot, I saw things, and did things that I thought weren't possible and when I went back to my battalion I was a whole lot wiser and fitter. I went right through to Germany, eventually after VE day I went into another battalion and finished up in Palestine where I finished my seven years. Good luck to your book Major and all the best to you for the future. I shall be 65 on 19 Oct 1985."

Meanwhile back on the outside. . . .

In general, the only contact that the locals had with the SUS was to see them marching from the station with their escort, sometimes handcuffed. They would also see them returning to the station on release.

Connie Turner, after a full day's work did her turn behind the counter in the YMCA canteen as her war work. Sometimes she had released SUS as customers, sometimes even SUS with escorts on their way in. On visiting days, the wives would gather for a cup of tea and would tell each other horror stories, one improving on the other.

Connie is now a pensioner, but is still as keen a dancer as she was then. The staff obviously also used the canteen and she was often invited to dances in the sergeants' mess (she sent me an invitation card for one of the dances, which she kept as a souvenir of those days.) She says that the coming of No. 10 MDB to Sowerby brought a little interest to a dreary wartime scene.

Mr Bairstow also remembers the dances. He lives at Pellow near Halifax and was then the drummer in the dance band. He was once shown around the DB by Sergeant JH Topliss and knew well three other members of the staff: Sergeant Tommy Miller and Sergeants Ward and Nash.

A charming letter from Lilian and Harold Watson, who in those days kept a butcher's shop. They lodged a Sergeant Max Silberstein, who later changed his name to Stilton and joined the Army Pay Corps. They too had many happy mess evenings.

Mr Barron, who now lives at Brighouse, used to volunteer for escorts to Sowerby Bridge as his wife lived at nearby Luddenden Foot. One time he was escorting a little Glaswegian. They were changing trains at Doncaster, when a train for Scotland was announced. The little Jock looked at him with pain and said "For God's sake hurry, Corp, afore ah forget masel".

Many of the letters from Sowerby Bridge have a recurring theme, one which has left a scar on the name of the MPSC: they insist that the cricket ground was concreted over to make a drill square and that the local council had much difficulty in post war years to snatch the pitch back from the military. Lew Butler insists that this is not so, but he left the town in 1942 and the sacrilege, probably perpetrated by a Lancastrian, may well have happened after this time.

Chorley is in Lancashire, not far from Leyland. The DB here, again, was a requisitioned mill, this time a bleach works. Lower Healey Mill still stands, now making carpets for a subsidiary of Tarmac. Mr Leonard Daniel was the first to describe it to me: ex REME, he even gave me its grid reference! Like Mr Bairstow at Sowerby Bridge, Mr Daniel had played at the DB as leader of a dance band. He wrote to me twice, the second time after he had walked the area to discover what remained of its wartime use. He was able to find the concrete base of the sergeants' mess hut and a few lower windows still bricked up. He described the surrounding area meticulously for me and pointed out that any escape from Chorley, if it were to stay clear of the town, would need to weather the Anglezarke Moors, one of the roughest areas in England.

But one at least did get away. . . .

Robert Connolly worked in Lower Healey Mill after he left school. One of his former workmates was brought to the DB as a customer – he had always been a hard lad, according to Mr Connolly. By a freak of fortune, he was accommodated in the cage located exactly where he had worked and, by night, lifted up a manhole cover and disappeared down the water ducts below the mill. He roamed free around Rivington for many days, until the civil police brought him in. An escaper at Sowerby, by the way, jumped from four storeys into the River Calder, not realising the cloying nature of its bed and was glad to be recaptured next morning.

Alec Rea, as a reservist member of the MPSC, remembered Chorley with affection, particularly "The Derby Arms", which I am assured is still standing and which then was a second mess for the MPSC. It was also the last pub that many SUS would see for a long time, as it was also the bus-stop where they debussed for the DB.

Again, as in Sowerby Bridge, the only contact for many of the local population with the SUS would be the time when they first arrived and when they were released. Many of the letters speak of seeing them arrive handcuffed. Mr N. Peel remembers two who attempted to escape through the emergency exit of a bus, only to be snatched back immediately. Mr BJ Walker remembers that his mother and others used to give the SUS and escort tea and cake as they savoured the last minutes of freedom. Often the SUS would leave valuables with the ladies for collection on release. Arthur House, ex King's Regiment, recalls being stopped on the station by an escort and asked the way, but the SUS under escort said "Never mind, Corp, I know the way – I've been there a time or two before".

I said that admission and release were the times when many saw the SUS, but there were other occasions, because Lower Healey Mill sat close to a public path and a favourite courting spot and Sunday walk area. Children played nearby and Maureen Hargreaves remembers her surprise as a child to learn that any of "our" soldiers were bad enough to be locked up. She and the other children wove tales that the men behind the barbed wire and hessian were really Nazis..Mr EL Moss, who now lives in Brentwood (as I said, local papers travel wide!) remembers that as a ten year old, waving at the "prisoners" was part of the Sunday walk ritual.

Mr N Peel and others remember the efforts that SUS would make to attempt to persuade cigarettes from the Sunday walkers. A favourite trick was to make a line of joined cotton strands, weight its end and fish for any cigarette that anyone would put on the end. Mr Peel also remembers a time when his girlfriend had managed to buy twenty Players – gold dust in those days – and lost the lot when she kindly gave one to a SUS, who had just been released.

Mrs Winefride Doyle, a very wideawake seventy four year old, rapped me on the knuckles for some geographical error I had made about Chorley, then produced a comprehensive map and a description of the area fit for a travel agent. She lived in a house, where Lower Healey Mill was visible from her back window and recalls that MPSC voices made "RSM Brittan sound like a boy tenor". Some things do not change!

Her near neighbour, Mrs D Sharpe, wrote to say that her younger brother had been a customer in Chorley, the black sheep in a family that had done more than its share in both wars. I hoped that I would be able to contact him for his impressions, but he had taken to the road after leaving the Army and had died young.

The late Alec Rea remembered the MPSC's assistance with Home Guard training on Sundays. The parade was held in a Chorley park and always ended with a noisy bayonet charge, much to the disgust of nearby residents. He also remembered that girls from a local munitions factory, with some local girls, would parade also on Sunday morning, this time near the DB wire to comment loudly on the doubtful antecedents of the MPSC. Hessian screens were finally erected on the wire.

As at Sowerby, another contact between staff and town was in lodging staff families in local houses. The parents of Maureen Hargreaves, already mentioned housed Sergeant James and his wife for a while and RSM Edwin Turbutt, who was later to settle in the area, was married from the home of another of my correspondents, Mr JE Ollershaw. Many went to mess socials and Hilary Bateman remembers attending a

Christmas party in the mess, where she was to enjoy the delights of bananas and sweets, that had not come from her ration card and were rarer than jewels.

Edwin Turbett was not the only staff member to settle in Chorley, of course. Ex RSM Nelson also settled there, as did others, but I would now like to take you back to my original statement that Northern locals travel far.

Early in the search, I received a letter postmarked Edinburgh. The head of the paper said that it was from a Professor of International Banking at Herriot Watt University – not exactly an immediate connection with a wartime detention barracks in Chorley, Lancs!

Professor G Home was 22 and a sergeant in the RAF Police when he was posted to Chorley. The RAF had heard tales of victimisation of RAF SUS and decided that RAF staff should serve in DBs. Professor Home found that the tales were unfounded. He goes on to say that the conditions for the SUS were far better than he was himself to meet in the Far East. The experience, he is sure, helped him to mature and the discipline and man management were to stand him in good stead later. On his leaving, a MPSC member said that he would have made a good soldier and without victimising the Blue Jobs, I would say that that was high praise indeed! Professor Home married a Chorley girl, qualified as a lawyer after the war; became a Deputy Managing Director of the Royal Bank of Scotland, then, as I have said, Professor of International Banking. I challenge any of the Old and Bold to beat that!

I enjoyed all the letters but one in particular subscribed "Sgt RAPC long demobbed" was particularly pleasant to read. Mr John Mould farms Lower Healey Farm, bordering the former DB. He recommended that I contact his predecessor's son, Mr Jim Alker to learn of those days. Tim Alker, Mr Mound wrote, "established a state of profitable symbiosis with the DB: he sold them his vegetables, then re-cycled them by collecting the swill and the night soil. For the full cycle he also used SUS labour on ditch digging and so on.

Obviously, I had to contact Jim Alker.

Jim fetched the swill from the DB and he worked closely with the working parties, many of whom put their main effort into attempting to scrounge cigarettes. Jim invariably refused their ploys because he knew that, if caught, they would pass the buck as quickly as possible. There were some pretty nasty characters amongst them, he assures me, mainly from the big cities. He remembers – a point not mentioned elsewhere in the letters apart from Mr Peel's disappearing cigarettes that the SUS had no hesitation in applying "aggro" to any civilian from whom they saw a chance of profit. Once also, he went into the DB to collect swill and saw a member of staff covered completely in lime, obviously having been thrown into an uncovered lime vat. It was not, he said, the only case of assault on the staff. On the subject of escapes, he remembers six SUS who escaped together, one wearing no boots! they were all caught at the station.

Lower Healey was to close in 1946. The huts that had been built around it were to house, at first Displaced Persons, then squatters. As I have said it is now a carpet works and the M61 runs past it, crossing the fields once larded by countless gallons of SUS sweat.

Stakehill correspondence started with a bang. The first person to write, as I think I have already said, was Mr Alex Holt, the editor of the "Middleton Guardian". He had gone to a great deal of trouble on my behalf, had sifted the archives and gave me leads that I was able to exploit from this end. This was followed by a long and detailed letter from Mr Frank Fletcher, who presented me with a potted history and geography of the area and of the mill.

Lew Butler was at Stakehill in 1944, when Wally Watson, by this time a major was Assistant Commandant and training officer and WOI Scott was RSM. He was to stay only a short time, then was posted to Langport, which I shall mention shortly elsewhere. Mr HW Vallins, formerly of the Corps, had Stakehill as his first posting after Aldershot and he gave me much detail of the running of the D.B.

Again, I had many letters from local people. This time, the focus was on an incident in 1945, which I shall deal with shortly. First, a little about the mill.

Again, it was a bleach mill, disused since the Thirties and known locally as Barlow's. It stood about half a mile from the main road running through the joint villages of Stakehill and Slattocks, two miles from Middleton and five from Rochdale. Mrs Agnes Smith remembers that it was first requisitioned as a barracks for the Lancashire Fusiliers, then was handed over to 92 Regt RA (this unusual ability of a civilian to remember a unit designation comes from the fact that she met her busband, when he was a Gunner stationed there.) It was able to accommodate 300 SUS.

The normal chaplain for the DB in 1945 was the Reverend A.V. Astin from nearby Thornton. He fell ill in this year and his place was taken during October by the Rev Urien Evans, Curate of St Martin's Castleton Moor, who conducted the services in the DB chapel.

After some short time of performing these duties, the curate wrote a blistering attack in his parish magazine. The regime in the DB, he said, was brutal and his parishioners should be aware of conditions more suitable to Nazi Germany.

The article was picked up by the national press, particularly the Mirror: Glasshouse Horror headlines were taken out again. Evans received, he said, almost 150 letters of support from ex SUS and their families. The Rev Astin wrote to "The Rochdale Observer" to say that Rev Urien Evans had never been inside the DB, merely in the chapel and could have no idea of what the DB was really like. He himself, as the regular chaplain had been often inside, visiting SUS in their rooms, had even married some of them inside, with a wedding breakfast laid on afterwards. One national newspaper picked this up, but it was not news, so the furore died down.

But only for a week. . . .

There had been attempted suicides in the DB before (throughout the prison reports and after, suicide more correctly attempted suicides, staged to ensure that a sensation will be created but with no real damage to the person-are regular features) The two previous attempts in Stakehill were fairly typical: an attempt to slash wrists during chapel and an attempt at hanging. The next suicide succeeded . . . A week after the press campaign had died down, Stakehill was firmly back into the national eye.

The Dubliner Michael Hanlon had, according to his wife Bridget, been in the Army "on and off" since 1940. This was his third spell in Stakehill, sentenced to two years for desertion.

His Pioneer unit was in Prestatyn and he had travelled up to Stakehill with another Pioneer, who was sentenced to ninety days. On the journey, he had told his mate that he would not complete his sentence and had made cutting motions with his hand at his wrists. His mate had taken him for a bit of a romancer, because he had also boasted on the journey that he had got two women in trouble one in Manchester, one in Birmingham.

On the 5th October, Hanlon had been sent to the Singles Block. Other inmates of the block were later to give evidence at Hanlon's inquest, that Hanlon had been beaten up by a member of the staff and two SUS cleaners, after he had attempted suicide. On the evening of the 5th, Hanlon was found in his room, hanging from a webbing strap. He was already dead.

At the inquest, evidence of a previous suicide attempt was a pair of scratches not penetrating the skin. Hanlon had a bruise behind his ear, which might have been caused by being beaten up, apart from the fact that the medical officer doing the post mortem showed that, to strike Hanlon in that particular place, a second person would have needed to hold back the ear and the bruise had more likely resulted from the hanging.

The coroner pronounced a case of suicide and said that it was not up to a coroner's court to examine the workings of the DB. The national press bayed and questions were asked in Parliament.

An inquiry was organised at the Drill Hall in Ashton under Lyne, the board including a KC and a psychiatrist. One hundred and ninety five witnesses were heard, including Urien Evans and former SUS. The House of Commons expressed itself satisfied with the result, but the DB was to close in January 1946, the SUS being transferred to Chorley and Sowerby Bridge.

As I have said, Lew Butler and HW Vallins spent some time here, but I had also two correspondents, who remembered the inside of the DB. Mr William Fuzzens was medical orderly at Stakehill in 1944 and sent me a full plan of the layout. At that time, the MO was a Captain Chandler, formerly of Wormwood Scrubs. Mr Fuzzens remembers that, as the DB had only a small utility vehicle as its transport "pool", all transport to a larger MI room at Fulwood, Preston was by bus, often with the "patient" handcuffed. Because of security problems, any SUS who was bedded down was sent to a mental hospital near Blackburn.

Mr P.G. Elgey, of Syke, Rochdale, used to volunteer for escorts as he lived nearby. Transport from the station was again by bus and hard men were handcuffed to "stanchions" in the vehicle, leading to much civilian criticism. Many of the well behaved SUS were taken home by Mr Elgey for tea and cake. Mr Elgey renewed his acquaintanceship with military penal institutions when he was posted to the Far East and served at Fort Canning, Singapore, when Indian mutineers were being held there.

I have rather banged on about the Northern DBs. I hope that the South of Watford Gappers will realise that it is not all Memory Lane!

Now for the other temporaries.

16
The Other Temporaries

Besides the milltown temporaries, there were others that were opened for the duration of the war only. The best known of these, of course, was Shepton Mallet. Another: Langport in Somerset, a former asylum, workhouse grain store – you name it – was to be handed over to the Americans after only a short period of use.

Headley Down was built as a Canadian prison and is remembered as a dreadful place by Ray Ganner, who was posted there when it reverted to British use. It was a cluster of concrete block buildings, where the opening of the cell doors was a permanent hazard, as the staff was inevitably left at the end of the unlocking with his back to a fixed iron grill door and the SUS between himself and the way out.

Ray considers that the sole comment needed on Headley Down was that of the farmer who owned the land – he considered that it wasn't much of a prison but would make a model piggery when the last SUS was released.

Major Sydney Harris was posted there for a short time and also remembers it as a dreadful place. He recalls one incident there, though, that had its lighter side. A soldier in the Queen's Regiment, of which Syd was also a member, had resolved on non-cooperation and fancied himself as something of a hard man. Everything had been done to him that the Rules allowed, but he maintained his stand. Saturday was visiting day and visitors arrived at the guardroom by bus. On this particular day, a formidable female figure stepped from the bus. She was brick-built and with a face that instantly revealed her as a relation to the hard man. Sydney, in his polite fashion, addressed himself to the lady and pointed out that her son was behaving in a regrettable fashion that was causing him, Sydney, considerable trouble. Sydney pointed out that this was particularly sad as the man was a member of the same regiment as himself. At that moment, the hard man was seen, marching with his escort across the square.

"Bert!" screamed the lady in a voice designed for fish selling and Sydney indicated to the escort that Bert should be marched in his direction. Bert was paler than normal when he arrived. There was a swish in the air and the thud of flesh meeting flesh and the hard Bert was reeling, the right ear clasped in his meaty hand. The escort steadied him. "You bastard", said his mother "You've been at it again, giving bother to this nice officer . . . and he's in your regiment 'nall".

From this time forth, Bert was a model prisoner and I'm sure there is a lesson to be learned somewhere in this.

Captain Lew Butler had wide experience in many of the wartime temporaries: Sowerby Bridge, Stakehill, Langport, Northallerton, but his first one was a Carrickfergus in Northern Ireland, where he reported with the original opening party. SUS started to arrive in November 1940. There were thirteen staff under a Major Clarke as Commandant and RSM Howes. During Lew's time here, there was no training and the SUS were employed on the creation of a drill square, the site of which was an apple orchard on a slope. The trees had to be uprooted, then the slope levelled. Regretfully, I have little information on Carrickfergus apart from Lew's account.

I am writing this in the early days of 1987 and every evening the television news is showing pictures of the prison riots at Barlinnie Prison, near Glasgow and Bill Flecknoe has much to say of Barlinnie in his account. As in the First World War, the military authorities had taken over two of the five wings, a main gate and a tarmacced area between the perimeter and the wings. It could hold 430 SUS and both Bill Flecknoe and Bill Bishop, who went there in 1944 say that some of the hardest and most evil were being held there (Bill Bishop remembers his posting there as being like "going from light into darkness).

In Bill Flecknoe's early time there, the Commandant, Lt Col Weare, used the old school routine. When SUS were caught fighting: he sent them to Dr. Poole, the MO, cleared them as fit and let them box it out in the gymnasium. In almost every case the tough who had started the fight came out the loser.

When Lt Col Weare left, he was replaced by Lt Col Taffy Lloyd, one of the legendary names of the Corps. A man of wide experience, Taffy was faced early with the kind of crisis, which would try the experience of any Commandant: a large intake of almost a hundred was admitted and, with the exception of a handful, refused to parade for allocation to squads. Taffy's address to them went something like this "You can be free men and do military training – that's your first choice – or you can be free men in close confinement on bread and water – that's your second choice. You will be dismissed to your rooms now and I'll give you 24 hours to make the choice". Next day, only six men refused to parade.

Fights were a common thing amongst the SUS, slivers of glass used as daggers being popular, then one day Bill and two others staff had to break up a scrap in the pioneer's shop, where both the SUS were using hammers, swung like mediaeval maces. On another occasion a SUS managed to climb a drainpipe and reach the roof four storeys above, where he broke the glass panes and showered all below.

The SUS did military training on infantry lines throughout the week and, as there were no specific training staff, all members of the MPSC were required to train SUS: "basic", according to Bill Bishop was the only word that could really be applied to it. He recalls that he was once reprimanded for allowing his squad to play leap frog after they had completed their exercises "They are not here to enjoy themselves" was the RSM's message.

Discipline was fierce . . . and not only for the SUS. No member of staff was allowed to call another by his Christian name when on duty and severe reprimands, according to Bill, "floated around like confetti". His posting came to the converted mills of Sowerby Bridge as something of a relief, I suspect.

A detention barracks with a difference was that at Downfield, near Dundee, where Bill Flecknoe served. Before requisition, it had been a remand home. It held 350 SUS and the training area used was in the Sidlaw Hills, where there was considerable military scope. Bill recalls one traumatic fieldcraft period, when a keen young, newly arrived officer gave the hearty cry "Right lads. The first man up to the highest point gets my haversack ration." There was a burst of SUS activity, with unsecured bodies everywhere and the staff sweated the proverbial little piglets . . . not a single SUS disappeared but it did not establish a precedent.

The instructor in bayonet fighting is remembered by Bill

as one of the great instructors he met in his service, a Staff Sergeant Findlater, formerly Scots Guards. He had been a member of the Scots Guards Spring Bayonet team and no single SUS ever answered his challenge to fight an exhibition bayonet bout with him.

Downfield became something of a "one off" detention barracks, when it ceased to cater for the British customers and became the Allied Forces DB. The British Commandant remained, as did the MPSC staff, but the SUS were Norwegians, Dutch, Poles French, Czechs and Greeks. Bill was a PTI here and physical exercises were taught by a great deal of example, with commands being given through interpreters. The Commandant, Major Melville, was a keen sportsman and soon there was an international football league and monthly international boxing matches. The staff, too, had a first-class football team, but there was also fierce international rivalry in the mess in the games of pokey die, crib, nap and pontoon.

I have before me a document from this period, which I consider to be worth reproducing here: It was addressed to the Inspector of Military Prisons and Detention Barracks.

DOWNFIELD, DUNDEE
the 23rd of June 1944

To Colonel Fraser DCM DSO
Sir,
Being informed that the departure of the allied detention barracks has been decided for yet unkwown destination, we beg you to throw your attention on the following application.

Major Melville who has been in command of the Allied Detention Barracks since the foundation has shown such an understanding and tactfulness towards the various nationalities he has had to deal with that he has undoubtedly been, with the help of Sgt Major James, the keyman of the establishment.

We would be most grateful to you if you could keep these two superiors in command of the Allied Detachments if you see yourself obliged to detach these detachments to another Military Prison.

On the other hand, we would like to inform you that Major Melville has always shown the most tactful perspicacity in his frequent contacts with the members of the Allied Detachments and also with the men under sentence.

This applies equally to Sgt Major James who has been so closely associated with that task for more than two years.

We regret to be obliged to importune you with this request but considering the importance that we are taking in this matter, we think to do for the best in submitting it to you without delay.

We beg to remain, your obedient servants
Lieutenant Straume Norwegian Section
Adjutant Chef Pollatschek French Section
Sgt Major de Pooter Dutch Section
Sgt Major Kujawa Polish Section
Sgt Major Schoonen Belgian Section
Sgt Major Zavazal Czech Section

I have tried without success to trace Major Melville.

Two of the wartime temporaries particularly intrigued me and it was by pure chance that I managed to get a lead on both. These were the most northerly outposts of the MPSC empire: Iceland and the Orkneys. I had a mention of the Orkneys DB in the transcript of an interview conducted some years ago by, I think, Sgt Major David Hood, the subject being an ex WOII White of the Corps. It was barely a mention and I wanted to know more. By one of those freaks of chance, an article appeared in "New Society", dealing with the Aldershot and Northallerton disturbances. The writer, Colin Ward, mentioned that he himself had been a SUS at Ronaldshay in Orkney. The next lucky stroke was that, on contacting him, I found that he lived up the road in Ipswich. A pleasant working lunch resulted.

Colin is now a successful writer on environmental subjects, but he was then a reluctant sapper. A touch of insubordination earned him 56 days in Ronaldshay Detention Barracks. Memory had dimmed somewhat, but he recalled a bleak group of windswept Nissen huts, surrounded by barbed wire. The morning was taken up with PT and pack drill and the afternoons were spent working alongside Italian prisoners on the construction of a causeway to help secure Scapa Flow.

My next source was an ex MPSC member, who appeared to have lost touch with the Corps, but still read the Journal. In a progress report, I mentioned that I had no information about Iceland and Mr FA Allen wrote from Newmarket. He had travelled widely with the MPSC, had been Chief Clerk at the Inspectorate and most importantly had been with an early draft to Iceland.

Here, the Detention Barracks was on high ground overlooking Reykjavik Harbour and the buildings had been used mainly for the storage of fish. Nissen huts had supplemented the original buildings and the staff lived in a house in a compound where fishergirls had worked (though these, writes Mr Allen, were not much in evidence when he was there!) CSM Arthur White, a Staff Sergeant and a sergeant opened the DB in 1940, then Mr Allen and Sergeant Urqhart joined in October 1940. They were locking up a maximum of 60 men from all the branches of the services. The SUS were heavily employed, loading and unloading stores from the ships, digging tank traps (!) and levelling out ground for parking vehicles. I have since been informed that they were later employed on airfield construction, fish gutting and the preparation of building blocks.

This is not an exhaustive account of all the temporaries of the War and I wait with anticipation further (belated) information from the Old and Bold!

17
Murderers of Poor Sammy Clayton.

When Napoleon had threatened invasion, Chatham and other naval bases were ringed with forts to prevent assault from the landward side. One of the Chatham forts was Fort Darland. Nearby Star Field was leased to a farmer but had been used by the Royal Engineers as an exercise area for the teaching of tunnelling. Later, spider huts were built on it and it became the place where RE boys were trained, then the Second World War and the shortage of DB accommodation caused it to change its role again and to become Fort Darland Detention Barracks. It was a bleak, threatening place but it would house 1000 SUS from all three services. It was to become notorious.

William Clarence Clayton, nicknamed Sammy, was a builder's labourer living at Enfield Wash until he was conscripted in 1940. He was a medium-sized, dark haired man, not over bright. At thirty eight, with a medical grading of C, due to deafness and frequent ear trouble, he was not the recruit of the year for the KRRC. His liability to go absent at the drop of a hat resulted in his still not having passed the training stage two years later and in those two years, he had collected a crime sheet, long as the proverbial arm. There were sixteen entries, absence interlaced with drunkness and he had been in detention three times: once at Aldershot, twice at Chorley before being sent for 112 days to Darland. This last sentence was to be the death of him.

The court martial was at Leighton Buzzard for his latest, extended, period of absence; he had been away a year and was picked up by civilian police in Mill Hill wearing civilian clothes. His MO certified that he was fit to serve detention but confirmed his category C.

Between the 12th October 1942 and the 16th March 1943, Clayton had reported sick seventeen times, mainly for ear trouble but on the 13th and 15th of March, he had complained of troubles with his breathing. The MO gave him Medicine and Duty and his reputation with the staff was that of a malingerer.

On the 17th of March, Sammy Clayton was one of a squad of forty six SUS who were marching under the command of Staff Sergeant Pendleton MPSC, with Flight Sergeant Chapman of the RAF as squad second in command. Already, earlier that day, Clayton had refused to tighten the straps of his respirator during gas drill and had been reprimanded. Now, as the squad marched over the parade ground, Clayton fell out of the ranks and said that he was no longer able to march. Pendleton ordered Chapman to take Clayton over to the RSM at the other side of the square and to inform him that Clayton refused to march and was probably malingering.

The RSM, WOI Culliney was with QMS Salter. Culliney ordered Salter to take Clayton to his billet, where the SUS was ordered to pack his kit. Clayton said that he was too weak to do so, but in time went outside with his Field Service Marching order. Outside Culliney was waiting and Clayton dropped his kit on the wet ground.

Witnesses later stated that it was at this point that the RSM punched Clayton and that Salter held the SUS from behind. Whatever happened – and some of the witnesses, seem after forty years to be very shaky indeed – Clayton fell to the ground unmoving. Culliney ordered Salter to fetch some SUS with a barrack cart (the tall wheeled variety long obsolete) and Clayton was loaded on the cart with the RSM's instructions that he was to be taken to the single cell block. The body, perched on the cart's load of salvaged rag and ashes, lolled without moving and Clayton's face was grey, apart from the red smear of blood around the mouth.

The NCO in charge of the single cell block was a reservist, Staff Sergeant Webber ex Coldstream Guards, ex Devon Constabulary. When Salter arrived with the still body on the cart, he went in to see Webber and shouted "One on for you, Staff" implying that Clayton was to be taken into cells. Webber refused the limp body, helped to remove it from the cart and threw water into Clayton's face. It was too late for water: Clayton was already dead.

The inquest on Clayton was held in the Royal Naval Hospital, Chatham. It established that there was a broken bone in Clayton's neck and other signs of his having been punched. The prime cause of death was tubercolosis at an advanced stage, but the beating had accelerated the death and the Coroner ruled that the two WOs should be tried for manslaughter. The medical officer and medical reception procedures were also heavily criticised.

Both WOs were later sentenced to terms of imprisonment in Maidstone Gaol.

During the inquest and the trial, there had been loud shouts from the public of "Gestapo" and "Hitlers". Anonymous and signed letters poured in, addressed to the Commandant, the coroner and to the two WOs. The one I reproduce here is fairly typical. I have kept the original spelling and punctuation because many of those received were similar. Some, however, were more literate but equally outraged. This one had photographs of the faces of the two WOs at the head of the letter:

Murder?

Gestapo! The day will come when these men are hunted down they will suffer and there families and you above all, you dirty low down swine, you are the lowest of the low, you will anser for these detention atrocities, study the pictures above, they look what they are, two real dirty barstards, hanging is to good, shooting is to good, the best methods for them razor blades over there faces, that will remove the grins, they will be pick up by gangs, the dirty swines.

Public outrage was such that the MPSC members at Darland were permitted to wear civilian clothes when they walked out: unprecedented in wartime. A paragraph in the Oliver Report, of which more later, sums up the feeling:

"Several of the worst of the stories in Group II of Appendix B have been published in the press and have gone before the public as examples of abominable treatment in these institutions. During the course of their local investigations, the Committee again and again came across evidence of the effect that allegations of this kind were having upon the lives and existence of the Staffs employed in military detention barracks. In some places, members of the Staff wearing as they do a prominent red flash with "MPSC" on their shoulder cannot appear in public without the risk of aversion, insult, and assault. Many of the best of them keep within their own precincts rather than risk the unmerited obloquy incurred by mixing with their fellow citizens outside. In this way men whose work is hard and thank-less enough in the nature of things are deprived of even reasonable recreation and relaxation."

Churchill was in Canada at the time, but reports of public feeling reached him and he ordered an immediate enquiry, to be headed by Mr Justice Oliver of the King's Bench Division, with the Bishop of Reading and a senior physician as members. The terms of reference of the Committee were to be as follows:

"To enquire into and report on the treatment of men under sentence in Naval and Military Prisons and Detention Barracks in the United Kingdom, and whether it is in accordance with modern standards and satisfies wartime requirements."

"The investigation will cover inter alia the supervision and administration of discipline, medical care, training, welfare accommodation, feeding and the suitability and adequacy of the staff."

The Committee was given carte blanche to visit, without previous notice, any military prison, detention barrack or Naval Detention Quarters. They visited all apart from the Orkney and Shetland DBs and Carrickfergus.

They kept to the same pattern for all visits. They would arrive in the morning, inspect the establishment, then would have the SUS paraded and would ask for complaints, assuring them of complete confidentiality and no repercussions. Of the 5200 then in detention, ninety one complained. I reproduce some of the complaints below without comment.

"Fifth time in detention for absence, impudence and disobeying orders. Complained of being jeered at by the Staff for effeminacy. Always in trouble in detention camps; can't do anything right. No one will help him, not even the MO. Was punished once for having cigarettes in his overcoat, and it wasn't his overcoat that they were found in. Feels weak and has lost weight.

(Note – because of this statement the Committee had him weighed and he was found to be a few pounds heavier than when he was admitted. Enquiries about the cigarette episode elicited that the coat concerned was opposite his bed, that it fitted him, and would not have fitted the neighbouring occupants of the room, and that every other man in his room had his own overcoat.)

First detention. Started at Sowerby but had trouble and was passed on here. Seventy five days ago sent in an appeal against his sentence and complained of being kept in handcuffs in his regimental guardroom. "The CO here said he would investigate that but nothing has happened." Complained about the food. "I don't think we get our proper rations at night. We do not get milk or sugar in the morning cocoa. We do not place any faith in the Visiting Officer."

(Note – The Committee enquired of the Commandant about the first complaint and were satisfied that he had done his very best to help this man)

Third time in detention. "I am 49 and can't keep up with the younger men. A Staff Sergeant said to me once, "Get along you old . . . you might have won the last war but you din't win this one." Complained on another occasion he was made to clean filthy latrine bucket. He also said, "I have not seen any ill-treatment here. The CO is just and good. I went sick this morning and explained to the MO that an old wound troubled me and he marked me fit. When the Committee asked how he knew that he said. "I don't know whether he did not not."

(Note – The Committee ascertained that in fact he had been marked for light duty.)

When asked if he had ever seen any brutality at the other places he had been at he said that in 1941 at a place which is no longer a British Detention Barracks, he had seen a young soldier frogmarched by four of the Staff. To prevent him from speaking they had put a wet towel in his mouth. They took him to the punishment cells. On the way along they had bumped his face along the floor. He also said that he had once seen a man "kneed" in the washhouse at Aldershot by the Staff.

(Note – An unreliable witness. No means of testing his statement as to an event in 1941.)

Third period of detention. Said some time ago there was an enquiry here as to "trafficking with the staff". "I was caught with some tobacco and was asked for a statement. I gave evidence and three members of the staff suffered. Two other soldiers under sentence also gave evidence. I complained that since then I have been victimised by the staff, they report me for trivial things some of which I have not done. A Staff Sergeant B blew smoke into my cell and then put me on report for smoking. I was admonished. Another time I was talking and if it had been anyone else he would have done nothing. He reported me."

(Note – This man has a very bad civil record. Staff Sergeant B is a non-smoker. The Committee did not believe the complaint.)"

In addition to the visits, announcements were made in all national papers and on radio to the effect that the Committee was prepared to receive written complaint and would interview complainants in London. The report contains the substance of many of these complaints and I reproduce two of them here for interest:

"No 8 was a witness with twenty years Army service and four years service. He was on the MPSC staff from December 1939 to June 1940. He said that there was unnecessary shouting and bullying by the staff, one or two of whom were really bullies and used filthy language. He said that a man who had fainted was slapped in the face by a staff sergeant who, in his opinion was bullying him not assisting him, although he added "He was trying to bring him round." He mentioned another case where a man who had fainted was dragged along the corridor to the washouse by a member of the staff who put his head under the tap. He said that he had protested against this treatment to one of the senior NCOs but that next day he was transferred to another Detention Barracks. He made no allegations of ill-treatment of prisoners there."

"No 32 had been serving a sentence in detention during January 1940. He said he himself was never physically assaulted, but that on many occasions he had seen men kicked by warders and that he had also seen men pushed about and punched in the back for lagging on parade, and that such things were done quite openly and anyone could see them. There was no ill-treatment when commissioned officers were about; which however, was not often."

The conclusions of the Committee were accepted without reservation and resulted in very significant reforms.

The unanimous opinion of all the Committee was that there was a shortfall of staff at all the establishments and that there should be a major recruiting drive. They then observed that recruitment had to be of the right kind of man.

Training up to this time had been a perfunctory business of two to three weeks attachment to Aldershot, where the probationer followed around an experienced man and learned the ropes. The Committee laid down that a proper training school should be established and that the probationers' course should last at least two months. Fort Darland, significantly, was chosen as the training school and stayed there until its move to Colchester after the war. Major Bob Firmstone was one of its organisers and many of the personal accounts we have collected start at Fort Darland. Many of them speak with admiration of the course and of the facilities at Darland. On photographs, the place has a grim and forbidding look, but much effort appears to have gone into making it a showpiece.

Many of the complainants had told the Committee that the only time that they saw a commissioned officer was when they went on Commandant's for punishment. Oliver decided that the establishment of officers would be increased and that they should be permanently circulating through the establishments.

In the Clayton inquest, the medical officer had been criticised and Oliver found that most DBs had part time MOs and that they changed very frequently. He recommended a permanent MO for each establishment and stated that the position should have some permanency.

On a material level, two things had appalled the Committee on its tours: the primitive night arrangements, where thirty men would share one open bucket and the SUS's rusty diet tins, which formed their sole crockery. Diet tins had originally been aluminium, but these had been collected in to melt down for the aircraft industry and tins only thinly coated and rapidly becoming rusty, had been substituted. The Committee ordered that all should be collected and recoated.

The Clayton incident was sad, should never have been happened, but it let fresh air into the system at a time when it was sorely necessary.

18
With the First Army in Africa

WE left Mr. Rea heading North for Chorley. After a pleasant stay there, he was posted to Fort Darland, which was soon to become notorious, deciding after a while to volunteer for overseas. he was sent to Aldershot and stayed there in transit.

He found Aldershot much changed, the grimness somewhat taken out of it and training much more to the fore. As he waited for his draft, he was allocated to the training team, where the most sought after subject to be taught was map reading. This consisted of the SUS in Field Service Marching Order being taken out into the countryside in green buses, then marched around an extensive park. The presence of two pubs near the park was a factor in the subject's popularity.

His draft finally came up and he went to Southampton, where a forty ship convoy was assembling, including the troopship Samaria and Nevassa, each with the staff of a Field Punishment Centre amongst the other troops. The journey took four days, with the Luftwaffe calling daily at noon but the convoy finally reached Algiers. No. 2 FPC was to be sited twenty five miles up the coast from Algiers and no transport was available, so the staff marched to the chosen location, which was close to the Mediterranean.

A French colonial official's house had been requisitioned as officers and sergeants living quarters and the FPC itself consisted of tent lines and a ten cell block, all surrounded by rolls of wire. Nearby was a small town, where coffee and cognac were popular outside duty hours.

In the gold of one evening, Mr Rea was sitting in the bistro, which had almost become a second sergeants' mess, when he noticed a British soldier sitting quietly drinking in one corner. He nodded a greeting and received a nod in return. The next night, the same soldier was sitting there and Rea began to feel that the face was familiar, but the lad was quiet enough. He finished his drink without undue haste, nodded to Rea's table and left the bistro. He was not there when Rea went into town again and the young soldier, who came in later in the evening was certainly known to Rea, being one of his training squad of SUS, whom Rea promptly snatched. This was the last SUS in No.2 Field Punishment Centre to win the nightly draw and to disappear down the tunnel, which emerged in the cane field next to the wire.

The Centre was faced later with the unpleasant business of housing a soldier condemned to death and Rea sat on the death watch. The man was a Pioneer, sentenced for the murder of a military policeman and two Arabs. He was a foul-mouthed creature and refused any kind of assistance, appearing to be completely indifferent to what he had done and to his fate. Rea remembers Vera Lynn's voice when she entertained troops nearby on the evening before the execution.

On the morning of the sentence, The Assistant Provost Marshal arrived in a truck with the firing squad. The Medical Officer was already there, as was the Roman Catholic padre. The padre went into the death cell and asked if the man wanted the comfort of the church and was spat on for his pains. The MO asked if he would like an injection and was told to stuff his injection. When his breakfast arrived, he threw it at the orderly.

When the hour of execution arrived, he was pinioned and put on the back of a truck with his escort and taken to a quarry, cursing all in sight. He was placed on a chair with a white patch as target and Rea insists that not a man of the firing squad regretted what he had to do.

As time went on, the FPC staff made many acquaintances in the French area of the town, helped by Rea's friend, Pip, another wartime temporary, who Rea remembers as one of the scruffiest sergeants he ever met but with the advantage that he was a Jerseyman and spoke fluent French. The population was mainly teachers and civil servants, many of them retired. The French police chief and chief jailer would also invite them to the local lock-up, where drunks were housed overnight, then made to do chores before being sent home. Arabs caught stealing would be bastinadoed, then released.

Other friends made were from the nearby American unit, where opportunities to trade existed. It was in their company that Rea heard Josephine Baker sing the Marsaillaise in Algiers on Bastille Day.

No.3 FPC was ordered to move to Bizerte. The move was

by freight train, with a goods wagon as sleeping accommodation and a flat bed wagon for sunbathing. Signals such as "meal stop" and "take cover" were sent from the cab, using the engine's whistle. At every stop, Arabs would appear to exchange eggs for tea; eggs, Rea suspects, that had originated with French colonial hens.

At Bizerte, contact was rapidly made with the local American units, where an exchange of rations and other commodities developed healthily. One American set-up was manned by the conscripted employees of an American restaurant chain and the FPC staff members were often regaled with a three choice and exotic lunch.

One American unit prided itself on its boxing record and had converted a French hangar into a boxing stadium. With the MPSC was one Taffy Baker, whom Rea insists would rather fight than eat. He was the little, slight-looking kind of Welshman of the kind that made the reputation of the valleys and he, of course, was aching to fight, particularly when he learned that the purse was $100 to win. The Americans were highly amused when they saw Taffy, particularly as their boys were mainly black and big. Betting was not easy running on the first bout. Six bouts later, Taffy had made $600. He increased this to $2000 in a poker game after the contest, then lost the lot.

As you will see, the late Mr. Rea could tell a story. We received his MPSC history on tape from Canada, where he went after the war and joined the Ontario Prison Service. Sadly, he died shortly after contacting us and we hope to send a copy of this book to his widow to show our appreciation for a well-told tale. We shall meet him again in Sicily and up the boot of Italy. Now let Tex Rickard take over the story.

"No. 1 Military Prison in the Field was formed-up in the Autumn of 1942 at the (Glasshouse) Aldershot under the command of Col. McKay Gordon and Major Winter, MC.

We left Liverpool per HMT "Otaranto" in the first week of January, 1943, for a destination unknown, which after 14 days' uneventful journey proved to be Algiers. Uneventful for us, but not so for No. 1 Field Punsihment Centre, who were in the convoy ahead of us, their ship was torpedoed just off Oran. All took to the lifeboats, no casualties.

On landing at Algiers we marched out to a place called Sur-

Coufe, Ain-Taya, about 25kms east along the coast. It was here that No. 1 Field Punishment Camp had been established. After a short period of waiting, which included plenty of long route marches drawing up of stores, etc No. 1 Military Prison moved to a place called Navarin, a small Arab village out in the wilds between Surtife and Constantine.

The camp was built by an advance party of SUS under the supervision of our own staff. It consisted of a few permanent buildings, Nissen Huts for Admin purposes and "singles" block and serried rows of sand coloured tents divided into compounds, housing two hundred, with each compound separated by coils of high barbed wire fencing, the whole camp surrounded by a 15ft wall of more barbed wire. Although the wire gave freedom of sight it was just as much a deterrent as the walls of Dartmoor.

A small railroad ran along the side of the camp, which supplied our requirements and also those of an American Flying Fortress base which lay on the plain about two miles away. Here were shunted every other day waggons containing petrol, SAA and bombs, which were later transported to the field.

One hot summer's day, with no hint of the unusual, we had issued dinner diets and patrols were posted, the Staff had completed their dinner, when suddenly an American soldier came running into the Staff tents shouting loudly, "Take off you guys, the gas is on fire!" At the same time there was shouting from the SUS inside the compounds, "There's smoke!" and one thousand men were clamouring for information, no doubt glad of a minor happening to break the monotony of such a camp.

True enough, there on the siding were five waggons standing together; more plainly now could be seen the smoke oozing out of the first one, which was quite plainly marked "Inflammable Petrol," the other four waggons comprised of three with bombs and the other with petrol, all these not more than two hundred yards from the camp.

Nevertheless, the situation was soon under control, the Commandant gave orders to open up every compound, whereupon 1,000 fear sticken men were doubled out over the plains. By this time the camp was clear, when it was noticed that the petrol waggon was now flaming. Fear lends wings, so the minimum quarter-mile necessary to escape the blast was done

133

in record time (Bannister, please note!) We flung ourselves to the ground watching the flaming waggon and waiting with pounding hearts for the roar of the explosion. A second later it came with a roar and a hiss, the petrol containers had exploded, a split second later there was yet a louder roar as the bombs ignited, sending our heads yet further into the sand and a prayer in our hearts, knowing that our timely action had prevented what might have been a serious situation with the loss of life.

The camp was completely gutted, there was very little left but charred and tangled barbed wire. Nevertheless, with improvisation, life went on, and a few months later we moved to Bone, a medium sized seaport of some distinction. Here we took over and converted into a prison an old disused French hospital. I must say it was indeed a great improvement to our last place. We worked on the docks unloading and loading ships, one of the shifts operating from 0600hrs until 1400hrs. This, of course, meant reveille for the staff at 0330hrs. Many were the moans and groans as we groped our way down the steps into the prison to awaken the SUS at this unearthly hour. Compensations were few, wines very cheap in the local estaminet, the French girls being known for their beauty the world over, so it was a case of "work hard, play hard" in that sequence.

Many amusing incidents used to happen whilst working on the docks. One day we were off-loading a NAAFI cargo which contained the usual beers and spirits there were 12 SUS working in the hold with one of the crew. Things were beginning to slow up, so on going down to investigate we found the whole party tottering about "drunk as lords". They had dropped a case of whisky, upended the case and were drinking it from their mess tins. It is left to your own imagination as to what happened after that and the trouble we had getting 12 fighting drunk soldiers back to barracks. Also that day the two SUS left the working party, stole the Brigadier's staff car-he was at the time inspecting the docks-put on a spare jacket and hat found in the back of the car, and drove away through the docks gate, only to be saluted by the policeman on duty. What the Brigadier said when found out should not be repeated in print. Was his face red!"

19
"Ginger' Gordon"

Before we start across to Sicily and up the leg of Italy, I would like to pay tribute to a man whose name appears repeatedly in the accounts wirtten by the Old and Bold in this campaign. The name of Colonel John Mc K Gordon is already known to you from the account of the MPSC with the British Expeditionary Force in pre-Dunkirk France.

Major Jock Swain, an old Cameron Highlander and a member of the MPSC Association until his death in 1987 stayed in contact with "Ginger" Gordon until his death at the age of 92. He had known him a long time, first meeting him when he, Jock, was a Lance Corporal and Ginger was his company commander. Specific incidents stick in a young soldier's mind and become, as it were, the summary of the whole person. With Jock Swain, the incident was on a Saturday morning inspection. The normal ladder of inspections had already taken place: Jock; the platoon sergeant; the platoon commander, then Ginger inspected. He turned to Jock and said "Laddie are they giving you too much to eat in the battalion?" Jock said that they weren't. "Then why are your platoon lines littered with food?" He pointed and there, undiscovered by all others were five baked beans.

It is the kind of thing that we can all remember, but the remarkable thing is that, all the accounts mentioning Ginger, recall some pawky Scots humour, tied to a sharpness of observation and an underlying understanding of what the soldier, however low on the heap, is going to remember and improve.

There are worse qualities for an Inspector of Military Prisons in wartime.

It is not surprising that Colonel Gordon should know soldiers. He had enlisted in the Camerons in 1908 and was commissioned from the rank of sergeant in the early days of the First World War. In 1916, he commanded a company of his battalion and won the MC at Bazentin Ridge, being wounded in an attack three months later. He served in West

Africa, the first BAOR and in the Irish troubles. He retired in 1936.

Someone was perceptive enough to realise at the beginning of the Second World War, that Major Gordon was a man suitable for the difficult task of organising a disciplinary service. As we have seen, he commanded the FPCs with the BEF, then later went to North Africa and became Inspector for the long slog up the leg of Italy. Ex WO I Rea remembers his old soldier's humour, once again summarised in one incident. When Rea's FPC was outside Naples, there was no electricity and no wicks were available for the issue hurricane lamps, so a long and bleating signal was sent to the Inspector, naming this and other deficiencies of the new location. Ginger's reply was "Your observations noted with concern. Improvise".

Tony Moore, who retired after many years regular and Territorial Army Service as a Lieutenant Colonel, knew Ginger Gordon well, as he served as the chief clerk of the Inspectorate for some considerable time. Tony's recollections are worth recording in full:

"The Inspectorate was located in the heart of Rome, in the Via Botteghe Oscura just round the corner from the Piazza Venezia. it was in a 5 or 6 floored office building, with Col Gordon occupying a top floor pent house and the office on the floor below, surrounded by a balcony giving a marvellous view across Rome. The staff consisted of 1 Chief Clerk (QMS), 1 S/Sgt and 2 or 3 Sgt Clerks, with 1 GD Man (Fusilier Barret) and the Colonel's Driver/Batman (Dvr Butcher) later charged and sentenced for "consorting with a known deserter" i.e. he gave a handout to a deserter on the run in Rome and was spotted by the MP. The Staff Lieutenant was J W Petts, ex QMS of the MPSC – and later Captain. I think he lived out. Col G had responsibilities for FPCs and MPs in Italy and Greece and later in Austria. He was very meticulous in the keeping of records and insisted on a very very high standard of work – letters had to be perfectly typed, no visible alterations and not even a comma omitted and he sprinkled commas around by the handful – a typical sentence would be "and, in this connection, it would appear, that the Sergeant in question, did, etc." He drafted his long policy letters in thick black pencil on duplicating paper, then dictated it to one of the clerks who took it down in longhand.

This was then read back to the Colonel, and after typing had to be "proof" read again before submission for signature. He was autocratic, and most people stood in awe of him; but he was scrupulously fair and had the gift of reducing a problem to a straight yes or no answer – particularly when dealing with complaints or disciplinary matters.

He always wore his regimental dress as a full colonel, and one was not allowed to enter his regiment as QOCH on any return it had to be in full – and most army forms did not allow space for The Queen's Own Cameron Highlanders. At the same time he always gave one your full rank Quartermaster Sergeant – never Q or QMS. He did not concern himself too much over the dress of the staff of the Inspectorate; but then he never saw us "walking out" where in Rome at least practically any combination could be worn: KD shirts and BD trousers, flannel shirts and shorts etc. Sgt Fayers, Grenadiers before transfer wore a blue New Zealand Issue shirt with BD slacks and I had a bottle green Indian Army pattern shirt. He was, however insistant upon medal ribbons, service chevrons and wound stripes, and having discovered from our documents that Fayers had been wounded in North Africa and I in Italy, insisted that we applied for authority for the award of a wound stripe – and I have an entry in my old AB64 to this effect, signed by Capt Petts.

As I mentioned earlier, we moved by train to Austria, all the goods, chattels etc in a goods truck, with the staff in situ, hitched on to a train bound for Klagenfurt. It was quite a pleasant and interesting 2 day journey and we were fairly easily established in Lienz. The staff were in billets with the staff of the Prison and Col G in the Dolomiten Hotel, also used as the Officers Mess. Col G carried out a long battle with the MO over his, the MOs, dress – he wore very short stockings and rather short shorts. For all his forbidding appearance Col G. did have a sense of humour. He adopted a kitten, and we prepared a complete file of documents for it, attaching it to the Inspectorate from the Royal Corps of Ratcatchers. One day it went astray, turning up some 3 days later, rather bedraggled. QMS Knott, the then chief clerk made out an AFB252 charging it with absence and sentencing it to 3 days PD1. Taking a chance he put the file in front of the Colonel, who had a habit of signing papers before he read them. This he did, then read the charge sheet. He made one alteration and, without a word handed the file back. Where it said on the bottom of the B252 "signature of OC Squadron, Battery or Company" Col G had altered the Battery to read Cattery. With the reduction in Penal Establishments Colonel Gordon had to revert to Lieutenant Colonel in I think early 1947.

During this period there were still gangs of deserters on the loose in Italy of all nationalities, and practically every issue of BTA ROs carried commendations for CMP involved in incidents with these people, generally a shooting match. All military trains were supplied with armed guards, and the road route from Austria through Udine was particularly dangerous, many hold-ups occurring. All individual vehicle passengers had to be armed, and Col G generally carried a shotgun and his driver a pistol."

Ginger Gordon was one of the prime movers in permitting a limited cigarette issue in MPs and DBs, but more important was an experiment in which he played a great part: the introduction of 3 Special Training Battalion. On this, I still have his original brief.

When Italy had been invaded, there was a sharp rise in the number of front line desertions and a consequent rise in demand for penal establishments. The expansion was made difficult by the extreme shortage of MPSC staff. By July 1944, serious consideration was being given to a suspension of sentence system, similar to that which had been applied during the First World War. Gordon, and many of the Commandants, were of the opinion that many of the young deserters were the victims of breakdown in the face of continued action and that many of them were redeemable as soldiers. They should be retained and given another chance to make good after suspension of their sentences. Gordon and the DAG, Brigadier R Ware discussed the matter in August 1944 and decided that the lines of the FPCs in the pre-Dunkirk BEF should be modified and used as the pattern for the new unit. The unit, named 34 Special Training Barracks was established at Cecchignola, near Rome, on 1st December 1944. It only closed with the arrival of VJ Day.

Selection of those soldiers who were to be given the second chance would depend on recommendations from their section sergeants, AEC instructors and Prison Sergeant Majors in whichever military prison they were confined. When selected, they would be known as recruits, not as soldiers under sentence.

The main staff of the STB was to be MPSC as far as this was possible. Qualifications for the task were to be:

All would be strict disciplinarians. They were to have proven expertise as military training instructors, with specialist qualifications in weapon training, Map Reading or PT. Any shortfall in MPSC instructors was to be made up from highly selected NCOs from neighbouring battalions and regiments.

The officers, also, were to be carefully selected and recommended, as were the AEC and APTC elements.

The barracks selected was a modern Italian construction able to hold 1000 to 1200 men, built next the the barracks which was being prepared as No. 1 Military Prison. Not all the capacity of the barracks was to be used, and Gordon estimated that full strength should be 300 soldiers, who should join in monthly batches of 100. Any soldier not measuring up to the training would be returned to his parent prison.

Three companies were organised, depending on stage of training and their time would be divided between training and labour, the proportion of training time increasing in each successive company. The most advanced: C Coy, would train for 80% of its time and would conduct some of its training outside the barrack area. Gordon's stipulation was that training would be varied, progressive but above all, active.

After some months of trial, it was decided to replace the MPSC element of the staff with soldiers from other regiments, because the MPSC badge was found to be too strongly associated with the military prison and because MPSC members were too thin on the ground in the theatre (at the high point in the campaign, there were five military prisons and six field punishment and detention centres to be staffed.) When the change to regimental staff was ordered, six of the MPSC volunteered to rebadge to their original regiments and to quote the report "they were accepted and rendered good service, two of them at least being amongst the best NCOs ever employed at the STB.

Did the experiment succeed? Of 1046 soldiers who passed through the system, 691 returned to their duty but the numbers whose sentence was put into execution after returning to unit are not stated. An appendix to the report consists of letters received from soldiers who have passed through the system and I think that it is appropriate to quote one of these: there is very little "fire in the belly" about it but it says a great deal, I think, about the "inner" success of the experiment. . . . and I find it appropriate that the lad who writes it belongs to Ginger Gordon's own regiment.

Pte XXXXX
B Coy, 2nd Battalion
Cameron Highlanders
CMF
28 10 45

Dear Sir,

Just a few lines to let you know how Pte Y and me are getting along. We have both settled down in the battalion and like it here very much. At present we are in Verona, N Italy and find it quite enjoyable place. We were at Venice a few days ago on a day pass it's all right but very expensive. At present the battalion is only about half strength and the quarter guards come around very often but we find no difficulty as we have kept up the standards of the STB. We are very grateful for the chance you gave us and we wish 34 every success in the future.

We remain Yours Obediently
Pte X and Pte Y
7th Intake.

20
Across the Straits and up the Leg

So many of the Old and Bold have memories of Italy that this chapter almost writes itself, but for a description of the corps in Sicily, I have to rely on the late Mr. (ex WOI) Rea, whom we last met in North Africa. On the way up the leg itself, the names of my contributors reads like a roll call of the old Corps membership: Bill King ex WOI; Captain (retd) Maurice Saunders, Tex Rickard, Bill Skinner, the late Les Fairweather. Of old Corps members, no longer in touch with the Association, ex S/Sgt HW Vallins helped me and also Lieutenant Colonel Tony Moore, whose service with the Inspectorate made a valuable contribution.

Mr Rea was on the staff of the only military prison I can trace in Sicily. It was near Catania and came complete with it own gaoler, Charlie. Charlie was near to pension age and appeared to have had a pleasant and easy life: there were geraniums around the cell windows and he carried all the keys of the prison on one large iron ring, until the MPSC convinced him that this was not good security policy. Feeding his prisoners had been the responsibility of the prisoners' families and they could eat and drink what they fancied, providing the families paid. The unfortunate prisoner, of course, was the one without a family.

The prison was escape proof, built of lava blocks. The MPSC staff lived in a large three storied building nearby. Business was not all that brisk and what training there was, was carried out on a small prison yard which could only be reached by squeezing sideways down a narrow passage.

A call from the military police introduced spice and variety to the routine. The CMP, said the APM, had just captured nine members of an organisation calling itself the Free Corps of Saint George, ranging in rank from private to colonel (the colonel was self-promoted from lance corporal). They were all deserters and had lived by theft and hijack, even taking over a merchant ship at one stage and selling its cargo. Their accomplices had been Sicilians and the "colonel" claimed that there were three hundred of them and that they would make every effort to free him. Could the MPSC, asked the APM, please take care of the free Corps and sort them out? They refused to wear uniform or to march and were due for court martial in ten days time.

The Free Corps arrived, chained together and with a CMP escort. They were dressed in every combination of tinker's mufti, were filthy and unshaven – they later proved to be syphilitic. They refused to march so the escort picked them off the back of the truck.

The cosy little gaol had one feature that had almost gone out of use: ten cells below ground level, with a narrow barred slit as the only source of light and it was these that were to become the home for the Free Corps for the next ten days. It was pointed out to them that non-cooperation was a two-way business: that even providing food was a form of cooperation. At the end of the ten days the Free Corps, shaven and wearing Army uniform, doubled to the gate to be received by their escort of thirty military policeman. Their sentences ranged from fifteen years to life.

Deserters in Italy were a scourge. Tony Moore mentions the Lane Gang, described, thinly disguised in Richard Llewellyn's "A few Flowers for Shiner". One of the Lane Gang is mentioned by Bill Skinner as being the subject of a Death Watch in Potici. This particular one had murdered a naval petty officer.

A string of military prisons and FPCs followed the Army up the leg of Italy. They were housed in a variety of buildings from a Roman Catholic orphanage to an agricultural college. The orphanage was in a small town outside Naples and was a bone of contention with the Poles, who had themselves wanted it for the same purpose. At one FPC, the church bell was the only signal for reveille, until a sergeant of the MPSC cut the rope, resulting in late rising, complaints from the Italian padre and a severe reprimand.

It was not all work. On Sundays, one MPSC football team played the local village and were beaten with monotonous regularity, much to the joy of the local youth and ex-Fascists. Their answer, possessing all the elements of British fair play, was to import four professionals from other regiments, deck them out as Corps members and field them on the following

Sunday. The 20-0 win resulted in a riot, which was put down by American and Italian police and one MPSC member spent the night in the local lock-up. After this, GHQ forbade international friendlies.

Bill King, as a colour sergeant in The Duke of Wellington's Regiment, was downgraded after being wounded and was transferred to the MPSC. There was no probationers' course and he was put to each duty in turn around the military prison in Brindisi with the idea of learning by doing. Brindisi was a civilian prison, in which the MPSC had taken two of the four wings, the others being reserved for women and men. The governor lived over the floridly decorated main gate in an extremely luxurious apartment, his needs being catered for by the female prisoners.

The main gate was used for admissions and releases only, the main traffic being through the back gate. Next to the back gate was a yard in which upwards of 350 SUS would be working at any one time, stripping and cleaning equipment salvaged from the front line.

One of Bill's early duties was on this back gate. He was busy and green. A truck hooted for admission and Bill, not yet wise to the evils of SUS, opened the gate in full, then was trampled to the ground as the yard full of SUS headed for the hole in the wall. The truck driver had the presence of mind to block the gate with his vehicle, but several of the SUS got through. They were captured later enjoying the town. This was the place where Bill first met Tex Rickards and they worked together to convert one of the larger rooms into a mess, complete with self-built bar. They both made Italian friends and were once invited to an Italian wedding, where a great deal of wine flowed and they enjoyed the succulent main dish of rabbit until they learned that it was cat.

Bill quickly found that life in military prison was not to his taste and he asked for a transfer to a Field Punishment Centre, where he would be able to use his military skills. He was posted to No. 2 FPC at Portici. Portici was just below Vesuvius. It was a tented camp, firmly dedicated to corrective training. There were four companies and they worked competitively, the aim being to motivate and develop, rather than merely lock away. They ran much on the lines of a regimental depot and an enlightened Commandant went so far as to introduce the privilege of a Saturday afternoon swim in the sea for the company showing best at Saturday morning inspection.

It was here that Bill met Maurice Saunders for the first time and Dinty Moore was Bill's friend and rival on the drill square. The amount of volcanic dust that a squad could stir up by its drill activity became the subject of competition.

The presence of Vesuvius was a permanent reality. Maurice remembers boot soles burned through during route marches on the lower slopes. There had been an eruption shortly before Bill's arrival and SUS had been killed in their sleep by a permeation of poisonous gas through the earth. As a result of this, it became routine for the Night Watch to carry a hurricane lamp, which had to be regularly placed on the ground to warn of seepage.

Bill Skinner was also at Portici, but attached to the military prison there. This was an old Italian cavalry barracks alongside the main road. It was flat roofed and the roofs were used for PT: there was no other military training apart from this. There were 300+SUS, many of them French Canadians and hard men. Most of the SUS were employed on the Naples Dock, loading and unloading, but also salvaging packing cases. These were cleaned, stripped of nails, then taken to a work shop near the prison, where they were converted into beds, chairs and so on. Bill says that much of the finished work was first class.

The staff quarters were in a large house outside the prison and still occupied by civilians, who very very friendly. One Sergeant Crome, who slept on the first floor, was twice robbed of everything apart from his bed – still a favourite Neapolitan pastime! Another Neapolitan method of passing time was to hang around the main gate, watching comings and goings. The urchins who did this were noisily ecstatic when a kilted Scot arrived as AVO. Sergeant Carr on the main gate was reprimanded for his slowness in opening and allowing the visiting officer to escape from his enthusiastic junior admirers. The main gate lodge, incidentally, contained a wide section of Italian donkey whips. Outside the prison was a steep hill up which the beasts of burden were encouraged by shouts, screams and liberal application of the leather or cord. One staff sergeant objected strongly to this and would dash out of the gate, use MPSC volume tones of reprimand then confiscate the whip.

The late Les Fairweather recorded a tape of his service for us immediately before his death. Les had started his service at Caterham and fought up the leg of Italy with the Grenadier Guards. He was wounded and downgraded, then transferred to the MPSC. His first posting was to No. 1 MPDB near Rome, where he found himself as one of the few military training instructors at a time when a military training programme was being introduced. His average squad was 60 SUS and he was on a treadmill of constant instruction. After a while, he asked the RSM when he would start to learn MPSC duties – he had had no probationary course – and was told that time would be found. After this, he did constant evening and weekend duties in a long, grinding row and admits that he learned MPSC duties quite thoroughly.

Tony Moore recalls two cheeky escapes during this period. In No. 1 in Rome, a course of instruction in vehicle maintenance was introduced. A "trusty" SUS had reassembled a motor-cycle under supervision and was told by the instructor to give it a trial run around the yard. As the SUS moved off, the ration truck arrived at the gate and was admitted. The SUS, a man of initiative, took the motor bike down the blind side of the truck and disappeared into town. Some hours later the motor cycle was seen in town, leaning against a cafe wall and investigation revealed the SUS in the back room, flask of vino, plate of pasta and girl friend on knee. He had not wanted to escape, he insisted merely to remember what he was missing inside.

The other escape was from the military prison in Florence, when three SUS drove through the main gate at night in a carelessly secured three tonner. They were picked up four days later in London "something of a record", adds Tony "when it took over a week to get home by the leave train".

The Italian Campaign was a hard one, but when it ended, the Army moved into Austria. One of the last penal establishments to close was at Casena. The staff were to move by rail to Klagenfurt, but the SUS were sent back to their units all that is, apart from one. This last survivor was a New Zealander, whose 28 days were nearly over and who was then to be shipped to New Zealand. As the only SUS on the premises, he was in a rather privileged position. It seemed pointless to keep staff on watch over him during mealtimes and the mess was a fair way from the gate lodge, so the Kiwi was given the keys and would let the staff in on their return from the mess.

Austria deserves a chapter and shall have one, but so also does one of the dream postings of the MPSC, the kind of which people can only dream. I speak of the MCE Trieste.

PART FIVE

Post War Blues

21
Woodbines and Players.

"Looking sea-ward from our Ante-room windows the view, particularly at night, is breath taking and inspiring. Far out to sea in the mist-laden air, the gigantic Adriatic rollers crash and tumble. Coming inland the water is placid and calm, and hundreds of little craft ply their trade fishing, dancing up and down on the smooth expanse of sea like minarets. The moon hangs low, like a big silver lamp in the water, casting her reflection in the glassy surface beneath and shedding a white glow over the everlasting ebb and flow of the tide. Overhead the sky is ablaze with the brilliant stars, whilst in Trieste itself, the city is twinkling with her millions of lights. Looking north-wards the dim outline of the hill stands out in bold relief, grim and foreboding, as if looking down on Trieste with disparaging view of her gaiety. On the hills themselves the houses flash their lights against the sombre back-ground and against it all the great white searchlight slowly swings in a great arc round Trieste, turning night into day. A picture to be remembered, a memory to take back with one, Trieste the beautiful, holding all things lovely gay and splendid, the prize of the Adriatic. That will be about all from the MCE Trieste this time. KEYS AWAY."

The passage is a bit purple and poetic but all the descriptions I have had of MCE Trieste share the enthusiasm.

But where, ask the younger end, is Trieste and why put a MCE there?

Trieste lies across the Northern Aegean facing Venice. From an obscure fishing port, it developed in the Nineteenth Century to become the main port of the otherwise land-locked Austro-Hungarian Empire. When Austria lost the First World War, Italy, on the winning side, was given Trieste, a fact much resented by the newly born Yugoslavia, of which it forms a logical part. The port became something of a ping-pong ball between the countries and the dispute carried on until well after the Second World War, when a compromise solution was arrived at: the city and an area around it were administered by a joint Anglo-American military government and the rest by Yugoslavia.

It is a sad fact that a military government needs troops and that where troops are, there will be sin, drunkeness and occasional uproar, all requiring correction and a Military Corrective Establishment.

Bill Flecknoe was sent to Trieste to start just such an establishment in February 1948. He found that the site was one, where he felt confident that he could happily soldier. It was an old Italian – previously Austrian – infantry depot on the highest point in the city: San Guisto, close to the cathedral. It had a surrounding wall, was brick and stone built, four storied and with accommodation for 25 SUS. This accommodation was to be on the lower storey, which was also to house the MPSC's other responsibility: a garrison Guardroom. The mess was to be on the top storey "living over the shop"!

No.3. MCE in Austria helped out with staff until six permanent members arrived from a still rationed, gloomy and austere UK. To them, the place was a wonderful land of food they had almost forgotten, goods in the shops, NAAFI and PX, sun and beaches. The only snag on the weather front, was the Bora, a fierce wind that could blow for days and could gust up to 70mph, knocking over trams and three tonners. They found that the city had ropes or chains at vulnerable points to prevent pedestrians from being blown into the street. . . . but the compensations outweighed the Bora.

Business was at its most brisk on Friday nights and over the weekend, when garrison customers were poured into the Garrison Guardroom by military and regimental policemen, to be kept overnight, then returned to their own guardroom, probably to return later for the MCE graduation course. Frank Bell was posted there from Shepton Mallet and regards it as the gem of all postings, though the training facilities were limited. There was one instructional room, a wood shed and a square "hardly bigger than a back yard."

He remembers the classic working party as two staff and six SUS sent down to the Married Families beach to clean it ready for the season. The exertions and the heat of training in summer, led to large intakes of Birra Dormisch, a potion mentioned also affectionately by Bill Flecknoe.

Barrack Square, Aldershot circa 1910. Garsia's reforms in operation.

Governor's office, Aldershot circa 1912. Major Henderson (?) in chair.

A workshop in Aldershot MP & DB.

One of a series of cartoons held by RHQ MPSC.

Governor and Civilian warders, Brixton Military Prison 1896.

MPSC staff on SS Immingham – one of the prison ships of World War I.

A typical cell at Aldershot 1939–45.

Colonel J McK Gordon MC, late Cameron Highlanders – Inspector General of Prisons, Italy and Austria.

Fort Darland – a barrack cart (see 'Murderers of Poor Sammy Clayton').

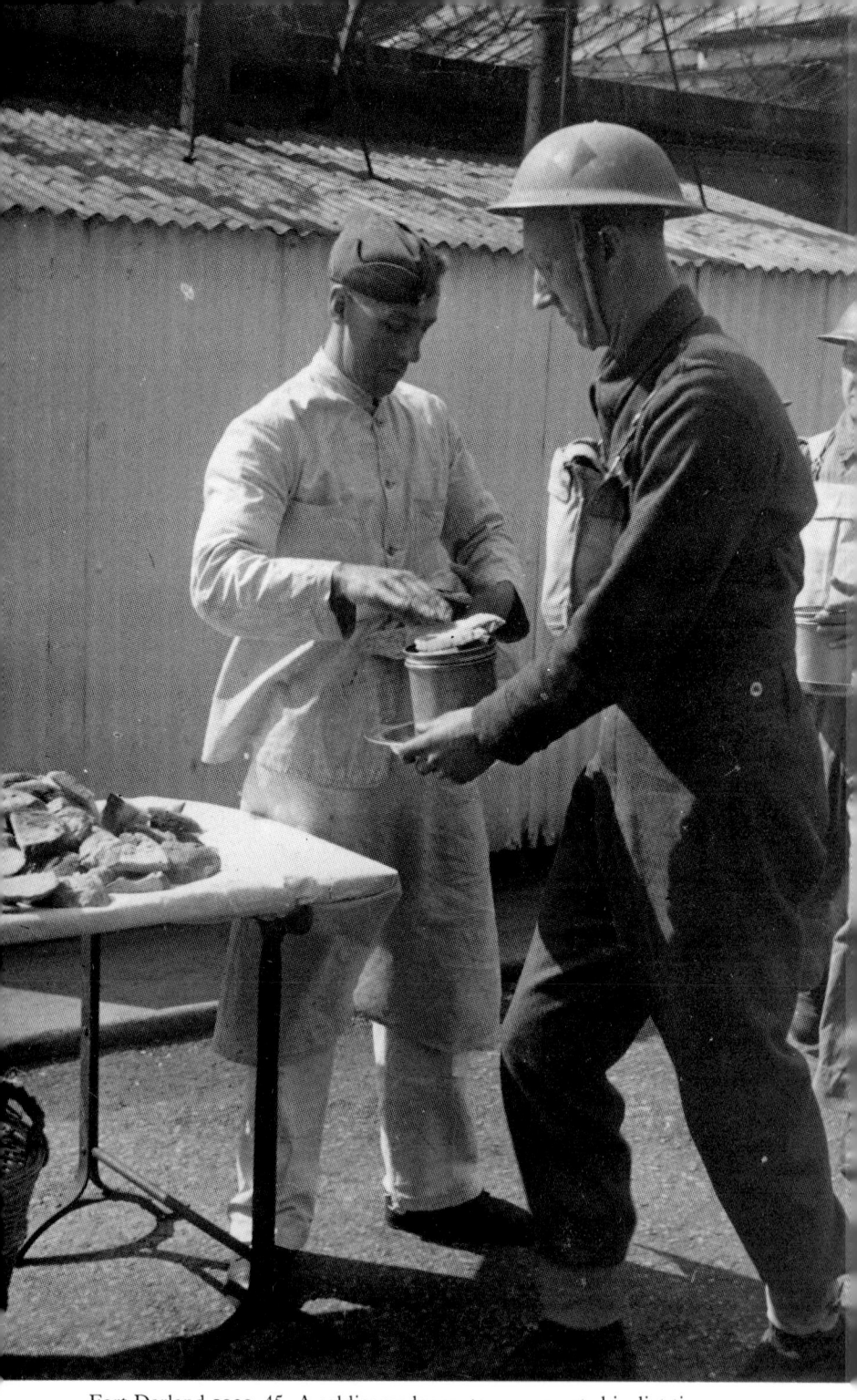

Fort Darland 1939–45. A soldier under sentence presents his diet tin.

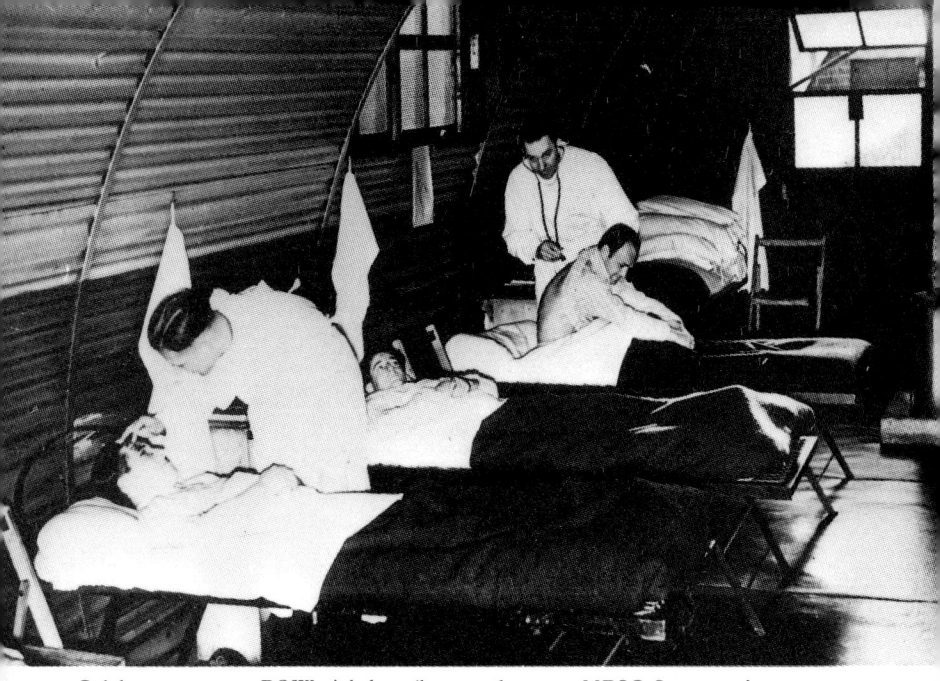

Colchester 1945 – POW sick-bay (later to become MPSC Sergeants' Mess).

The Mallet.

Interior of a cell, mat making.

Navy rum also comes in for favourable mention, for the city was a favourite visiting place for the Navy and the MCE saw much of them: petty officers were always welcome guests on the top floor and ratings often visited the bottom floor.

Bill remembers another member of staff – unnamed – who also enjoyed the view from the mess window. He would sit, strumming his ukelele and looking out, then would often put down his instrument and quietly leave. Observation revealed that his main attention was on a window visible from the mess and that occasionally the window was decorated with a plant pot, that the ukelele player left only when the plantpot was on the sill. Time revealed that the plantpot appeared when the husband of the "Plantpot Lady" left the house.

The garrison and the fleet did not supply the only customer for the MCE. Trieste sat on one of the hot spots of the Cold War and was a favoured crossing point for those who were opting out of life beyond the Iron Curtain. The line between the Yugoslav Zone and our own was manned by check points and the MPSC were required to work in close liaison with Anglo-American Intelligence. There was a twenty four hour standby in the MCE, waiting for a call from the check points. When a call arrived, the duty staff went to collect either the Players or the Woodbines.

Players were the higher grade refugees, whom the Intelligence saw as possible infiltrators or as deep intelligence sources. They were held only for a short time at MCE, then taken for interrogation.

Bill remembers the Woodbines as poor devils: "They were the sad dregs of humanity, some military, some civilian, often with rags as their only footwear, clothes ragged and stinking from days and nights of constant wear. Searching them was an awful task. The military refugees often came in with the strangest collection of weapons, which were checked by a WOI RAOC, who was always on call for the task.

Before collecting from the check points, the cooks of the MCE were always alerted and a meal would be waiting. A RAMC orderly was also on standby for delousing. The Woodbines were showered, fed, then placed in a room for first interrogation. Many broke down and cried when they found that a bed with clean sheets and blankets was prepared for them, a luxury they had almost forgotten. The CQMS of the MCE, Colour Sergeant Jock Campbell of the Royal Scots, held a stock of condemned, but clean, uniform for reclothing them and, after satisfactory interrogation, they were sent to a camp in Austria for resettlement.

"Once, a group of German POWs, who had escaped behind the curtain and who had walked many hundreds of miles, was held by us for about three weeks. They were very grateful chaps, glad to be with us, and they gave us absolutely no trouble at all."

Bill Flecknoe handed over to Sid Rumney and finally left Trieste in 1952, sad to go and "with a bloodstream mainly running Birra Dornisch and Navy rum". A statement was made that the Anglo-American Military Government would leave in 1953 and in October of that year, the Married Families of MCE left. Appropriately, the 5th of November started with a Chinese cracker of small arms fire in the city and the Trieste riots had begun. The action swirled around the streets outside the MCE, which was almost in a state of siege, armed guards travelling with ration vehicles. When the time came to mourn the riot dead, the place chosen was the cathedral directly opposite the MCE and there were something like 5000 mourners around the main gate. Two MPSC members: Sgt Scott MM and Sgt Harkins repelled boarders and were given the title of "The Defenders of San Guisto" by grateful colleagues, who with the SUS, had occupied tactical positions with fingers crossed.

It was only in October 1954 that evacuation finally took place and the MCE closed down. A contributor to the Journal at the time wrote "The married men sighed with relief. So also did the single men but for different reasons: those signorinas had to be seen to be believed!"

22
Austria – The Lienz Mutiny.

Movement north from Italy was by train, the Military Prison at Florence being the only presence left. Many of the staffs were leaving for the UK and the only two old stagers from FPC Portici to move into occupied Austria were Bill King and RSM Arthur Bishop. Bill Skinner also moved up from the Military Prison, Portici.

Bill King and Arthur Bishop were to set up No. 25 Field Punishment Centre in the town of Klagenfurt. They were given a woodyard in the Feldkirchnerstrasse and POW labour to convert the central building into a secure barracks. Bill Skinner was to do receptions.

Also in the Feldkirchnerstrasse was the British Military Hospital and a field bakery but more important, perhaps, was the sports stadium opposite the FPC, which originally could seat 150 to 200 spectators, until the harsh winter made it necessary for the wooden tiers to be used on FPC stoves. Bill King remembers his time here as the golden days of his service, mainly, I suspect because it was here that he met and courted his future wife. He had to ask permission to marry, then waited nine months for clearance and was finally given a day off for the ceremony.

Bill recalls one interesting SUS who was brought in. He was carrying the normal army kitbag, but also two suitcases. On being told to open them, they were filled to the brim with foreign currency from a number of different countries but he carried documentary proof that all of it legally belonged to him.

The MPSC's main presence in Austria was in No. 3 Military Prison in Lienz in the East Tyrol. It was a civil prison standing in open country near the tourist town. The Inspectorate, under Colonel Gordon, also moved to Lienz and requisitioned the Dolomiten Hotel, where the offices occupied the bottom floor and Colonel Gordon had an apartment above.

No. 3 became the concentration point for all the bad-hats,

who were to be transferred to UK, mainly to Dartmoor. They were serving sentences between ten years and life and had little to lose. Bill King was posted here after Klagenfurt and remembers it was a boil waiting to burst. Every day there were minor riots or punchups and he remembers his time here as the worst part of his service.

During one of the disturbances, a SUS called Balfour was hit upon the head and his scalp was opened. Bill was on Night Watch and had to stand by as the MO stitched the wound. By this time, SUS were allowed two cigarettes per day, to be smoked under supervision, but Bill, against the rules and feeling pity for Balfour's pain, gave him a cigarette to douse the pain. Bill reckons that that cigarette saved his life.

It was a young staff at No. 3, mainly NCOs newly transferred to the Corps to replace the experienced, whose release number had come up. They were assisted by regimental NCOs temporarily attached and were dealing with old lags with rape, murder and armed robbery as common entries on the crime sheets. The situation was potentially explosive.

When the explosion came, it was a Saturday evening. Bill King was on duty on the top landing of the prison, when the whole place burst with the din of breaking furniture, clanging of bars and howling SUS. He found that he was alone, the only member of the staff on the landing, the only man wearing MPSC flashes and a MPSC badge – he says that he felt more vulnerable than he had felt in the front-line. He took off his battledress blouse and his cap, then in his shirtsleeves made a play of smashing furniture, trying all the time to edge towards the gate.

On his way down, he came face to face with Balfour, who was obviously a ringleader. . . . and Balfour recognised him. He pushed Bill into a cell and ordered that he was not to be touched.

Many of the prisoners, particularly those on short sentences, wanted nothing to do with mutiny and their release was negotiated. Balfour filtered Bill in amongst them, so that he was able to reach safety.

Thirty or forty mutineers were in control of the prison. Attempts were made to regain command, including the use of the fire hoses of the local fire brigade but all sorties were repelled, the SUS at one stage launching what amounted to a bayonet charge, armed with lengths of jagged pointed wood broken from the bunks. Tony Moore remembers a boot swinging at him in the melee and he himself replying with a kick to the knee which appeared to break a leg. Latrine buckets became missiles and one Staff went down when he was lashed by an arm in a plaster cast. Tony remember Captain Petts, a former Corps member and Assistant Commandant shouting "Hit them on the shoulder, not the head", but nobody on either side appeared to take much notice.

A detachment of the Royal Ulster Rifles was called in from the local brigade and was ordered to pile arms and surround the main trouble area. No arms were allowed into the prison and reports of shooting appearing in British national papers were quite inaccurate.

As may be imagined, the local population had watched the whole business with interest . . . and some incredulity. They could not understand why the German method of pacifying such a situation was not used: the ordering up of artillery and systematic destruction of the prison.

Without artillery, the mutiny petered out after almost two days and the mutineers emerged to be loaded by the RUR onto trucks and taken down to the town gaol. The MPSC retired to the mess for a drink they felt they had earned. Bill was halfway down his glass of beer when the phone rang and an excited Austrian voice shouted that one of the mutineers had snatched a warders' pistol and had freed the others. There was a general rush into town, Tony Moore this time carrying a quite illegal shotgun. Some – few only – of the escapees had managed to get away in a fifteen hundred weight truck, which had been left unsecured and, worse, with a Sten gun aboard, but all the rest were rounded up. The Austrians, not surprisingly, wanted nothing more to do with them, so they were handcuffed in a long line and taken to the local dance hall, where they spent the night . . .

Next day, they were loaded into three tonners, into which cages had been quickly built and they were taken to Klagenfurt.

The mutiny had been reported in the British national press, with a statement that an enquiry would be held by the High Commissioner in Austria, Lieutenant General Sir James Steele. The General drove to Klagenfurt to talk to the mutineers but they hurled so much abuse at him that he ordered them to be gagged. Strips of inner tube were used for the purpose.

It appears that the mutineers were not court martialled, but were shipped off to England to start their original sentences and that they had their final moment of glory when they rampaged through the ship.

Bill King goes back to Austria regularly but another member of the Corps, ex Staff Sergeant Peter English wrote of a return there fairly recently in the Journal. He enclosed a photographic view through a barrier of a handsomely pitched roof one of the buildings of old No. 3. It looked idyllic.

23
Number Three and Before

As I said in a previous chapter, the dreaded Number Three loomed large in my young soldier nightmares: ""You'll be up the road to Bielefeld" was enough to keep me and countless others in that sloppy army of the immediate post-war period enough on the ball at least to get some work out of us.

Number Three was the end of a line of FPCs and MPDBs, reaching from France to as far East as Brunswick, following in the path of 21st Army Group.

In the planning before D Day, one military prison, capable of accommodating 500 men and five Field Punishment Centres had been mobilised. They were to follow the advance and to cater for all soldiers sentenced to under one year's imprisonment without suspended sentence. Those sentenced for longer periods were to be evacuated to the United Kingdom.

By September 1944, the military prison and FPCs were established on Continental Europe. Later, a second military prison, also to take 500 soldiers was opened.

I have been unable to trace locations and information about these establishments during the time when the army group was fighting through France, but three of my correspondents had memories of Belgium. Captain Harry Boulter's first MPSC appointment was at No.7 FPC at Purres, an underground fort South of Antwerp, from which he went to No.25 MPDB, near Brussels and to No.23, Antwerp. He was to be one of the early staff at No.3.

The movements of the late Doug Brinkman illustrate pretty well the situation when military penal establishments are following an army in the advance. Doug trained at Fort Darland, then did a short tour in the United Kingdom before being drafted to Belgium. His route was via Tilbury and Ostend before he finally reached No.8 FPC in Dieste, where an old Belgian barracks housed the FPC. He was with them here for only two months, then the FPC moved lock, stock and barrel to Ijsselstein, near Utrecht in the Netherlands.

The FPC was here allocated a group of old huts in open country, over which a tank battle had been recently fought: the huts were pierced where shells had passed through and the ground was pitted and bloodstained. The huts were surrounded by a water-filled moat out of which the first batch of SUS were to recover German bodies. Doug at this point caught influenza and was sent to hospital in Eindhoven. When he recovered, he was required to take three SUS and their escort in a three tonner to the FPCs new location, which was given to him as Sodersdorf, near Lueneburg a considerable jump in the FPC's progress. I do not need to tell the Old and Bold that second line transport was fairly well clapped out by this time and they will not be surprised to learn that the journey took longer than a week. All the SUS were delivered.

The late Les Fairweather, whom we last met in Italy, was in a draft for Belgium, where they were required to start a FPC from scratch at Bierken, again near Antwerp. They were given an old Belgian fortress prison. It was moated and very secure, but rolls of dannert wire were dropped into the water of the moat to ensure even greater security. It was a forbidding place and discipline was fierce for both SUS and staff – a movement of the head on parade was counted as an attempt to communicate and was immediately punished by close confinement. The staff were watched almost as closely as the SUS and it was here that Les earned his first severe reprimand. He was on night duty and had religiously "punched the clock", but was caught sitting down by the RSM and was charged with lack of vigilance. From here, he was posted to No.6 MPDB in Muenster – a semi derelict barracks with a great many security problems and a hard core of evil men amongst the SUS. There was no real mess here, a mere stable of a building, where the atmosphere amongst the staff was not good. He was posted, with relief, to No.3 at Bielefeld at the end of 1945.

Doug Brinkman, when he finally arrived at Sodersdorf, found a camp deep in the woods, the main activity of the SUS being tree-felling. The staff found life here a pleasant change from the gypsy existence they had been living across Belgium and Holland. There was swimming nearby and, despite Monty's non-fraternisation order, the occasional local dance, to which a charged Smith and Wesson was compulsory wear. Sometimes, there would be a three tonner, its back lined with requisitioned arm chairs, as a liberty bus into Hamburg, where any hotel not blasted in an air raid became a British club, usually with its resident three piece orchestra, paid in soap, Major Jimmy Deeble was an officer at the establishment to which Doug next moved: No.8 Military Prison in Neumuenster, to the north of Hamburg on the Kiel road. This was an old German cavalry barracks almost in the centre of the town where two blocks had been surrounded by barbed wire and converted for prison use. The former officers' mess became a luxurious sergeants' mess and the administrative chores were in the hands of a complete battalion of German POWs.

Jimmy Deeble recalls the great number of death sentences passed in Germany at this time and one in particular has stayed in his mind: two young Irish Guardsmen had been sentenced together. Jimmy was in the Commandant's office when they were marched in to be told that the sentence had been commuted to five years imprisonment. He was standing behind the Commandant when the two were informed of this and will remember their faces for the rest of his life.

Another of the condemned was less lucky. He had been an SIB sergeant and had murdered his girl friend. His sentence was confirmed and he was sent to Bielefeld, then taken to Hameln Gaol to be executed. A guardsman also killed his girl, but the sentence was quashed on a technicality. He returned to UK and murdered again. This time he was executed.

All roads are by this time leading to No.3. Neumuenster closed in 1947, Muenster already in 1946 and NO.23 in Brunswick (about which I would like to learn more) closed in 1948.

Number 3 MPDB, later to become No.3 MCE, was now the only British military penal institutions in Northern Europe. As the British military presence in Germany increased and became permanent, so the need for No.3 increased, until the 1953 location lists show a staff there of 72 MPSC, including many names that appear elsewhere in these pages.

Why Bielefeld? The British Zone of Occupation was a rectangle of North West Germany, spreading from the Dutch and Belgian border in the West, to the line in the East, which was soon to become known as the Iron Curtain. To the South the line of the rectangle was drawn just North of Kassel. Bielefeld was almost in the exact centre of this rectangle, with several barracks and close to the East West Autobahn, perfectly sited, then, for all potential customers to be in convenient reach.

It had been a Wehrmacht barracks and already had a four metre wall and an iron gate. The accommodation was mainly barrack rooms in three stories, with the typical German attics, used for wet weather training. It had a gymnasium, assault course, miniature range and grenade range, all within the walls. It was centrally heated and had showers on each landing. Bill Flecknoe, who did a short tour here before returning to Colchester, wished that the complex could be transported bodily to Berechurch Hall Camp. The mess took up the best part of one three storied building and had its own hard tennis court.

When Les Fairweather went there in 1945, there was already a highly comprehensive training programme in operation and Harry Boulter recalls that the long termers were employed in dismantling wartime bunkers and in shoe repairs.

As I write, I have before me an article, which appeared in "Soldier" in the issue of July 1949, a very fair and comprehensive account of life in No.3 MCE as seen by a civilian staff writer. There are doubtless some readers, who will recall the visit upon which the article was based. I would very much like to reproduce it here, but it ran to four closely printed pages of "Soldier" and space would not allow for it. I hope, at least, that we shall be able to produce some of the illustrations, with the white-looking 1937 webbing worn over battledress and the stage brassard on the arm.

As I said, the report was a fair one, but all old soldiers know that no press report ever catches all the story. Les Fairweather remembered a discipline pattern for the staff that has much about it of the Aldershot of the war's beginning: severe reprimands for two minutes late at the morning gate, amongst other things and how an absence from a mess function could damage the promotion prospects.

Discipline for the SUS was, of course, even fiercer and PD 1 and 2 were much applied. This was also the first time that Les had ever seen a silent cell, no window, a gridded light and absolutely no furniture.

The previous paragraphs suggest that Les Fairweather

found No. 3 MCE a place out of which a posting was to be welcomed. Not so: Les was a committed trainer and he found that the training in No.3 was the best he had encountered in any establishment. It was infantry based but aimed to take the SUS well past anything that he would have covered in his primary training. On the educational side, too, the SUS was able to work up to the standard of the recently reintroduced Army Certificate of Education at First Class Level. At the other end of the scale, there was a highly effective series of classes for the many semi-literates found in the army at that time. Les himself helped such a soldier and wrote of the satisfaction he felt at changing the man's whole outlook.

Major Sydney Harris went to No.3 as Assistant Commandant in 1953 and stayed there for two and a half years. It was during his time that the most publicised of No.3's inmates was having his brief period of notoriety: I refer, of course, to the case of Sergeant Frederick Emmett Dunne.

Emmett Dunne had been a sergeant in REME, stationed at Gladstone Barracks, Duisburg. He had become infatuated with the wife of his next door neighbour, Mrs Watters, the wife of Sergeant Watters and a former German night-club singer, Emmett Dunne killed Watters with a blow to the Adam's Apple, then, helped reluctantly by his half brother, who was serving in the same camp, arranged Watters body so that it looked as though he had committed suicide. A suicide verdict was, in fact, recorded and Emmett Dunne later married Mrs Watters. He then boasted in his cups about what he had done; the body was exhumed and he was courtmartialled for murder. He was found guilty and sentenced to death on the 7th of July 1955.

The date is important. On the 5th of May 1955, Germany had regained her sovereignty and the British forces in Germany were no longer an occupying power, their rights and obligations as guests in a sovereign country being laid down by the Status of Forces Agreement. In certain cases they were subject to the German Basic Law and Article 102 of that Law states that "The death penalty is abolished."

During the wrangling, Emmett Dunne was lodged in No.3 and treated as a person sentenced to death, the sentence having been confirmed by Sir Richard Gale, the Commander in Chief of BAOR.

The Sunday Pictorial, indulging in what we now call cheque

book journalism, had "bought" Emmett Dunne's story and Emmett Dunne's new wife, accompanied by a Pictorial journalist, came back to Germany and took an hotel room in Bielefeld. By this time, the death sentence had been commuted to life imprisonment.

The Night Watch NCO one evening was called by Emmett Dunne, who asked for a visit to the toilet, as his pot was full. By chance, Sydney was on his rounds and he instructed the Night Watch NCO to check how Emmett Dunne was dressed. he reported that the prisoner was fully dressed. Sydney immediately phoned the SIB and asked for one of their sergeants to go to the street behind the MCE. Sure enough, a Volkswagen was waiting there, with the Pictorial's reporter and Mrs Emmett Dunne. They were promptly removed and Emmett Dunne found himself having to make do with the sanitary facilities more immediately available to him. He left No.3 spent some time, I am informed, in Shepton Mallet, then went to serve his sentence in Norwich Gaol.

Emmett Dunne, then, was the most publicised customer of No.3. My mate Danny was the one whom I knew, but it is interesting to consider how many people, now all civilians, passed through those trim iron gates and to wonder what they now recall of the old Wehrmacht signals barracks. The last word goes to a satisfied customer, writing, you will note, from the Korean Campaign.

Dear Sir,
I sincerely hope my letters finds you exceedingly well, I have long wished to write to you, to express my appreciation and many thanks for your faith in myself and other soldiers who were undergoing corrective training in No.3 MCE., under your very able command, my name is Bell, Sir, and I was at that time a member of the 101 Provost Company and used to drive Major Jones, officer commanding that same company. After I left the MCE I volunteered for Korea and later joined the 1st Bn Argyle and Sutherland Highlanders, unfortunately after only eight months in action I have been wounded in the left leg, and will be flying home to England soon, but what I really wished to say, is I would be grateful if you could express on my behalf to Instructors staff, and to Mr Church of the Salvation Army organisation, my thanks for the help they gave me whilst I was at the MCE. I am rather proud of the fact that the training I received was far better than I have ever received during my Army Service, and I think if we are to have an Army fit to put in the field, I would recommend No.3 as its training school. Well,

sir, I do hope you won't disapprove of my dropping you this short letter. I would also be grateful if you would pass on my regards and thanks to Staff Taylor and others I don't remember. May I also add my best wishes, respects and regard to you sir, and Mrs Dobson.

I am Sir,
Your obedient servant
L/Cpl R J Bell

Need we say more?

24
Trouble at Northallerton

After the bombing at Hull Gaol, the soldiers under sentence were marched from there to nearby Hassle, where they were temporarily accommodated before being moved to the old gaol at Northallerton.

During the evening of the 7th of August 1945, a youngish captain in the Queen's Regiment arrived in the North Riding town and booked in at the Red Lion. He spent an uncomfortable night, apprehensive about his new posting, which he was to take up on the next day.

When the next day arrived, he presented himself at the grim Nineteenth Century gate, which, instead of the normal Home Office sign, carried a small black and white painted board, announcing that it was now No.11 Military Prison and Detention Barracks. A tight-faced Staff opened the small wicket gate and Captain Sydney Harris began his association with the MPSC: an association, which is still maintained.

Inside, the SUS were on muster parade and being detailed to the task of the day. Amongst the lines of GS caps and plastic badges, Sydney spotted the Paschal Lamb and flag of his own regiment and he knew the face beneath the badge very well: it was the face of one Private Francis; who had been in Sydney's platoon in India. It should have been acompanied by another face, that of Private Jackson, for the two had been inseparable throughout their service, forming a Kiplingesque partnership much given to evil. Seeing the face and talking to Francis gave some comfort to Sydney, who felt that he was not totally leaving the Army as He looked across the square at the grim pile that was to be his home unit for the next year. It was a forbidding grey stone structure, tiny windows all barred. Clustering around its walls were ten or twelve Nissen huts.

Sydney reported to the Commandant, a gentle ex-schoolmaster, Lieutenant Colonel Lee, and found that he was to be company commander of A and B Companies.

He learned that A Company had a strength of 180 SUS, all with sentences ranging from six to fifteen years. They were housed in single cells in the main block. His other company occupied the Nissen huts and were men who had been sentenced for up to two years. Another company: C occupied the old women's wing of the gaol.

Routine for the SUS was hard and unchanging: not hugely different from the routine described by Clenshaw in an earlier chapter. At six a.m., cells were opened in sequence and slopping out began, then the soldiers filed past the kitchen counter and were issued with a tin plate, a mug and a spoon. The breakfast diet was invariably tea, porridge, a slice of bread with a pat of margarine and a spoonful of jam. This was taken to the cell for consumption, the utensils cleaned and placed outside the cell door for collection. At 9a.m., they paraded for work, which involved the weaving of coir PT mats, breaking up of equipment to salvage the brass, remaking mattress biscuits (the sectionalised mattresses, three to a set, which made up the normal soldier's bed), and the boot repairs from Catterick Garrison. Only B Company did any military training: rudimentary drill and some marching on a field behind the gaol.

At noon, the SUS came in for lunch. Again they formed a queue to process past the kitchen counter, where they were issued with a diet bowl, a canlike affair into which potatoes, cabbage and meat were piled. Into the lid went a dob of rice or tapioca. As they left through another door, the Orderly Officer and the duty staff would be waiting. "Report your diet" was the cry and the standard response was "Diet correct, Sir". Sydney remembers occasions when the response was a diet bowl hurled in his direction.

Back to the cells again to eat. The cells had wooden beds secured to the floor, a wooden stool, a galvanised bucket and bowl. By standing on the bucket, a SUS in the upper stories could see out of his cell windows. It was not unknown for them to wait for a civilian to come in sight, then to yell through the bars "Help, help, the bastards are bashing me" and other similar communications for the outside world.

After lunch, the SUS returned to drill or work until four o'clock, when they ate bread, margarine and jam with the occasional treat of raw onion. After this, they were locked up until cocoa at seven, then again locked until reveille.

Sometimes, the long period of confinement led to some SUS breaking up his cell equipment and tearing his uniform. This would spark off an epidemic of mug banging throughout the prison.

Escapes were rare, but in February 1946, one SUS rushed the back gate using stools to break through it, then disappeared into the North Yorkshire countryside. Winter in North Yorkshire is not the best time to live off the land and all were recaptured or gave themselves up.

From December 1945 onwards, regular large drafts were returning from overseas and arriving to continue their sentences in Northallerton. It was the job of Sydney or another company commander to parade the draft on arrival and read the regulations. He was disconcerted to hear from draft after draft that they had been informed before departure from overseas that Northallerton was a mere staging centre, where they would be documented and then discharged. Sydney considers that this misinformation had much to do with what later happened.

March the first 1946. Inside the main building of the gaol, the layout was typical of most Victorian prisons: three landings climbing around a central well; bridges across the well connecting landings; the inevitable netting over the well to prevent suicides. In the centre of the bridges sat a highly polished dustbin. It was the rattle of one of these dustbins hitting the safety net that signalled the start of the rampage.

Two tons of cell doors, stools, broken beds crashed onto the wire. The stairs were barricaded and the door of the armoury on the first floor was smashed. Soon howling rioters, armed with fixed bayonets, were touring the landings.

Eleven of the rioters found a way onto the roof. Slates were stripped and were soon being skimmed in the way that boys play ducks and drakes over a pond. Soon, they found a new outlet for their energies. The roof was coped by huge blocks of stone and they found that the mortar could be worked loose to allow the blocks to rain down on the Nissen huts below.

When the din had first started, Sydney had been in A Company office. He came out to look around, but somebody had been waiting for him. Two open paint tins one red, one black, hit the netting above him. For the rest of the day,

Sydney wore a raincoat over a rapidly stiffening red and black battledress.

The SUS not involved in the riot had been marshalled to a corner of the square, where they stood shivering but contained. Soon, smoke started to curl from the main building and the National Fire Service was called from Northallerton. They doused the mess of burning wood on the safety net, then turned their hose pipes onto the eleven on the roof. Water in March in North Yorkshire rapidly becomes ice and the SUS on the roof demanded to see the Commandant. Sydney, speaking for the Commandant, said that they could drop any idea of talking terms, but that they could have dry clothes and a meal if they came down. A flurry of slates exploded around.

Meanwhile the SUS on the square were quiet, properly formed up, interested, no doubt, in the break from prison routine but anxious for it all to be over so that they could get out of the cold. Then, around the corner of the main building marched a CMP detachment, red capped and commanded by a sergeant. The orderly ranks broke and a swarm of SUS had soon surrounded the detachment and were loudly informing the military policemen of their various but unanimous opinion of the Corps of the Military Police. Sydney, doubtless with the tact for which he is known throughout the Corps, indicated to the sergeant that the detachment could be better employed elsewhere. The SUS cheered and returned to their places in the ranks, some shouting "Well done, Queenie" – a reference, doubtless, to Sydney's regiment.

At nine o'clock, in suits now resembling cold armour, the eleven came down from the roof. They were issued with dry clothes and given a meal, then locked in cells even barer than before.

The court martial was held at Catterick and lasted four days. There was a full courtroom: there were eleven mutineers, each handcuffed to a double escort and eleven defending officers. The mutineers had been issued with new battledress for the trial the day before, but when the escort turned up at the prison on the morning of the trial, all eleven had already ripped their uniforms and were standing grinning in gaping ribbons.

In the court itself, they did not enter into the solemnity of the occasion. At an early stage, the president adjourned the court and demanded the services of a male shorthand writer, as the language of the accused was too blue for the ears of the lady writer who had been first appointed.

When Sydney was giving his evidence, he described how one Private Rann had charged him with fixed bayonet, only stopping when the blade was within inches of his chest. Rann shouted in the court "Next time I won't stop, you bastard" – a fair example of the attitude of the accused. The sparkle left them, however, when they were awarded sentences ranging between four and fifteen years. The ringleader, a Private Hogan of Queens Regiment, who had been rather proud when the prosecuting officer had had described him as the Evil Genius, received a fifteen year sentence.

As you will read, Shepton Mallet and Aldershot were also having their troubles at that time. The practice was to run a kind of merry-go-round for the "bother boys" in the three prisons, so that each shed its unholy load to the other, thus ensuring that trouble and news of trouble spread round the circuit. The systems was so effective that Aldershot, the original Glasshouse, finished its rioting season fit only to be used as a coal-yard!

Northallerton closed on the thirtieth of June 1946, by which time Lieutenant Colonel "Taffy" Lloyd, another name long associated with the Corps, had become Commandant. He and Sydney closed the military prison, then went to Shepton Mallet. For his part in the control of the riot, Sydney received the King's Commendation.

25
The Glasshouse Goes

After Northallerton, Aldershot, the original glasshouse, was next on the mutiny list. Six trouble makers, who had been transferred from Northallerton, were at the bottom of it. They were to inspire a mutiny, which was to leave MPDB Aldershot as a shell, fit only for demolition.

As so often, the time of tea was to be used as the start of the uproar. There were three staff only on duty. The action was obviously planned and started with the throwing of diet tins, then the overpowering of the three on duty. Soon, all the cells were open and all three hundred SUS were on the rampage. The Commandant arrived and used a loud hailer to warn of the penalties for mutiny but he was shouted down. The staff were withdrawn and the main effort became one of containment.

The night of the 23rd of February 1946 was to be a noisy one and for the three hundred mutineers a cold and hungry one. Predictably, they took to the roof – that same skylighted roof that had given this and all DBs the "Glasshouse" title – and they set to work to destroy the skylights as though destroying a symbol. Soon the cordon, which had been called in, was being pelted with glass, slates, bed frames, even Bibles, according to one of the many reporters who had arrived by this time. With what must have been considerable effort, cell doors were wrenched off and brought to the roof for launching. The mutineers sang "Don't fence me in" repeatedly and shouted to the reporters, whose presence they must have welcomed:

Bread and water for laughing.
Bread and water for going sick.
Five years hard labour for ten days AWOL.
One hundred and sixty days bread and water for slanging a sergeant (one wonders how he had the strength to shout!)

It was a field day for reporters and the Mirror, in particular made a meal of it.

The Army Fire Service was called and kept hoses trained on the mutineers throughout the night, with a troop of searchlights to illuminate the scene.

On the Sunday morning, Lieutenant General Sir John Crocker, the C in C of Southern Command and Major General RK Ross, Commanding Aldershot District arrived and talked to the mutineers through a loud hailer, agreeing to meet a deputation. The deputation made the following points:

The food and cigarette ration is too small.

The war is over and we want our freedom.

Sentences are too severe.

Sir John Crocker said that he would do nothing until the mutiny was ended. There would be no mass punishment, but the ring leaders would be court-martialled when they finally surrendered, as surrender they would. Almost two hundred of the mutineers came down and were taken to a gymnasium near the Glasshouse, which had been surrounded by barbed wire. Here they were fed and given blankets. Reporters who spoke to the guard, were told that they were having no trouble "all they seemed to want to do was sleep".

The rest were still on the roof, though the howling was not now so loud. Slates and a few pieces of the skylight still came down, though more as a gesture than anything. Impetus seemed to be lost. Suddenly the watchers, who had now been joined by a crowd, mainly women, who had arrived for the Sunday afternoons visits, saw smoke and then flame rising over the now almost roofless building. The hosepipes came into play again. A detachment of military police, helmeted and armed with sub machine guns arrived and stood by. They had not long to wait. Soon the mutineers started to leave the roof and to come down to surrender. They were handcuffed and moved quickly out of the area, some going to Reading Gaol, where the Canadian Army still had a detention wing; others went to Wormwood Scrubs and some to Headly Down. The last we hear of these latter, is a Mirror report saying that they are spending the day howling and that the Canadian staff are shouting for assistance.

The inevitable questions were asked in the Commons and soon began to focus on the whole question of the long sentences for desertion, particularly those awarded in the Normandy to the Baltic advance. Finally, considerable remission was given to most, so in a sense the mutiny had been successful.

A court of inquiry was held and nineteen men were named the ring leaders. The court martial on these was held at Headly Down, the charges being mutiny and the destruction of property to the value of £9073. Ten of the accused were acquitted and the others were given sentences ranging from 3 to 5 years. Almost the last we read of the Glasshouse Destruction is a short paragraph saying that the nine have departed for Dartmoor.

Not the last report. In 1958, when the ruins of the Glasshouse were about to be demolished, the Evening News carried its obituary. There are journalistic flights of fancy, but it is worth a few lines in this book:

GOODBYE GLASSHOUSE – And Good Riddance
By Denis Foley

Aldershot Thursday

I was the last "prisoner" in the Glasshouse to-day. The Old Aldershot military prison scene 12 years ago of one of the worst riots in British Army history, is being knocked down next week.

My tour of inspection revealed that the £9000 worth of damage has never been repaired. The riot was the death knell of the notorious detention centre.

In the whole of its 90 years of history, the Army claims not a single saint went marching in. And every sinner that entered its grim portals did so at the double. Then he did his work at the double . . . and left at the double.

Hefty Warders

It was the prison where, they say, "they never went back". Its barrack square rang to some of the most blistering language that ever tripped off an NCO's tongue.

The warders were the heftiest sergeants and warrant officers in the Army. Inside the atmosphere of the rigid Army discipline still prevails. The prison has a Sing-Sing layout with long galleries running along both sides of the three storey building.

The glass roof, which gives its name to all detention barracks, has only a few panes remaining.

Scribble

The damp has ravaged the iron stairs and foot walks which, in the old days, were burnished for hours by prisoners. The floor which you could "eat off" was littered with debris.

Inside the cells I found the scribbled inscriptions of the cooped up inmates on the white-washed walls.

One read "They died with their boots on 1940". Another: "Five years to go. Wait till I get out."

Marks of Riot

Every cell shows the marks of the riots. Steel doors were ripped off: wooden bed planks shattered; bread – and – water solitary confinement cells, with their steel grilles and peep holes ravaged.

Outside in the exercise yard, where the men were made to double for an hour at a time with 56 lb packs on their backs. Preparations were being made to day for the demolition job. It will take six months.

Goodbye Glasshouse. And on behalf of everybody who has broken the Queens Regulations – Good Riddance.

26
The Mallet

I have been dreading this one. As an outsider, but one who has been in Corps circles for some years now, I have noticed how the Old and Bold are polarised between Colchester and Shepton Mallet – all I need is the Association membership list to prove this. Tour within a ten mile radius of Colchester and Shepton Mallet and you could visit half the Corps retireds. The reason why I am dreading this chapter is. . . . I have never been to Shepton Mallet.

All you will read in this chapter is what I have gathered from the accounts of Old Corps members and from newspapers so any error is in my interpretation. If I am wrong, you are the person to tell me (but before you do, ask yourself if you wrote to me before the book was written!)

My historical background came from neither old members nor newspapers. It was cribbed from a book, which I recommend to all who wish to learn more about the Mallet than I can offer in this meagre chapter. I refer, of course, to the excellent book published in 1986 by Mr Francis "Walt" Disney, "Heritage of a Prison". The launch of this book was attended by the last serving officer of the Corps who had been on the staff of the Mallet: Major Peter Andrews and a copy of the book signed by the author, was presented to the Corps Library by Doug and Pauline Moody.

This was not the first time that the Mallet appeared in a book. Lightly disguised, it appears in Nathanson's "The Dirty Dozen", seen through the eyes of an American, when it was the dreaded Stockade. But more of that later.

Its form, when the British Army took it over on 15th October 1939, was that of the typical Nineteenth Century prison: single cells, set like orderly books along the cast iron shelves of the landings. Its origins were older than the Nineteenth Century, however. In the Seventeenth Century it had been Cornhill House, standing in an acre and owned by a clergyman in a nearby village. When the justices needed a house of correction, they bought the house and land for £160. It was on this site that the Mallet grew.

It stayed as one of the few prisons in Somerset until 1930. It became something of a white elephant then and the County at one point thought of selling it off so that its yard thick walls could be quarried for their stone. The emergency changed all that. Memories of the shortage of prison space during the First World War and the knowledge that the Second World War was to be a conscript's war from the first, convinced the authorities that an empty prison, however dank from age and disuse, was a desirable property. Aldershot, the last MPDB at home, was certainly not big enough to house all the "gangsters in uniform" that the wide net of the national service acts would trawl in. How right they were!

You may recall that Wally Watson had been given a storeroom in Aldershot as a base for preparing to take over Shepton Mallet, but was then posted off to the British Expeditionary Force.

The War Office was not the only government body interested in the Mallet at this time. The Public Record Office was keen to find a safe place outside London for the safekeeping of the documents that together made up the core of Britain's history. Finally it was decided that they would be allocated to the women's wing of Shepton: the part later to become D Wing of the MPDB. In all, three hundred tons of documents were trucked to the little Somerset town, including the Domesday Book, Little Domesday and a copy of the Magna Carta. During the course of the next few years, the American and British service authorities were to complain about the wing, closed off behind barbed wire, they thought should be holding the evil, not the historical.

As I have said the Mallet was used by the British in the early parts of the war, but it was handed over for American use in 1942 and was to become their main stockade in the United Kingdom.

On taking over, one of their first tasks was to build a brick execution shed. This was a two storied structure. In the upper storey, a strong beam ran across the room, with large hooks driven into it. There were two hooks, as this was to be capable of double executions. Beneath the hooks, the floor was pierced with a trapdoor, heavily weighted with sandbags and operated by a lever. In the room below, there were two slabs upon which the executed men were instantly postmortemed. My old colleague John Blueman, who was Schoolie at Shepton Mallet for some years, recalls that his library had been the room where Pierrepoint had donned his official dress before conducting an execution. There was a small door between the shelves leading to the shed. John also remembers that Major Eric Milton, then the Quartermaster, was keen to have the lower storey of the shed as storage space, but this was not allowed. Bill Bishop remembers that the lower storey was reached by a flight of stone steps and was on the route of the Night Watch patrol. The second step from the bottom was loose and there was a permanent drip from a faulty roof immediately above "many a nervous NCO felt the touch of rain on his shoulder, just as the step wobbled and thought that Old Nick had finally got him."

During the time of the Americans, there were 21 soldiers hanged and two executed by shooting. The scars of bullets were still visibile on one wall.

When the Americans moved out, Mr Disney tells us that they took with them or burned all the equipment they had used there, apart from one grisly object: a coffin marked: PROPERTY OF THE UNITED STATES ARMY. PLEASE RETURN.

In 1945, the prison was repossessed by the British Army and became No 12 MPDB.

On admission the SUS started in the bedding shed and choked in the floating dust of hair – a most unpleasant task and only by good behaviour could he earn his way into one of the more congenial kinds of labour.

Escapes were few and I have no record of any successful escape. Ex RSM Dolly Gray recalls one attempt, where a hosepipe was used to reach the top of the wall. The escapee jumped from there and broke both ankles. John Blueman had heard of another attempt made by scooping a hole in a ceiling with a spoon, but John had no further details.

As Bill has said, there were villains in the Mallet and I have the impression that "keeping the lid on" was a constant struggle. Ray Ganner recalls a near riot in 1955 or 1956 caused by a new NAAFI manager issuing oatmeal instead of rolled oats and I suspect that violence was always under the surface. There was certainly some kind of riot at the time of the

Northallerton and Aldershot unrest. but I have not been able to trace references to it.

The lid finally came off in 1959, when Bill Bishop was RSM. On the 10th of March, he was with the Commandant, Lieutenant Colonel Morton-Clarke of the Royal Berkshires, when he heard an uproar coming from B Wing. It was about midday.

B Wing had collected their meal, parading by landings and had begun to eat, when Staff Sergeant Mc Andrew, one of the three staff on duty, made the announcement that all extra library books were to be handed in. This, one would think, was not the most inflammatory of orders, but the announcement was met by hullaballoo. Mc Andrew shouted for silence and things quietened for a moment, then a voice yelled something to the effect that they were not standing for this and there was a crashing wave of upset tables and the rattle of thrown diet tins. At this point, two of the duty staff were attacked: Flight Sergeant Pitt was head butted and Staff Sergeant Marsh was bleeding heavily from a cut on the head, both were stained with thrown food.

When Bill Bishop arrived, the riot had moved to the landings. Furniture and kit were being thrown onto the safety nets and there were howling SUS everywhere.

Many of the SUS were not taking part in the riot, merely standing sheep-like around and Bill ordered them into a nearby room. On his arrival, the rest of B Wing ran up the steps to the next landing and some to landing number three. The rioters on No2 were entertaining themselves by throwing kit into the net.

Bill went upstairs. He ordered the three at the top of the steps into Room 13 nearby, but they ignored him. One of them, Williams, swung a bucket at Bill's head, whilst another, Doran, stood behind him yelling encouragement. Bill blocked the bucket with his left arm and surged forward, pushing both into Room 13 and slamming on the bolt.

Up to landing No3. There were twenty men here, all yelling abuse. Two of the rioters stood in front of the others, blocking the stairhead, whilst those behind were yelling "Kick him in! Kick him in!"

When he was three steps from the top, Bill called for quiet and told them that, if they had complaints, this was the wrong way to go about having them heard. He promised them an enquiry if they dispersed to their rooms.

They started to shout their complaints. A Wing, they said, had more television viewing and more indoor games; A Wing were not forced to polish their work boots. They seemed trivial complaints. Perhaps the prison atmosphere had inflated them into major issues, but there was another theory mentioned by Bill in his account (which, incidentally, covers the mutiny in a few lines, mainly devoted to a tribute to the staff, with little or nothing about his part in the thing). Bill's theory is that the whole riot had been engineered as a cover up for an escape, though no escape attempt was made.

Whatever the underlying reasons, the rioters moved away after voicing their complaints. Some ran to room 18 and slammed the door. As Bill locked it, he could hear the sounds of a barricade being built inside. Four of the others went to Room 15.

The Commandant arrived and ordered men in the rooms to come out. They refused, so the staff used a railway sleeper on the door of Room 13 as a battering ram and soon had the rioters out of there and handcuffed. They had started a fire in the ventilating shaft, but this was quickly doused..

Room 18 was still occupied.

The Commandant ordered them again to come out. Someone inside shouted to ask if they would be mishandled if they came out and they were told that this would not happen. There was a good deal of muttering, then the door opened and they gave themselves up. Later, when the cell was examined, several knives made of glass and sharpened metal were found.

The thirteen mutineers were later put before a court martial held in Shepton Mallet drill hall, their escorts being provided by the Somerset Light Infantry Nine received sentences ranging from three to five years. The rest were acquitted. Not one of them was over the age of 24.

Bill Bishop and Marsh received Queen's Commendations for their part in the suppression of the riot.

Inevitably, the Press went to town on the story. Inevitably, they also got many things wrong, but what impressed me on reading the accounts was that Press sympathies were with the staff in most cases: usually, the poor underdog of a prisoner becomes the hero. A former padre from the Mallet was interviewed by the Express and told of damp, discomfort and boredom. Phrases like "Hell Hole" and "Prison a disgrace to Britain" made good headlines. Questions were asked in Parliament, predictably by Gerald Nabarro and Bessy Braddock. Mr (later Lord) George Brown asked if there was no stately home available to use as a substitute prison. There was an extensive correspondence in the columns of the Times, Mainly concerned with the status of SUS who were to be discharged after serving their sentences. There was a great deal of mileage in the Mallet Mutiny.

I particularly enjoyed two articles that appeared after the dust had somewhat settled. The Press had a Godsend: one of the accused who had been acquitted, left the Mallet a day or so after the court martial. His release had been held up, pending the trail. Robert Thomson, self-styled mouthpiece of Shepton Mallet Glasshouse, did not seem at all reluctant to be interviewed by the Daily Sketch. Under the head "I'll blue ten shillings on Army bull", he told the newspaper that he would gladly fork out that sum to buy one of the buckets he had been forced to polish so often. He would take it home to Edinburgh for fetching the coal. The picture of the young man in his sharp, wide-boy's suit and Army boots, does not really lend itself to the touchingly domestic scene of lugging in coals for mother. This is borne out in the Sunday Mail, when Robert's widowed mother sits waiting anxiously for Robert's return home. The mother of nine tells the reporter "I've heard he's in town. but he hasn't been to see me yet". Her expression then softens and she says "Robert was always such a quiet reserved boy at home". Bob finally gets home at tea time, grip – no bucket – in hand. He stays for 45 minutes, then goes out to meet a pal. He was there long enough for his mother to see that "he has changed dreadfully – so thin, pale and worried. He was never like that."

That was the last immediate Press response to the mutiny. Nine months later, the newspapers are invited in to look at the Mallet. Most are impressed with the regime and with the staff, but appalled by the buildings. In Parliament, it was compared unfavourably with Colchester.

The mattress stuffing and so on, described by Bill Bishop in the early days had, by this time, given way to a whole series of vocational courses, a range far wider than that we can afford to provide today. Also, a range of crafts was being taught and the standard reached by many of the SUS was so high, that the Mallet several times won the Army Arts and Crafts shield. As John Blueman says "It was always an odd occasion for the GOC when he had to come to the nick to present the shield". In fact, some of the work produced in Shepton Mallet is still in use and is valued property. In the HQ Mess of my own former Corps, Eltham Palace, there are two "Nick" produced wrought iron standard lamps. HQ South West District mess at Taunton has a fire basket from the same source; Guy's Hospital has an iron jardiniere produced there. The teak benches presented to the town of Shepton Mallet on closure were produced in the workshop and still stand, I believe, outside the town hall.

After the publicity, closure was almost inevitable, particularly as National Service was ending and the lease of the prison was running out. It was finally handed back to the Home Office on 31 March 1966. There was a civic reception at the town hall and it was here that Lieutenant Colonel KPP Goldschmidt, the Commandant, and the last RSM, WOI Watt handed over the teak benches already mentioned. The sergeants' mess held a commemorative dinner in the Red Lion Hotel, where they were joined by Major General Sir Gerald Duke, the then Colonel Commandant of the Corps and the then Provost Marshal, Brigadier Davenport.

It was not a complete severance of the Corps' ties with the town. As I have already said, many Corps members chose it as their place of retirement and it is still very much alive in the conversations of Corps Weekend.

Postscript to the Mallet
some odd Rooti Gongs

The thing I noticed early on in my association with the Corps, is the value placed by its members on their Long Service and Good Conduct Medals – more value, I felt, than in any other corps or regiment with which I had served before. Since starting my research for this book, I have begun to see why: to soldier one's way through the "eighteen years of undetected crime" was for the MPSC member, like crossing a mined obstacle course. Bill Bishop at one stage, you may remember, says that severe reprimands were flying around "like confetti". There is at least one pillar of the MPSC establishment, whose excellent row of medals is not rounded off with "the mark of the beast".

In the accounts I have had of life at Shepton Mallet, two of my correspondents recall presentations of the LSGC that were somewhat out of the ordinary.

Doug Moody became eligible for the award in 1958 and was particularly pleased that the Provost Marshal, who would present it had been the Commanding Officer of his battalion of the Queen's Royal Regiment in Italy. Shortly before Brigadier Richardson was due to visit, Doug took pneumonia and was rushed to Shepton Mallet Hospital. The Commandant, Lieutenant Morton-Clarke came to visit him in his ward and asked to do the pinning on. Doug said immediately that he would like the PM to come to the hospital and he explained why. If any other member of the Old and Bold can claim to have been presented with his rooti gong, pinned to his dressing gown in a matron's room, then he should inform me.

Unusual presentations of the LSGC seem to have been common. Ray Ganner was there when Lieutenant Colonel SLAS Rudd-CLarke, an old screw gunner, was Commandant. One year, Remembrance Day was approaching and in the Commandant's safe were nine or so medals, with a corresponding number of recipients keen to complete their row before the day. Ray was appointed to pester the Commandant into action.

Action there was. Ray had his handed to him over the Commandant's desk; Joe Upton received his along with his keys when he came on duty and so the informal – very informal – presentations went on. Sergeant Spatchurst was to receive his in a manner suited to make a story for over the bar for the rest of his service: got his rooti in the Commandant's toilet.

It happened like this: the administrative inspection was approaching and Spatchurst had missed the battledress matching parade (for the benefit of the younger end, this was an attempt – usually futile, to match the colour of BD trousers to the colour of the BD tunic). Light in the Commandant's office was bad, so the Commandant, and Ray Ganner trooped into the loo, where the light from the window was better, as they went in, the Commandant clicked his fingers, tutted and said "Wait, I've something for you" He opened the safe, took out the LSGC and, with a flourish suitable to the occasion, pinned it on.

At least Spatchurst got his rooti. . . . did you?

PART SIX

The Big Wide World

27
Egypt and Beyond

The Corps maintained a major presence in Egypt long after the Second World War. To see how major, one needs only to look at the MPSC distribution list 1953:

50 MCE, Moascar. . . . 31 all ranks.
51 Fanara. . . . 41 (including 8 temporarily attached from 50 MCE)
57 MPDB, Suez. . . . 13.

This was a formidable chunk of the Corps' strength and it is not surprising that the Corps' stay in Eygpt is well documented, ranging from Wally Watson's account of the pre-war Citadel in Cairo, to Colonel Jim Robinson's "wrapping up" tour in 1955.

The Second World War started with the Citadel and a minor branch in Khartoum as the only MPSC presence in the Eastern Mediterranean. With the Suez Canal as our main East-West link and with Mussolini's new Roman Empire along the North African coast and on the horn of Africa, it was obvious that Egypt was set to become the major base for the British effort in this part of the world. The cosy little 52 room Citadel was not going to be able to accommodate the rush of "customers" inevitable when the build-up came.

During the First World War, the Citadel had been supplemented by a detention barracks in Abbassia, one of the garrisons east of Cairo, but this had closed in the Twenties. On the 8th of August 1940, the Citadel DB finally closed and again a DB was created in Abbassia as part of the Polygon complex. Families from the Citadel moved first to Palestine, then South Africa. The decks were cleared for action.

The figure behind the move was Colonel CD Belton, who was the Inspector for the Eastern Mediterranean. He it was who decided also that the Field Punishment Centres, which up to then had been the responsibility of the CMP, should be handed over the MPSC. Major Bob Firmstone was one of the first MPSC members in the area to be associated with the

FPCs, serving first at 27 FPC near Beirut, then at 24 FPC in Ikingi, ten kilometres distant from Alexandria. He remembers this as a very tough camp: no beds, iron discipline, the afternoons spent carrying rocks for the Royal Engineers.

The new MPDB at Abbassia was numbered 50 and this number was to be used in various places throughout the area, until Britain finally left Egypt.

The first Commandant of 50 was Lt Col Bisset and one of the first staff was Mr (ex RSM) W Fitzsimmons, who had transferred to the Corps from the RA in 1939 and who sent me a meticulous account of all the MPDBs in the Eastern Mediterranean.

Two of the well known Corps names were early associated with 50: Bill Flecknoe and Bob Firmstone, both people who had wide acquaintance with other military penal establishments. Harry Barker was also there. All are unanimous in their conviction that No. 50 was one of the best organised MPDBs they had encountered.

The camp covered approximately fifteen acres and could hold more than 700 SUS. It comprised ten dormitories and three large single room blocks, a prison block and a consular block. SUS in detention rather than imprisonment would start their sentence in single cells and would graduate to a dormitory only by good behaviour. The long sentenced were employed on stripping telephones and cables for the Egyptian Post Office. Some worked dismantling engines and equipment for Ordnance.

50 had more than its fair share of hard men amongst the SUS and Bill Flecknoe recalls many of the touch and go incidents that seem to have been common to most wartime DBs. One morning, for example, when the SUS were washing and shaving, Bill had cause to check a rule breaker. Suddenly he was deluged with buckets of water from two sides, then three SUS held him as the man he had checked unscrewed his razor and started towards him. He was saved from a great deal of nastiness by the arrival of big Jock Sneddon, one of the leading footballers of the Corps.

Desertion, theft and cowardice were the main offences. Captain Harry Barker recalls one SUS who was serving a sentence for cowardice, a man Harry had known in the desert – the kind of soldier who would drive anywhere, anytime, but who had finally cracked under the strain. Harry was able to intercede for him and he received maximum remission, returning to his unit to become again one of the most useful members. Another "coward" escaped. A few months later, a member of staff saw him outside the RA Reinforcement Depot and picked him up. It transpired that he had escaped to rejoin his unit and had been wounded, was sitting waiting at the RHU to return to the desert. These were some of the accidents of war. It is well worth while to remember that they happen, but that places like 50 also contained the "gangsters in uniform", who found the attractions of Cairo and Alexandria infinitely preferable to the flies, sands and dangers of the Western Desert.

After 50 MPDB, the next one to be formed in the area was numbered 54 and was at Heliopolis. Mr Fitzsimmons provided me with some detail of its opening and its makeup, but for greater detail, I have to thank Mr Reg Degavino and his account starts only in 1946, when he was posted there after a probabtioners' course at 50. The establishment was built as a square, the rear walls of the cells forming the outer wall and with a central parade ground. Reg recalls a whole row of painted regimental badges at the side of the square. He did not know who had produced them, but they were, he says, excellent pieces of work.

When he arrived at No.54, all the inmates were from Cypriot Regiments and had been sentenced for mutiny – they had been promised release as soon as the war ended, then had found themselves having to work on the same demobilisation system as the rest of the Army. They spent most of their days cleaning their own equipment or polishing buckets, kitchen utensils etc; using sand, water and bath brick.

At one stage, they all refused to shave and troops were brought in from the nearby transit camp to cordon the perimeter, then the staff started in to dry-shave the SUS. After the sixth had been dry-shaved, most of the rest decided to drop the protest.

Visitors were allowed on Saturdays and Sundays and a tent was erected on the square to act as a visiting room. Most of the Cypriots appeared to have relations in Egypt. One SUS, in fact, escaped by using his cell door as a ladder, went to Cairo to see his relations, then came back at the end of the day, to knock on the main gate for readmission.

A popular pastime with the SUS was to catch kitehawks

with a baited string, then release them with a message to the family tied around one leg. It is not recorded how successful the method was.

In addition to normal duties, staff were required to patrol their living area armed with tommy guns in an attempt – often futile – to keep away Arab thieves.

No 54 closed at the end of 1946 and an amnesty was granted to the Cypriots. Reg was then posted to 50 MPDB with Rupert Leedham, another young sergeant. Here they were taken under the wing of Staff sergeant Paddy Nolan (not, I think, a relation of the Paddy Nolan in my introduction!) and it was here that Reg met Ron Wall, with whom he later served in the Essex Police.

Another acquaintance he renewed when he joined the Essex Police, was a SUS called Grainger. Grainger was Irish, bullet headed, barrel chested, long armed and standing about 5' 4" – not a form easily forgotten, particularly as he extended his original sentence of twenty eight days to two years by a series of mindless escapes and a refusal to wear uniform. In 1947, Reg was coming home on leave and Grainger was aboard, being moved to the United Kingdom. The ship put in at Salonika and Grainger, of course, escaped, swimming to shore and stealing a boat, which he rowed back to collect a mate who could not swim. Needless to say, he was recaptured.

Reg Degavino left the Army, joined the police and, in Romford, arrested a short bullet-headed Irishman for breaking and entering. The name he gave was not Grainger and he suspected the forces of darkness when Reg addressed him by that name. Bail was not allowed.

It appears that 50 at this time catered for "customers" other than the normal run of the mill SUS. At one point, South Africans occupied one of the singles blocks, tall men with brown boots and leather equipment, giving no trouble and patiently waiting to be sent home. I suspect that these had been the last occupants of a South African detention barracks, which Mr Fitzsimmons had visited at Helwan in the middle part of the war and where he had trained the South African prison staff.

Other unusual customers were thirty or so Merchant Navy sailors, who were imprisoned for mutiny in the consular block. Life was not too tough for them: most of their time was spent sunbathing and "Aye aye, sir" replaced the more formal "Staff".

Kitehawks, to use the formal term, were a considerable hazard for the newly arrived SUS. At mealtimes, the SUS formed a single file, collected their meal, then marched back to their rooms to eat it. Until they learned wisdom, the SUS would often find that a kitehawk would swoop, snatch the meat ration and disappear to eat it.

The first time that cigarettes were permitted became something of an occasion. The SUS were lined up in two ranks, with a bucket of water between the ranks and RSM Fazackerley said a few words, then ordered the staff to issue the precious smokes. A strict time limit was set, so the cigarettes had to be taken in long draws. This turned out to be unpleasant for the long sentenced men, whose long abstinence from the weed caused an instant high; and for the non-smokers, all of whom had accepted a cigarette rather than be left out, and who turned green.

No 50 closed at Abbassia around the end of 1946 and its subsequent moves have caused me some headaches – I am still guessing!

Reg Degavino insists that the MPDB to which he was next posted – at Nuserat, Gaza, was also numbered 50. Mr Fitzsimmons opened a detention barracks at Nuserat in the early forties. He has a vivid description of a derelict lock-up miles from anywhere and a night of mosquitoes from an unemptied cess-pit, his party's introduction to the MPDB which was to be numbered 57. This was to take in a wide range of nationalities: Jews, Arabs, Indians, Rhodesians, and also British. It was to preserve its international flavour when it later moved to the Canal Zone and became the domain of Major Sydney Harris. I am assuming that both 50 and 57 were at Nuserat and am waiting anxiously for some member of the Old and Bold to tell me otherwise.

Nuserat, it appears, was a great distance from anywhere, though Reg Degavino vaguely remembers a RE camp and a tin shack of a garrison cinema. Eating out was literally this: a dusky gentleman owned a mud hut at the roadside and cooked chapattis and chips over a paraffin stove which produced so much black smoke that all eating was done outside.

It is easy to forget that Palestine, too, was a British Station and the original No 57 had been a part of Palestine Command.

Until 1947 and the start of withdrawal from Palestine, another MPDB existed in the shape of No 51, then in Jerusalem. This had opened in 1941 and had the local troops and long sentence SUS from Paiforce, about which I shall write later.

My information about No 51 MPDB comes from an interesting source: an ex SUS, who is now a poet of some eminence, though I will not print his name. One of my regrets is the lack of SUS (ex) material in this book.

As a young lance corporal in the Black Watch, my correspondent was serving in 1946 in Palestine. For some reason – and I did not question his motives – he was caught in possession of six ABs 64 (this, for the younger reader, was the old army's pay book and identity document.) For this, he was sentenced to two years imprisonment, which he partly served in Jerusalem, then in Fanara. He is obviously a man of considerable intelligence, so his impressions of his time "inside" are particularly valuable to me. I asked him a series of questions when I wrote to him and I have taken the liberty of joining the answers together to make a continuous passage.

"I was taken from Acre Central Prison by fifteen hundredweight truck to No 51 MPDB in Jerusalem, arriving there in the dusk. It was a smallish building, probably built in the thirties.

As a person who likes solitude, the thing that most oppressed me was having people permanently around me and this, even more than the humiliation of such things as slopping-out, was the thing that bore most heavily on me.

There was no real work, just a multitude of tiny jobs: dig this, clean that, polish this, tidy that.

By and large, the staff treated me very fairly, there were even one or two acts of kindness, certainly no brutality, though there was always talk of it by the SUS . . . how so and so was kicked to death, how such and such would wait outside the prison and get revenge . . . that kind of thing. In retrospect, I can see how a career spent working amongst men, some thoroughly bad, some seriously bent, some maybe dotty, must inevitably strain the patience.

Fanara I liked more than Jerusalem – more like a POW camp, tented, wired open and light. The labour was tedious – making bricks, but more positive than the endless chores in Jerusalem".

With the name "Fanara", the next phase of the Egypt story

is evoked, but before we move to the Canal Zone, I would like to tidy away two widely cast outstations: the MPDB in Tripoli and that with Paiforce.

Tripoli

The first mention that I have of Tripoli comes from Major Bob Firmstone, who went there in 1943 as Commandant of No 56 MPDB. It was then a converted Italian military hospital and had been manned before his arrival by NCOs from surrounding units. There would appear to have been little real training in that time, merely imprisonment and an attempt to make life more uncomfortable than the SUS would experience outside. Bob regularised the regime, introducing PT and military training in the mornings, then camouflage net and sandbag making in the afternoons.

By the time that Bill Flecknoe went there – and I have unfortunately no date for this, the influence of Bob Firmstone seems to have died off and Bill Flecknoe tells of MPDB Tripoli run much to seed. By this time, it housed British and West African SUS and the staff was of the same mix. The RSM spent most of his time out of the camp and the staff arranged their own rosters. The only people working were the African staff and the white staff went fishing or swimming. It appears that Flecknoe's boot was size eleven and was quickly and efficiently applied.

Bill was later relieved by WOII "Dolly" Gray, another of the Corps' legendary names and he continued the work of restoration.

Major Bill Bishop was posted to Tripoli in 1952 and I make no apology for printing his account in full:

MCE Tripoli

I was posted to MCE Tripoli from 51 MPDB Fanara about February 1952 and flew along the route taken by the 8th Army a few years earlier. We flew in a Dakota and seemed to stop at every battlefield recorded. I eventually arrived at Castel Benito Airport. The name was shortly changed to King Idris following Independence Day.

I travelled through the city and a few miles along the road to Tunis and arrived at a very modern prison, built by the Italians during their occupation. We had a section of this prison, including what used to be the Governor's House. It was reached from the main road by a magnificent drive which went right round the house. Half of the house was my married quarter and the other half was single staff accommodation. My part consisted of a very wide passage about 8' wide with lounge, dining room, kitchen, four bedrooms and two dressing rooms and bathrooms leading off. The single staff had similar accommodation.

The entrance to the MCE was across the drive from my front door, with Gate Lodge and Main Office adjacent to the main gate. SUS accommodation consisted of three ten man dormitories and three single cells. The parade ground was bounded by SUS accommodation on two sides, the perimeter wall of the prison and the Sgts Mess on the other two. It was quite a large square more than adequate for the few SUS we held. One part doubled for use as a miniature range. The Sgts Mess entrance was across the drive at the other end of my quarter, with an emergency entrance in to the MCE at the rear.

The Commandant during my tour was Major CTC Wharton RAOC whose main job was CRAOC at HQ Tripoli District. He paid weekly visits for routine administration and as required for office parties. At other times, "I was in charge" I was WOII at the time, and had a staff of 1 S/sgt, 3 Sgts, 2 L/cpls attached from local units. We were served by a ACC Pte and names I remember from those days are "Happy Harry" Smithers and Sammy Clayton. We were established to hold (I think) 25 SUS, we rarely had double figures, but we were never empty.

I don't recall any untoward incident in my tour, but we did have one young Medical Officer who did not believe in dietary punishment. He refused to pass any SUS as fit for punishment. A quiet word with the DAPM was sufficient to get a new doctor.

This was one of the "plum" postings of the Corps, and it was with great sadness that I received orders to close it down in the Spring of 1953. I believe it reopened elsewhere in the city of Tripoli when we left the Suez Canal Zone in 1955.

Among the benefits of this station was the location. We were about 5 miles West of the town on the Tunis road, and 5 minutes walk from a very nice sandy beach. There was an excellent bus service to town, and the families spent a lot of time there. Because of this facility we were very popular with other messes. A regular Sunday activity was picnic lunch on the beach, with swimming in the afternoon. Children were taken home to bed, and the parents returned for a evening whist drive.

For the benefit of staff who served there in later years, we were about one mile beyond that popular resort known as Piccolo Capri.

Another MCE was also established along this coast at another place which figures in the history of the Eighth Army. 60 MCE opened in Benghazi on 1st January 1950. It had two wings: one British, one Mauritian. There were two MPSC staff and four Mauritian, then attached staff from the RA and 16/5th Lancers. More details of this MCE are not at hand.

Paiforce

PAIFORCE? you ask. Everybody has heard of the Eighth Army, but the Persia and Iraq Force is not one of the names to conjure with. It was established to protect one of the supply routes to Russia and to protect the oil wells of Persia. Captain Harry Barker served there and his is the only acount I have of this little known area of military activity.

Harry was serving in No 50 at Abbassia, when he was detailed to move to Bagdad, overland by truck, via Palestine and Syria. It was a three week journey and the object of the exercise was to open two FPCs: No 41 in Bagdad and No 42 in Tehran. He opened No 41, then found that 10th Army already had a small FPC in the holy city of Qum, run by the CMP. Harry left the establishment of No 42 in abeyance and attached himself to the CMP. The FPC was small, the average number of SUS being roughly 40. It was a tented camp with huts as staff quarters. His stay there was short as 10th Army left the area and he was posted to No 1 MPDB at Shaiba, near Basra.

Shaiba had British and Indian SUS, mainly short stay sentenced people, as the long sentenced British went back to Jerusalem and the Indians were returned to India. There were also a consular prison within the perimeter and Merchant Navy and NAAFI people were often guests there. Apart from Harry, the staff were drawn from the units with the force.

The most interesting group that No 1 locked up, was a party of Chinese, who were employed by the Royal Indian Army Service Corps, with whom they had mutinied. Every one of them was loaded with huge sums of cash and quantities of gold when admitted. They served three weeks, were released, and then returned to prison after three days: they had mutinied again and burned down their tents.

For the permanently Colchester based Corps, Tripoli and the Holy City of Qum are unlikely postings, but for the Old and Bold, the mystic names of Suez, Moascar and Fanara are still very real. It is there we go next.

28
In the Canal Zone

The Old and Bold know the background, so they can skip, without bad conscience, the next two or three paragraphs, but the younger end may need a short history and geography lesson.

The last paragraph showed how Egypt occupied a key position for the war effort, the Suez Canal in particular making it vital for us to hold this corner of the Eastern Mediterranean. We had been there since 1882, although technically Egypt was still then a part of the Turkish Empire. It was ruled by a Khedive, a kind of vicreroy and in 1922, the pro-British Khedive, became the first King of Egypt of modern times. In 1936, he signed a treaty with Britain, the treaty recognising Egyptian independence, but guaranteeing to Britain, amongst other things, the right to garrison the Canal Zone.

In 1952, the Egyptian King, Farouk, was deposed by a group of officers and British influence from that date begins to fade.

Already, British troops had begun to concentrate in the Canal Zone. Headquarters Middle East Land Forces was at Fayid and British garrisons were strung like beads along the Suez Canal.

To catch something of the "feel" of the Zone, I can do no better than to quote from Jim Robinson's account of his journey from 51 MPDB in Fanara, to 50 MCE in Moascar.

"Number 50 was just outside Ismailia, close to the Canal and to Lake Timsah. The journey there by truck was fascinating, like going back into Biblical times. We travelled down a road parallel to the Canal through rural areas where the houses where made of mud, sometimes with a coat of whitewash outside, sometimes not. In the fields, oxen drew the plough cutting a single furrow, while the wife picked out the weeds or stones after the plough. There were whole fields full of water melons and they needed water in plenty, so donkeys, oxen or sometimes a man would be seen turning a pump to lift the water from the irrigation ditches.

Another means of irrigation in this area was the Sweetwater Canal. This was a narrow canal of the most foul water you could ever see or smell. Occasionally you would see a dead donkey or dog floating on it. Always there was a shimmering of oil or grease on the water, no doubt from the boats that also used it. It was used as a public latrine and youngsters using the canal would flash their backsides at passing troops or their families. The canal also provided the drinking water for many people including the Army. At least the army water was purified first at the El-Firdan filtration plant. Washing was also done in the canal but I dread to think what the clothes looked like when finished.

Further out from this was sand, which went for miles. The only trees around were date palms and they were only in the areas of irrigation ditches and canals."

At Suez, Major Syd Harris was commanding No 57 MPDB. He had been posted there in May 1948 and left there in 1953. He therefore spanned a large part of its history in the Canal Zone (you will recall that No 57 had started life in Gaza)

Sydney called 57 the League of Nations and it did, indeed, cater for the miscreants of a surprising number of nationalities: West and East Africans, Cypriots, Swazis, Zulus, Mauritians, including Chinese Mauritians. Sentences ranged from 28 days to life and crimes from theft to murder. During Sydney's tour there, twelve to fifteen of the inmates were sentenced to death, but none of these sentences was confirmed and all the sentenced were shipped home to their own country.

There were of course problems. Sydney recalls one Cypriot officer, who arrived still wearing his rank badges and immediately started to attempt to organise the rest of the Cypriot SUS. This was not enthusiastically viewed by Sydney and met with little success.

Obviously, labour for the SUS was vitally important and a woodworking shop became the pride of No 57. The major difficulty was finding wood to be worked, until the value of the telegraph poles was appreciated. A sawpit was constructed and the poles were then sawn . . . by hand and longitudinally. They became the basis for a flourishing furniture industry and a welcome source of revenue for the PRI.

Even in the Canal Zone, there was only limited quantity of

telegraph poles and a shortage of material crisis appeared to be looming, when a reconnaissance by Philbin, a man of infinite resource, revealed a railway siding, no longer used but with sleepers still in position . . . ninety sleepers. These were promptly loaded and disappeared into the hungry maw of the furniture factory, to emerge as coffee tables, stools and desks. Some years later, when Sydney had been posted to Cyprus, he was invited to lunch by the Governor. Conversationally Syd asked Lady Harding if she still had the coffee tables from the Canal Zone. She said that she had them indeed, but considered them too good to take around on postings. Sydney, in the tactful manner so characteristic of him, then pointed out that the Governor of Cyprus was a receiver of stolen property.

Later when evacuation of the Zone loomed large, planning officers from HQ were surprised to find that a siding shown on their maps no longer existed.

Ray Degavino had moved from Gaza to Suez in the year before Sydney and his memory of No57 in its new home is "a great deal of sand and a barbed wire fence holding rows of tents". He mentions a cell block near the gate, always highly illuminated at night, from which a Greek or an Arab, who had been sentenced to death had escaped shortly before Reg's arrival, never to be seen again.

Reg's other impression of the place is an echo of the social life of the Army of that time, rather than a purely MPSC memory. At the time of the shapeless lumps called battledress, the most sought after loot was an Australian Battledress: fine cloth in tasteful green. The staff of 57 managed to find a source not stated, for these attractive items from Oz. They were obtained in large sizes, as No.57 had the advantages of a SUS tailor, who would then unpick the seams and produce a confection cut to the body and flared tastefully at the trouser cuff, perfect dress for home leave.

Ray Ganner joined British Troops Egypt in 1948 in the largest MPSC draft ever. There were about forty of them, with WOs Vic Bint, Syd Rumney and Bert Mullings as the warrant officers. The Depot and Training Establishment, MPSC for the whole of the Middle East was attached to 50 MPDB in Moascar and it was from there that the large draft – and one of approximately thirty later on in the same year – were allocated to the penal establishments of the area. In charge of the Depot was RSM Cripps, with WOII Betteridge in support.

50 MPDB, soon to become 50 MCE, was another tented camp with interior wire compounds and a perimeter fence. The feel of it in winter is caught very well by an extract from the April 1949 Journal and it is salutary to quote it here, to ensure that the younger end appreciate that BTE members, whatever they remember now, were not entirely on a Cook's tour:

Camp Life in winter at 50 M.C.E.

"As was reported in our last contribution we are stationed in the open desert outside the "Treaty Zone" of Egypt.

During the winter season the Khamsoon winds are most persistent, and, as the desert sand is by no means static; we suffer accordingly. When the winds blow a fog of sand and dust rises up to a height of some 50 feet, and in consequence reduces visibility to an absolute minimum.

The sand is indeed very cruel, filling the eyes, nose, ears and mouth, and creating an unpleasant outlook on life, leaving us with the one ambition of getting home to wind, rain, and snow, which are certainly an improvement on this peculiar desert climate.

Meals are a nightmare – sand serving as the main condiment, and does in fact render salt and pepper useless. Some children revel in putting soil from the garden to their mouths, but try them with sand, and you will cure them for the rest of their natural lives.

Regardless of these difficulties, however, Summer (or I should say Spring) is fast approaching, and short breaks of leave at Timsah, by the lake, or at Port Fouad (holiday resort at Port Said) will more than compensate us for the climatic adversities which we have tolerated in the past three months."

The weather and sand were not the only snags, for this was a time of boiling unrest throughout Egypt, finally coming to its head in 1951, when the families living out in Ismailia (and, for No57, those living in Suez and Tewfik), were forced to evacuate their quarters and to live, uncomfortable but secure, in tented accommodation. They were allowed to bring the minimum of possessions with them and the things that we left behind fell to Arab looters.

Jim Robinson arrived at 50 MCE in 1953 and I reproduce here his account of his stay:

Accommodation at 50 MCE was the same as elsewhere – tents – four men to each one. Conditions were primitive and the tents were hot during the day, but just right in the evenings except during the cold weather when we had to have an Aladdin stove to try and keep warm. We had just one bulb in the centre of the tent and this supplied all the power we had. The wiring was primitive and often blew the fuses. I think that we were lucky that there were so few fires. We did have one tent fire. It happened early one morning, the tent was burnt up in about two minutes. Those who were around and had water, threw it on to the adjacent tents or their own. There was nothing they could do about the burning one.

My first job was on discipline, It was not very tight at the time. The Commandant, Lt Col Mills or Nutty Mills as he was known had gone overboard on the new Stage System that had started just a couple of years before. All admissions went straight to Stage II, then if they misbehaved in any way they were downgraded to Stage I. There was no cell block and in those days of National Service and reluctant soldiers, you can imagine the problems we were faced with.

Solitary confinement when it was given, was carried out in a tent sited on its own. This gave the SUS constant contact with other SUS, even if it was only visual.

Lt Col Mills was replaced by Lt Col John McDonald KOSB (Big Jock). He did nothing for a fortnight but walk around the camp, watch and take notes. Then he called everyone together, told them what he had seen, what he thought of it and what he planned to do in the future.

The first thing he insisted on was a tightening up of discipline – for SUS and staff. For instance, you were to give an order to an SUS only once. If he failed to carry it out he was to go on report. The staff would be backed up to the hilt. If any member of the staff was found to be at fault then God help him!

Discipline as I have already stated was strict. SUS who had been remanded for Commandant's would hand their kit into the CQMS store, knowing quite well they would be in the cells soon afterwards. There was often a scuffle when the SUS would refuse to march in and had to be frogmarched or one would not move fast enough.

I remember one very hard man who had escaped. He was found about five days later hiding in his old unit. They phoned to say they had found him and could we go and collect him. Two NCOs went and found eight RASC NCOs standing around the SUS who had refused to move. He was brought back to the MCE on the back of a 15 cwt truck. On arrival at the MCE he was told to get down, but he refused to do so and said, "you get me down". The Commandant was at the side of the truck when this was said, so he decided to leave and merely said, "I want to see him in 30 minutes". The SUS was removed from the truck by the same two NCOs S/sgt Les Osborne and Bill Ingram, but he continued to resist and struggle all the way to the cell.

There were plenty of other strong characters amongst the SUS and the staff but they were not necessarily unpleasant.

One SUS was a man named Coogan who came from somewhere in Ireland. He was serving a two year sentence for refusing to soldier. He was a National Serviceman who had no intention of serving his two years National Service. He ended up serving more than three.

He was always in trouble yet he was always pleasant – a likeable rogue, he lost every day of his remission and served the full two years.

If you told him to dig a hole a mile wide, he would do it, but if you told him to clean his brasses he would refuse. He was on Company Orders every day for report and would march himself there without bother. One day having done this he was seen by S/sgt McAughy, another Irishman, who asked him was he on report Coogan replied "Haven't you nicked me today, Staff" to which McAughy replied, "Not today". Coogan's retort to this was "Well, you big Orange bastard you have now, haven't you Staff". And he was nicked.

The next thing to be done was to build a cell block, 12 cells, then a revised training programme with a more rigorous attitude to be adopted. Big Jock then explained his own attitude to Mess life – which was to say, do as you like, providing you do not bring the unit or the army into disrepute. You can even take the roof off the Mess if you wish as long as you put it back by the morning. Finally, whatever you do, make sure you are able to do your job properly or I will bust you. In fact I think he busted eight sergeants whilst he was there and posted several others. It must be admitted he never did take anyone to task for high spirits in the mess. An example of this was John Gabbet an A/Sgt and as such very vulnerable. One Friday night when mess caterer, he got himself very drunk. He took a sabre off the wall of the mess and placed himself outside the Commandant's sleeping quarters. Then he started to shout at the top of his voice, "You Scottish Shylock you, if you want your pound of flesh, then come and get it". He raved in this vein for about an hour, he didn't repeat himself much either, though he sometimes used stronger language. The Duty Officer did try and shut him up, but failed hopelessly. Nothing was said that night but the following morning the 2 i/c was told to check the Bar Stock and Cash. It was found to be correct.

Nothing else happened, except that Gabbet repeated his tirade from then on every Friday night.

The staff spirit rose considerably and everyone made an effort to improve the camp, particularly their own tents. The building of the cell block was an ideal opportunity to effect this until finally the Arab contractor had to complain that the losses of material – mainly corrugated iron sheeting was too great even by Arab standards. Instructions were given by the CO that this had to stop. As we were not quite finished, we then had to raid the CO's supplies. He was most upset but he never did find out who had taken them.

The situation in Egypt at that time was very unstable. Often there would be trouble in Ismailia or Port Said or somewhere else in the Canal Zone. Then all civilian towns would be put Out of Bounds. Sometimes a soldier would be killed as he walked around the town, or perhaps an Egyptian. The air in the towns at these times would be electric and sometimes really frightening. The Arabs would become very aggressive even as you passed them and God help anyone who fell into their hands. Normally it would be severe mutilation. It was always necessary to be armed whenever you went outside the Garrison by vehicle and needless to say this in turn led to other serious incidents.

The other problem we had was thieving: the Arabs would steal anything. Occasionally however some soldiers would work it with the Arabs to have all their stores stolen from their trucks. The soldiers would stop at some pre-arranged spot, then go and answer some call of nature. On their return they would find their truck empty. They would obviously have gained a few hundred pounds, which would have been a fortune then to a National Serviceman on 35 pence a day. They must have been found out later and after they had been discharged at the end of their service. Many were arrested, brought back to the army and to Egypt, where they were court martialled and sentenced.

We had a signal one day in late 53 or early 54 telling us to evacuate all SUS and be prepared to take in 2000 natives as detainees. We were given 24 hours to be ready. Everyone moved very fast. Some SUS moved to 51 MP & DB at Fanara, others with just a short time to do were given remitted sentences, whilst others were sent to unit guard rooms to finish off their sentences. Some of the staff were posted on a temporary basis to Fanara to help them cope with extra SUS they had. Others, myself included, were left behind to face the expected 2000 detainees.

The following day the Arab detainees started to arrive, but something must have gone wrong: instead of 2000, we received 25!

With these numbers all the staff would soon become bored. The Commandant therefore decided that this was a good time to replace the entire perimeter fence with a double apron fence. From somewhere he obtained materials including hundreds of telegraph poles. The staff wearing PT shorts, boots, socks and jungle hats started work. The fence had to be buried to a depth of two feet in what was very hard sand. I can remember digging part of the trench and grumbling about the digging and the Commandant to the man next to me, then I realised it was the Commandant I was talking to – he was digging as well. All this work eventually paid off because we soon had a first class secure perimeter fence with a catwalk all the way round.

Whilst all this was going on, the normal duties of the camp had still to be carried out, patrols, nightwatch etc, and with these low numbers of detainees we soon had the SUS returned to us.

The Arabs were put in a special compound with a fence of corrugated iron around them. Nightwatch consisted of four NCOs, one in a tower by the SUS gate one in a tower at the edge of the Arab compound, but as this was outside the camp perimeter you were armed with a SMG. The other NCOs patrolled the SUS lines and every two hours we changed around.

On the first night of one of my nightwatches, I was in the tower by the Arab compound, when one of the Arabs started walking from his tent towards the fence. Knowing that two Arabs had escaped the previous night and that if this Arab got near the fence, I would not be able to see what he would be doing. I told him in my pigeon Arabic to stay where he was and use the latrine bucket by his tent. He said, "No, I'm going to use the latrine by the fence". I again told him to stay where he was but he refused and continued to walk towards the fence. I warned him I would shoot if he did not stop, but he shrugged his shoulders and said, Ma,alesh' or so what. I cocked the SMG and having warned him again, which he ignored, I fired a shot into the sand in front of him. He must have then realised I was serious, because he went back to his tent a little faster than he left. Everyone in his tent started praying and I heard Staff Robinson mentioned quite a few times.

I had a ticking off for this, a very mild one, but never again did I have trouble from them, except about 6 weeks later when a recently admitted Arab tried the same thing. He too ignored my warnings and was starting to walk on when the other Arabs must have told him that I would shoot. He went back straightaway.

These Arabs were really in limitless detention. They had no idea when they would be released and had no visits from their families or relatives, mainly because the relatives couldn't get into the restricted area of the Canal Zone.

I was patrolling in the Arab compound one day, when I noticed one of the Arabs was unconscious and had failed to eat his food. The doctor was called in who checked him and said to leave him. After three days he had still not eaten and was still apparently unconscious, when we noticed blood coming from the corner of his mouth. The doctor decided that he should go to hospital. The Red Crescent ambulance was called for and it took him to hospital, the civilian one. We didn't see him again.

The next day another Arab was found unconscious and after a few days, he too had blood coming from his mouth. He was also sent to hospital, and was never seen again. Then we had a third one unconscious. This was too much of a coincidence so he was segregated. This time he came too and started eating. When he was put back with the others he became unconscious again.

This time we segregated a Sudanese detainee and soon the unconscious man came too and began to eat.

It was then discovered that the Sudanese had been hypnotising them and drawing blood with his finger nail. Once they had gone to hospital they recovered quite quickly and went home – no more detention.

I also remember one of the Arabs attacking the Commandant with a short length of angle iron. The Commandant however, was just a bit faster than the Arab realised and he disarmed the Arab very neatly with a sharp blow from his fist. No one ever tried that again.

Soon agreement was reached between the British and Egyptian governments for the withdrawal of all British troops from Egypt. As a result we were told we had to close down on December 31st 1955.

Incidentally this was also the last day for Military Corrective Establishments: they were to be known as Military Corrective Training Centres from the 1st Jan 1956.

No 51 MPDB in Fanara is well documented in the various accounts I have received: amongst others, those of Ray Ganner, Bill Bishop, Lew Butler and Reg Degavino.

It was another tented camp but the mess was modern brick built and decorated with handsome murals by German POWs. Next door at No51 was a POW camp, holding hardline Nazis, who once burned down their tents and ran home made swastika flags up their flagpole.

Main labour for the SUS was the making of concrete slabs for use in married quarter building. Obviously with a slab-making "factory" on the premises, all camp paths were paved and tents had firm floors. Brass stripping from old equipment was another SUS activity.

One account speaks of German war criminals being brought to No51. Certainly Polish and other foreign offenders were locked up there and a Polish officer and staff sergeant were attached. Ray Ganner informs me that the staff sergeant's wife had escaped to freedom by swimming a river with her baby. She had set up a business in Rhodesia and had prospered.

Lew Butler had already done one tour at No51, when he

returned in 1951. It was about the same year when No51 was to be the scene for the hanging of four British servicemen. Three of them had murdered an Egyptian taxi driver, had fled and had been captured in a cinema. The fourth was a former corporal who had murdered his Commanding Officer.

These were to be the last hangings of British servicemen and the impact on the minds of the staff, not only those concerned with the death watch, but all staff in the MPDB, comes over in all reports.

Albert Pierrepoint, the British official hangman, was flown over from the United Kingdom to carry out the executions. Staff Sergeant Mick Riley was detailed to assist him. One of my informants tells me that the experience made Mick ill for several days after the event.

The three who had killed together were hanged on the same day and the corporal on the next day. The bodies were handed over to the RMP and were buried in consecrated ground in the Moascar British Military Cemetery, the graves being angled differently from the rows of graves of those who had died with less disgrace.

No 51 closed early in 1955. With the movement away from the Canal Zone, Cyprus became the British foothold in the Eastern Mediterranean and it is to Cyprus that we next turn.

29

Cyprus

The stubby end of the British presence in Cyprus is still there and the centuries old enmity between Greek and Turk is ever-present, polarised now, so that Cyprus to the British soldier means the sovereign bases and the Green Line. To some it is only a brochure at the travel agents.

The Cyprus with which we are to deal in this chapter is the Cyprus of EOKA and Enosis, Grivas and Makarios, a Cyprus where there was one British soldier for every fifty Cypriots, where soldiers and families were shot on the streets; where one member of the Corps was shot down in the presence of his son.

Major Bill Bishop was sent there as RSM in 1955 to open a MCE around the nucleus of a three cell block in Waynes Keep Camp outside Nicosia. He went without other staff at first and was attached to the RMP, one of whom was a young officer later to become Brigadier B. Thomas OBE and to loom large on the MPSC scene.

Other Corps members arrived, as did also twelve Turkish labourers and a quantity of barbed wire and fence posts. Captain "Dusty" Miller arrived and Reg Avery as Chief Clerk and Sergeant Maggs, whom Bill classes as the most wily procurer of stores on the island. All that was needed was a MCE and some customers.

The Turkish labourers were willing enough, but unfortunately spoke no English, so it was a classic case of teaching by example. Bill thinks that six MPSC sergeants worked harder than they had ever worked before, learning much of the science of post hole digging. Soon there was a MCE with compounds containing tents, eight foot fences topped by dannert wire and tents for the SUS. The Greeks blew up the British Council Building in Nicosia, the garrison was reinforced and the customers began to pour in. The original concept had been a secure place for holding 25 SUS and this was soon woefully inadequate. A leapfrog situation developed with staff numbers frantically attempting to keep pace with admissions.

Although the fences were high, food began to disappear mysteriously from the ration stores and it was only after a while that Bill learned how it was being done. Two Royal Marine SUS would regularly scale their own fence and the fence of the ration compound, pick the lock of the ration store and then return with the loot to their own tent for a midnight feast. Bill was so impressed that he ordered them to demonstrate and says that "it was a credit to their marine training, more suited to a circus than an Army".

When Major Sydney Harris arrived in 1957, the situation had reached an extreme pitch and it became necessary to enforce the curfew regulations in a nearby pro-EOKA village.

This could only be done by using SUS, so a nightly patrol of two MPSC and ten SUS, armed with rifle and bayonet, was instituted. The sight of such a patrol, a mixed bag of Navy Army and Air Force SUS so startled a senior officer that his car skidded off the road.

The extreme of under staffing came when Operation Matchbox required the MCE to become a detention centre for 100 Turks to be held for three to four months. To patrol the perimeter, the SUS had again to be armed. The system worked amazingly well until two SUS leaned their rifles against the perimeter fence, shinned over and made their way to the Lancashire Fusiliers barracks – one of the SUS was a member of that regiment. Here they obtained rifles and ammunition from the guardroom, made their way to the British Military Hospital, shot themselves in the foot and handed themselves in.

A little known fact is that several ex members of the Corps were called back to work in a civilian capacity in Civil Detention Centres in Cyrpus. The group was led by Lt Col "Big Jock" McDonald and ex RSM Fazackerley. I would like very much to know more about this.

Ray Ganner remembers the Turks as a very aimiable crowd, who spent some of their time producing model sailing boats in the pioneer's shop, all the boats being named SS Waynes Keep. One of the Turks admitted was a village headman, who brought with him all the village treasury, including IOUs, all of which had to be accounted for. The detainees were visited often by Turkish dignitaries, including their Mufti.

On the SUS side, there were the ups and downs inevitable in a reluctant National Service army. A dirty protest was staged before the IRA had even thought of it, though it was short lived. Another SUS threw his whole equipment down a deep latrine and claimed with misguided satisfaction that it had gone where it could no longer be cleaned. It took on its pristine state again shortly after he had rescued it and he wore it thereafter with no protest of a similar nature.

1959 saw a British Turkish Greek Agreement about Cyprus, which solved very little of the real problem but laid down the right of Britain to keep at least a toehold on the island. The MCE became a Military Corrective Training Centre, still numbered with the original 52 and it was in these latter days, in 1961 that Major Bill Humphries did his apprenticeship with the Corps, under the tender tuition of RSM Bill King and Staff Sergeant Len Conning. Bill Humphries was to return to the island on a six month emergency tour in 1964, but he was not returning to Waynes Keep. When 52 MCTC closed down in 1961, the Cyprus Detention Centre was established in Pyler Camp, Dhekelia. This had a Superintendent instead of a Commandant, a skeleton MPSC staff, finding the rest of its staff from the garrison. Customers came from the sovereign base areas and the British element of the UN forces. This was the last remnant of MPSC staffing on Cyprus.

30
Corradino and Windmill Hill

The Corps today is Colchester-bound and a posting in the sun is a scarcity product, so the possibility of a tour in Malta or Gibraltar seems like a tourist agency dream.

They were always plum postings (though there was some discomfort in a Maltese posting between 1941 and 1944!) The "plumminess" of the postings is even echoed in the Victorian letter books, where the warders are applying, particularly from Stirling and from Halifax Nova Scotia, for a tour in the Mediterranean. They are seldom successful.

The old MPSC members were more fortunate, having Windmill Hill in Gibraltar and Corradino in Malta. Windmill Hill closed on 31st October 1954 and it is to Doug Moody, faithful informant, that I owe my information about it. With Eric Milton, Doug was destined to be also the rear party to close Corradino.

Gibraltar was never a big station for the MPSC, but Doug served there from 1948 to 1951, sailing out in SS Eastern Prince.

He found a military prison of the old style: a main block with three landings, each containing single cells only. There was still a huge shot drill yard, used by this time for training, the whole thing surrounded by a high wall, which the Rock Apes often used as an observation point. The quarters were built onto the prison, so that the children going to school had to shout "Gate Staff" before they could leave. This became something of a game with them.

There was no fresh water on the Rock and all the roofs of the prison were flat, draining water into a central tank. A daily task of the SUS was a few hours on the pumps, then the distribution of water to the quarters. Without the daily call of the SUS, the quarters had to rely on the sea water from the tap. In one drought summer during Doug's tour, water was shipped by tanker from the United Kingdom.

Staff at Windmill Hill was a RSM and nine staff sergeants

or sergeants. Training was the responsibility of all the staff and was very basic, consisting mainly of drill and PT. There was no Commandant, but a Superintendent was appointed from a resident regiment and visited daily.

The MCE was on the upper Rock and was in a security area, patrolled by the War Department Police, who were mainly Gibraltarians. The area also included a Heavy AA Regiment and two emplacements for 9.2 inch guns were directly above the MCE. When they fired a practice, all windows in the MCE had to be opened and the shot was fired over the MCE itself. The HAA also fired occasional practices and during this time the atmosphere was more battle zone than corrective establishment.

A bigger bang occurred during his tour, when from a magnificent viewpoint near the sergeants' mess, he was looking down on the harbour and Europa Point. An ammunition ship, the SS Bedenham was unloading and suddenly exploded, taking out all the windows of Main Street and lifting furniture and lino in the quarters.

Falling numbers of admissions led to closure, but shortly before the last days, Gibraltar was visited by the Queen and the MPSC were required to line a short part of the route.

As I have already said, Doug formed half the rear party when Corradino closed after almost exactly one hundred years as a military prison, detention barracks, then finally as the Combined Military Establishment.

It was built on Corradino Heights, to the south of the Grand Harbour and was inside the bastion surrounding the Dockyard. There had been a defensive point on its site, which had been used during the defence of Valetta by the knights of Malta.

Corradino opened in 1866 and this date appears over the main entrance under a carved Royal Arms. The stone building had been built for the Admiralty to house 159 prisoners. It was handed over to the army in 1871 and was extended by running out the leg of a T from the main building in 1901. This last data I am able to give with such complacent certainty because I have in front of me as I write, a well preserved blueprint, produced in the old way on linen, and dated 1930. It schedules alterations and costs as well as offering a plan of the whole complex and doubtless will find a place in the Corps museum, for the schedule of changes is in many ways, the illustration of the early chapters in this book. Let me show what I mean.

In 1897, a stone-breaking shed is erected and alterations made to the hair picking shed and to the laundry at a cost of £538. The space for these is taken from the shot drill yard. We can see here that shot drill is losing ground – figuratively as well as literally – to the claims of productive employment. From the letter book, we know a little more of the background. There had been problems with the working of stone under the strong Maltese sun for some time – the Medical Officer complains in the prison reports about this and recommends the issue of straw hats for stone breakers, then some kind of roof. There are also complaints that prisoners working the stone are able to communicate too easily with each other. We can assume, then, that some kind of roof is put over the stone breaking area and we know – again from the prison reports – that stalls as in a stable, were also set up. With the hair picking shed, a side of the building is removed, again on the MO's orders, to allow the air to circulate and to lessen the amount of floating fragments of hair breathed in during this extremely nasty job. Notice how closely the advice of the MO is followed. The stone shed was dismantled in 1904 – obviously to allow space for the newly introduced military training. The hair picking shed, incidentally, stayed as garages and stores until Corradino closed down.

In 1902 and 1903, eight married quarters are built along the road leading from the dockyard gate to the prison at a cost of £4320. They are clearly visible on the 1930 plan: bungalows with a verandah and small garden. Some of these have already been dismantled by 1930 and I am informed that some were destroyed in the bombing of the island during the Second World War. There were two officers quarters with stable accommodation for four horses and a report in an early copy of the Journal speaks of these as also having been bombed. A new Commandant's quarter was built in the late Fifties outside the perimeter. When it was being built, an underground passage was found, running a hundred yards into the moat flanking Corradino. The passage was pierced with loopholes for small arms and there was an emplacement for a heavy gun.

Garsia's influence is felt in 1907, when a modified gymnasium is built, costing £400. In the prison report, mention is made at this time of a miniature range constructed in a "subway" of the prison, possibly in a passage similar to the one already mentioned. The floor of the gymnasium was still visible in the early sixties. I apologise to the reader for what is probably a hunk of totally uninteresting detail to them, but Corradino was the last of the old prisons, so the detail particularly interested me.

The main "customers", of course, throughout the history of Corradino, were the soldiers who were garrisoning Malta – including occasionally the Royal Maltese Artillery and other Maltese troops. Trade was usually good during the nineteenth Century, but in 1894 became so good that some long term prisoners awaiting ships for the United Kingdom had to be farmed out to the Civil Prison in Valetta at the cost of one shilling and sixpence per head per day. During the Boer War, prisoners from South Africa were accommodated and there were several complaints about their lousebound and ragged state on arrival.

The other good customers were the Navy – there was a strong RN and Royal Marine presence on the staff right to the very end. Relations with the navy were not always cordial. The main customers were stokers and other hard men and it is a permanent bleat by the Admiral that conditions are easier in the military prison than they are aboard ship. He demands the return to shot drill and the crank and the argument goes right up the line to "Head Office". From there it is passed to the Commander in Chief, who gives the Admiral a flea in his ear.

In more recent times, inter-service relationships appear to have been excellent and the Corradino mess was a favourite watering place when the fleet was in. A report in the Winter 1963 Journal shows that it was not only the Royal Navy that was attracted there. When the US 6th Fleet was visiting, the PO's of one ship managed to get permission to hold a party in the mess to entertain their officers, with the Corradino Staff invited. I quote "They put 90 dollars behind the bar to cover the cost of the drinks and the caterer was kept busy working out the exchange rate. They also supplied their own American style buffet and the mess was eating baked beans for weeks afterwards. They put on a good party and were very well behaved. The skipper complimented the RSM on the "good club" he was running". I suspect there is a short story somewhere in the events of the evening!

There were other interesting foreign guests, remembered by Vic Bint from his time as RSM. One evening during 1958, there was a knock on his quarter door and the Commandant, Major Roberts informed him that civilians were to be admitted to the establishment for a period. Vic, aghast, said that this was totally illegal, but the Commandant had the Governor's order (there was a state of emergency at the time) and a wing was cleared. It was put in the hands of the Maltese police and housed the next day Dominic (Dom) Mintoff and other members of the Malta Labour Party. They stayed there for two months, guarded first by the Malta Police, then some policemen from Gozo. I had thought of writing to Dom Mintoff for his impressions: it certainly goes some way to explain his aversion to things English!

It goes without saying that the staff of Corradino saw regular visitors from the Corps at home – we could use a firm base in the Mediterranean now! Items submitted to the Journal through the years have all an undercurrent of smugness. They regret that the 50 degree temperatures outside have driven them back inside the mess to roaring fires. They describe the facilities of St. George's Lido, then say that they prefer the seclusion of one of the nearer bays for their swimming and sailing; the Casino is expensive. It wasn't going to last for ever.

Maltese independence put the black spot on Corradino and the duty frees. Admissions had already begun to fall with the end of National Service and the run-down of the fleet. Bill King, the last RSM, sent me a copy of the final signal received from Commander PRG Smith, the Naval Advisor to the CME and I think it sums up the feeling at the closure of this, the last of the military prisons.

To: C.M.E., Corradino.
Hang up the thumbscrew, dismantle the rack,
And send me my Warders and Cook Ratings back.
   Thanks for the hours of penance well spent,
By the Rates who have gained from instruction well meant.
Though the building may moulder, we will raise up our vino,
And drink a last toast to C.M.E., Corradino.

Close the cell doors and hang up the keys,
But send me the Warders and others back please.

31
Kure

The interested reader will now be thumbing through the atlas to pinpoint Kure. When they find it on Japan's Inland Sea, they will possibly be puzzled as to why the MPSC should be serving in Japan.

The answer is, of course, that Japan was the main base for the United Nations forces, who went to the aid of the Republic of South Korea.

This may be the place to outline the background of this campaign for the benefit of the younger reader.

Up to the end of the Second World War, Korea had been occupied – almost colonised – by their neighbours, the Japanese. At the end of the war, the Americans occupied the Southern area of the country: all the area South of the 38/th Parallel of latitude. The USSR, who had declared war on Japan at the very last minute, occupied the North of Korea: after all, it was perks like this that had made them declare war at all!

In 1948, the Americans handed over their occupied zone to the South Koreans, leaving on 500 military advisers and a Korean Army only lightly armed and half trained. On the 25th of June 1950, the North Koreans invaded the South and rolled up the Southern army like a carpet.

The Security Council of the UN asked for a force to aid South Korea. Many nations responded but the main effort was American. The British Commonwealth sent troops from Britain, Canada, New Zealand and Australia.

The war went up and down the Korean Peninsula like a yo-yo. Inevitably, as throughout recent history, penal institutions follow the drum, so a Field Punishment Centre was established, moving behind the Britcom Division. It must have been located in many odd places during the seesawing action, but we have information only about its situation in one location, in Pusan.

Major Jimmy Deeble was Commandant in Kure – of which

I shall have more to say soon – and was required to examine a site in Pusan, with a view to adopting it as a FPC controlled by the MPSC. He found a derelict hutted camp, already in use by the Canadians as a FPC and subject to a most brutal regime. MPSC staff were moved in.

A report in the 1952 Journal from the Pusan FPC reports that the camp is now "in a much better state of repair: a few windows have been put in and most doors are now in place". In the same report, extra woollens are being issued ready for the Siberian winter, which they expect to last from November to March. They are delighted that the tour in Korea has been shortened to eighteen months and they send – rather forlorn – greetings to the MPSC staff in Malaya. There are two MPSC in Pusan: WOII CW Pullen and Sergeant L Poole. Two others have been posted to No. 25 Canadian FPC and some have already gone home. The main staff under them is drawn from the KSLI and the Gloucesters.

Compared with Pusan, Kure was certainly more comfortable. It was housed in an all wooden camp, surrounded by a 14 foot palisade, also of wood. There were guard towers let into the perimeter fence. . . . because Britcom Corrective Establishment had been a Japanese POW camp. Doug Moody writes of the unpleasant feeling of doing guard in the towers, when one remembered the past use of the place. During the occupation, the Australians had taken it over as No. 22 Combined Detention Barracks and the Australians were to administer it throughout its time as Britcom MCE.

Inside the perimeter, there was a good spread of wooden buildings, the SUS accommodation being single rooms, opening from a corridor. There was a large exercise yard, nicknamed, with some lack of originality, the Bull Ring. The camp was well situated, high on the hill to catch the breeze in Summer – equally well situated, though, to pick up the Arctic winds of Winter. Earthquakes were not unknown.

From its opening in January 1952, Britcom MCE was scheduled to take in SUS from Britain, Canada, Australia and New Zealand and the mind boggles when one thinks of the variations in dress, drill and attitudes to discipline implicit in such a mix. It is to be remembered also that the mix would be further enriched by the presence, not only of Regulars and National Servicemen, but also members of the called-up reserve.

The mix was also present amongst the staff. The Commandant, Assistant Commandant and the RSM were British, but a photograph I have in front of me shows peaked SD caps, berets, wideawakes in Oz and NZ format, then a scattering of Canadian field service caps. In the picture is a younger Jim Deeble and a fresh faced Major "Jimmy" James, then a staff sergeant. The RSM is WOI Lou Staley and the RQMS is WOIIPearson.

The RQMS must have had a nightmare job on the clothing side, but rations were uniformly Australian. There was, surprisingly, a great deal of mutton issued, but also fruit juice and ice cream. The rations were so generous, that Jim Deeble decided early that the SUS were eating better than the troops in the line and altered the ration scale. This led to one Australian ex-customer complaining to his MP and a ministerial enquiry resulted. When Britcom MCE proved that the complainant had actually gained weight during his stay, nothing else was heard.

An issue that Doug Moody remembers is the free sixty cigarettes per week – staff only, of course! They were Australian products, camouflaged under the name of Players and Capstans, but awful. They were known as Bush Fires, not only because of their taste and aroma, but also because each packet contained a warning that cigarette ends could start a bush fire.

Reading between the lines, one gets the impression that the problems of training were so great as to be shelved in the early stages. It was only with the arrival of Jim Deeble that the nettle was grasped. The problems are outlined in the 1955 report on Britcom MCE and I think that some points in it are worth quoting.

"It is worth commenting on the low standard of discipline amongst the SUS when they first arrive. This is not true of all, but of far too many. Some of the most common faults are failing to stand to attention when addressed by an NCO and the inability to stand to attention correctly. Noteworthy is the filthy state of body and clothing of many of the admissions – many boots have been worn down beyond repair. Some of the SUS have not been inspected by their officers for as long as a month before admission".

Widely experienced, Jim Deeble did a rapid appreciation and had soon organised a training programme appropriate to the abnormal situation. Based on a short sharp shock of twenty eight days, there was also a continuation programme for the longer sentenced. Proof of the pudding is that there was a sharp drop in the numbers returning for "second helpings". Discipline was fierce but fair and, to quote Doug Moody, "a twenty eight day man had lost four days remission before he reached Reception. If they stepped out of line, they had the book thrown at them. The state of play was understood by all nationalities and most worked hard and well". All staff had to do their part in training. The 1955 report has the following to say about this:

"This was most unpopular amongst the least efficient members of the staff, who considered that MPSC work entailed turning keys and supervising bucket polishing. However, the majority of the staff have developed into efficient instructors and in some cases into excellent instructors".

He introduced an assault course and training films into the syllabus. Education was restricted, but many gained their educational qualifications before they left Kure. The stage system was made to work effectively, Stage Three being given one shilling per week, though not allowed parole.

The things that interested me most was how the "nationalities" worked together. Talking to Jimmy James and reading Doug Moody, I have the impression that the relationships were excellent. Doug Moody actually bunked with an Australian Provost Corps sergeant and both became firm friends. In the mess, all mucked in, Staff Sergeant King of the APC even using his own film projector to present films three times weekly. International shooting competitions were popular and the Commonwealth spirit even managed to survive games of cricket! Britcom MCE was often visited by officers of all nationalities, including American provost officers, who went away impressed and keen to copy.

In the September 1956 issue of the Journal, the Britcom MCE is preparing to close. Some members are quoted as needing only five minutes' notice to pack and the situation is summed up as "a necessary interlude we could well have done without . . . so it's farewell at last to the Monkey House".

As something like 3000 SUS had "graduated" and as most did not return, then there certainly was a job to be done – and it was obviously done well.

32
Stonecutters

There is something of Alcatraz and Sing Sing about the name of Stonecutters Island, making it the perfect place for a military penal establishment. One can imagine the tremor of horror when some young SUS was told "It's twenty eight days on Stonecutters' Island for you lad". As a Work Study report of 1969 says – somewhat more imaginatively than such reports usually are – "The ordinary SUS during his ferry journey to the island is given a feeling of remoteness which decreases the risk that he will attempt to escape". It didn't always work, but that's the story for later.

The original name of the island was Ngon Shun Chau and its more threatening name resulted from its use as a civil prison, where hacking at granite for sea walls was one of the labours allotted. There are watch towers and wall sections still on the island from these times.

Readers may recall that the APM in 1914 reconnoitred the island to examine its possibilities as an internment camp, but it never came into use as such. In the Twenties and Thirties, it became a rest camp for the artillery and the name of the MCTC: Battery Camp, was a relic of that time.

Its use during the Japanese Occupation is given variously as a rest camp for officers and a snake farm for collecting the anti-toxins needed in the jungle. Members who were on Stonecutters assure me that there were no relics left over from any rest camp as they understood the term, but that the variety and nastiness of the snake population of the island suggests that the latter use was the case. Jim Robinson recalls an occasion when a young SUS from the Welch Regiment had escaped. The RSM Jim Leedham, CSM Jim Robinson and Staff Sergeant Larry Wright were searching a particularly thick piece of bush, knowing that young Taff had to be close. One of them finally said loudly "Ah, well, if we don't get him the snakes will" and one SUS sprung like a Jack in a Box from the bush, praying them to take him with them.

The island was about half an hour by boat from Kowloon. It was a military island and also held a Royal Naval wireless station and a warren of tunnels in which were stored much of the ammunition of Hong Kong. The ammunition depot had its own kind of jetty and a detachment of WD Police, who were mainly Sikhs.

The Combined Military Establishment of Hong Kong had not originally occupied the island. It moved there only in September 1961 from Murray Barracks on Gordon Street, a barracks originally taken over from the Australians after the war and which had been used by them to confine Japanese POWs.

Battery Camp was small, with accommodation for, at most, 42 SUS, a number rarely locked up. As guardroom accommodation in Hong Kong was so limited, Stonecutters usually populated by short sentence SUS, often serving less than twenty eight days. The accommodation was self-contained, having toilet and bathing facilities in the same block as the rooms.

They were a mixed lot, the SUS. The average was the daft young 20 year old, very much the same style as our best customers today, carried away by the delights of Hong Kong to drunkenness, a punch-up or absence in the arms of Suzie Wong. There were also, of course, their naval equivalents. To add leaven to the lump, there were locally enlisted Chinese and the odd Gurkha. When the CME was at Murray Barracks, Jim Deeble recalls a customer of a different kind. When the POWs freed in Korea left ship in Hong Kong and went on the rampage, they were rounded up and put inside to cool off. Stonecutters saw some of the Americans' Vietnam veterans. Hong Kong became for them a R&R base and five were caught by the Hong Kong police in a drug "scenario". The US authorities had the feeling that waiting for trial would be extended leave, so asked Stonecutters to take them. They were treated exactly the same as the British SUS and didn't like it, so demanded a phone call to the senator. Obviously, this was not on, but they did receive a visit from a very young, very frightened US officer and settled down thereafter to await trial.

Training was on a twenty eight day cycle, as sentences were usually so short. All the basic infantry weapons were covered; there was an assault course and a miniature range. During the Sixties, I have reports of a rough terrain route march competition, noted down as Adventurous Training. Swimming and life-saving instruction were given also in the programme, though they had to stop during 1963, due to the extreme pollution of the sea.

One man who obviously benefitted from the swimming instruction was a young Chinese SUS. It was the day of the Annual Administrative Inspection and the Commandant had been able to report with pride – and relief – that there had been no escapes in the year. The General caught the boat and the Commandant went away to prepare for his leave in Malaya. As he reached the gate, the alarm sounded. He was able to see the Chinese figure booted and fully dressed, as he shinned over the ten foot fence, ran down the steep hillside and plunged into the sea, with a member of staff in hot pursuit. Staff Sergeant Dick Searle, who was the staff in pursuit, was a strong swimmer, but the SUS was going hard at it and the staff had to turn back to shore. A passing yacht did a smart tack and an immaculate "man overboard" drill, but the swimming SUS waved him away. As the Commandant watched, the swimmer was picked up by a sampan and was heading away to freedom, only to be stopped by the harbour police launch, which had been alerted. On Commandants Orders, the young man stated that he had only tried to escape to draw attention to his leg, which needed hospital treatment. Could any MO have ordered better therapy than a climb over a ten foot fence, a run down a steep slope and a touch of endurance swimming?

Educational training was non-existant, with each annual report attempting to find an excuse. The compromise usually reached was for staff to give lectures themselves and one feels the relief in the 1971 report, when the introduction of EPC allows the bluff to be dropped.

Distance from the mainland was the excuse most offered by the Schoolies, but in fact the half hour boat journey was a severe limiting factor on many things. The doctor, for example, could only visit twice a week and medical cover came from a Corporal RAMC or from a Chinese medical orderly. For some time in the Sixties, the island had the services of a medical sister, wife of one of the RN at the Wireless Station, but this facility went, when the sailor was posted. It is only in the 1973 report that mention is made of helicopter evacuation of SUS.

The ammunition depot had a fire fighting service, mounted on Land Rovers and these tenders doubled as ambulances, I assume because of the presence of sirens and flashing lights: though the island's single road, on which it was almost impossible to engage third gear, would not suggest a pressing need for warning equipment.

Children's schooling depended on the ferry, as did mainland visits to other messes and shopping. All depended on the ferry running. . . .

And there were certainly times when it didn't run. Lucy, Rose, Shirley, Lola, Mim and Ora were not charming associates of Suzy Wong, nor was Mary. The typhoons so named were regular features to be dreaded. Rose, for example, beached thirty ships in the harbour and totally scrapped one US Navy warship, then wrecked the Macao ferry "Fatshan" taking 70 lives. On Stonecutters, Rose drove a ship onto the ammunition jetty and up the steps behind the jetty. S Sgt Frank Simpson of the Corps found himself without a front door and spent the night attempting to block the gap with the heavier furniture. All the quarters in Stonecutters kept four days' food supplies in preparation for the typhoon season.

The forces of Nature were not the only hazards. In 1966, the year when Princess Margaret came to Hong Kong to open British Week (but completely unrelated to this happy occasion) the Star Ferries decided to put up their fares and the Chinese population exploded into riot and looting. The MPSC found themselves on VP guards and assisting with ammunition movement until the riots cooled and the status quo was established – for all apart from the Services, who lost their concessionary rates on the ferries. In the next year, the Cultural Revolution was imported from Mainland China and Jim Robinson recalls one occasion during the rioting, when Bomb Disposal went to examine an object and found, not explosives, but a highly venomous snake in the box. Product of Stonecutters?

The isolation from mainstream Hong Kong meant that the little community on Stonecutters had to work together. One of the advantages of the posting was that most staff had a quarter waiting for them on arrival, some, it would appear, pretty grotty and up a 200 foot slope. It needed much resolution, on first arrival from the UK, to drag family and baggage to the front door. Occasionally, flats were taken in Kowloon, with disadvantages and some advantages. The ferry journey was a snag, but the relucatant worker had an advantage when the typhoon stopped the ferry. Another advantage was that he could not hear the alarm bell, which was clearly audible from the quarters on the island. Reports repeatedly recommend the posting for the young married staff member. He had the advantage of an instant quarter but also the opportunity of learning his trade in a small establishment where he would be required to do a wide variety of jobs and where he had good opportunities to complete his course. He could train with the units of the garrison and in 1971, the report could claim that a staff of 12 had completed a total of 41 courses. The MCTC also ran regimental provost courses for the garrison and helped out with the instructors on camps.

The isolation led to a strong mess, where a San Miguel could be had on the self-help patio under the Nuffield Trust awning. This awning, I suspect, had been the subject of much heated discussion in mess meetings, as a school of thought favoured concrete patio furniture, fitted for removable umbrellas as better provision during the typhoon season.

Wong Shing was the Number One Boy, whose English, it is claimed ran to a perfectly enunciated "a small beer, please" – not a commonly used phrase in a sergeants' mess. The Chief clerk's brother, He Che Sang, kitchen hand and tea maker and Old MPSC China Hands will remember his "Hey you, where you go?". There were two cooks, one of them Wong Cheung having been with the MPSC in Hong Kong for twenty nine years. The other cook was Wong Ah Kam, helped by Sui Tat, who spoke no English at all but was a master of mime. At closure, they and the Chief Clerk and Big Fixer, Robert Ho, were taken out by the MPSC staff for a meal at the Gallant Restaurant in Hung Hom, where they first settled to a game of mah-jong. The game was joined by S Sgt Tommy Thompson of the Corps, who made the unlikely claim that he had actually won money.

Religious life on the island was again restricted by the isolation, though some padres appear to have overcome this obstacle more efficiently than others. The church was used for Padre's Hour, but it is late in the sixties before services are regular. In 1967 the church is proudly reported to be redecorated and carpeted, with a portrait of the Rev. Bayley Hardy VC DSO MC as "an attractive feature". In 1973, the church treadle organ (a scrounged item from the pre-Stonecutters period) is replaced by an electrical organ "played by an extremely adept member of the MPSC."

The Corps' only Lieutenant Colonel, Jim Robinson, served on Stonecutters' three times, showing an initiative and wangling power that makes him a suitable Corps Secretary. Major BO "Jimmy" James formerly senior major and Lt Col Peter Andrews were RSM in their time and a fresh faced young WOII Graham Harris appears in one of the group photographs. Of the Old and Bold, amongst others, appear WOI Leedham, WOI Charlie Barber, WOI Colin Smith. Lew Butler and Harry Boulter both did a stint as Commandant there.

The late Eric Milton, a name recurring throughout the post war history of the Corps, and a man whose passing is much regretted, left as Commandant in 1966. He and Mrs Milton were dined out in style at the Mandarin Hotel Buffet Supper Club, with something of a wing-ding tour of night clubs to follow. One member vaguely remembers seeing a cabaret with Bruce Forsyth as star, but this may well be a duty-free figment of the imagination. In the month following, Spud Taylor dined out before leaving for Australia and S Sgt Johnny Brazil left the service for permanent employment in Hong Kong. . . . the ferry journey obviously could be made if the spirit moved!

During Eric Milton's tenure of office, apart from typhoons Lola, Mim and Ora, the island had another interesting visitation: the Japanese Embassy requested information regarding Japanese war graves on the island. A grave was, in fact, found within the danger area of the rifle range and six skulls, with hair and teeth, two jawbones, a variety of other bones, a Japanese fountain pen and a shoe were unearthed. If this disinterment formed part of a SUS training period, one assumes that these SUS made sure never to return to the CME.

Admissions were falling throughout the early Seventies, so that the annual figure in 1975 was 86. This – and air trooping – put the black spot on Stonecutters and 31 August 1976 saw its final closure as a military penal institution and the MPSC's foothold in the fabulous East. Immediately before closure, it housed an Adventure Training group of the WRAC and flimsies hung drying from window bars. Its ultimate fate was to be a centre for the Duke of Edinburgh's Award condidates from Hong Kong schools.

I have a photograph before me of Jim Robinson ceremonially turning the key of the main gate for the last time. The same key, rescued from the already mentioned fresh-faced (but predatory) Graham Harris, is now contained in a mounted map of the island and hangs on the wall of the MCTC Colchester Officers Mess, to inspire damp-eyed military reminiscence.

33
Ipoh Kinrara Tanglin

The 1935 Journal has a reference to a small MPSC detachment in Tanglin Barracks, Singapore as a small Military Detention Barracks able to house 32 SUS. It was staffed until the Japanese Occupation, when the MPSC element suffered the same dreadful fate as the rest of the garrison, apart from RSM Munday, who had been in hospital and was evacuated to Australia. It is my great regret that I have no records of the ones who did not get away.

For the period immediately after the war, I am more fortunate, as a Mr Wilson wrote an extremely lucid account of the period. Mr Wilson was infantry and was in a group given the duties of the MPSC for Singapore and Malaya. They ran FPCs up country and had charge of Tanglin and the infamous Changi Gaol, then under the GDC's command. Apart from military evildoers (and at this time of flux there were many!), they were responsible for the custody of Japanese war criminals. They were also called upon to assist at their execution.

Escort of the war criminals to court, according to Mr Wilson, was a dangerous occupation, as the escort often received the missiles from the crowd that were aimed at the prisoners. Before I say almost my last word on war criminals, I must mention another informant on the subject. My appeal for MPSC information in soldier led to a Monsieur Petitjean of Vanves in France sending a set of photocopies of the major war criminals in Changi, which I cannot use here, but will put in the archives.

Mr Wilson and his colleagues found that they were doing the job in the dark, so to speak, without any course and without the accumulated experience contained in the blue book. Three of them were rebadged to MPSC, but had no training until an RSM and a MPSC detachment were sent out in August 1947. Again, I would like to know more of this and can only hope that the Old and Bold can fill this gap for me. They immediately organised training and put the organisation on a professional footing.

At this time, incidentally, six Indian mutineers were being held in Tanglin under sentence of death, but they were pardoned and repatriated when Indian Independence was declared. Another Indian also due to be executed had been held at Tanglin the the previous year. The last entries in the condemned soldier's diary read:

0700 Given a cigarette.

0715 Absconded.

He had been taken out for a wash, jumped onto a laundry truck and was never seen again.

Before the MPSC arrived, No 1 FPC was at Ipoh. Its Commandant was a Lancashire Fusilier and he, with his RSM, took local release and started a pig farm. The experience was already there, because when the MPSC arrived in Ipoh to open No 3 MCE (yet another!), the compound had the look of a farm, with goats, pigs and ducks wandering in what is now called free-range. They were used for the multiplicity of diets associated with a mass of castes and religions. The new RSM, WOI Jock Turbet and his CSM Spud Murphy, felt that a more secluded compound, to segregate SUS and animals, would lend tone to the new establishment. He did however, keep one ram, which was shampooed in Lux, horns shined with boot polish and supplied with a brass name tag for its neck. It lived Mr Wilson says, "better than a general", with a diet of grass, potato peelings and beer. It had a short and happy life as a mascot.

Captain Maurice Saunders, whom we first met as a newly transferred infantryman in Italy, was in an early post war draft to Malaya and served at No 3 in Ipoh. His main memory of it is a Turkish bath humidity and a constant drip of beetles and other Oriental fauna from the attap roof into any food or drink being consumed. The original joy of pineapples, coconuts and bananas soon began to pall.

No 3 MCE was two miles outside Ipoh, the capital of Perak in the foothills of Uneng Tahar. It was a pleasant place apart from the humidity, which made a towel into formal after duty wear. Bill King spent a short time there before being medically evacuated with the foot rot so prevalent in this kind of climate. When he was there in 1948, Japanese war criminals were still being hanged in Ipoh and a MPSC sergeant was acting as hangman.

Relief from the dripping monotony and the boredom of a small mess came from the frequent visits of rubber planters and tin miners, who were working the Ipoh area. Several of these later moved to Kinrara area, so many lasting friendships were made.

In 1951, the MCE was to move to Kinrara, but the new camp at Kinrara was not completed when Ipoh closed. Maurice found himself organising a move of staff and SUS into a tented camp at Kluang. It was to be temporary, but No 3 MCE found themselves occupying it for nearly five months. It was not uncommon to be washed out of one's tent during the monsoon. Clothes and equipment moulded overnight.

Finally, however, the new camp was ready for occupation. It was hutted and had been built in an area of coarse jungle grass and the first task for the SUS was the clearing of the area, using hand sickles. The next task was to carve out a parade ground from the side of a hill, using picks and shovels only.

The camp was located a few miles from Kuala Lumpur, the Malayan capital, but the nearest civilian settlement was Petaling Jaya, originally a "Templer" village, but one which grew into a considerable town. To remind the younger reader, General Templer was High Commissioner in Malaya during the emergency. To deny the Chinese Communist guerillas the food and intelligence that made their jungle life impossible, he concentrated the population in endangered areas into defended villages and PJ, as it was normally known, was one such village. It was to become something of a boom town and the MPSC members in No3 usually had their quarters there. Some quarters were later built near the MCE. Grass fires sometimes occurred and one of these to windward of the RSM's quarter caused some anxiety. . . . and speculation.

Doug Moody remembers a Night Watch on Christmas Eve 1956. He was quietly patrolling – and totally sober – when the strains of "Silent Night, Holy Night" drifted through the sky, causing thoughts of heavenly choirs and instant conversion. The music came, in fact, from one of the voice aircraft used more normally to broadcast propaganda and surrender demands to the terrorists. Programmed with new recordings in honour of the occasion, it was still a reminder that the Chinese terrorists had not yet been beaten. They were still around and the road near Kinrara was a favourite ambush site.

Jim Robinson went to Kinrara in 1959 on an accompanied tour. After one of the nightmare journeys associated with the early days of air trooping, the Robinson family was met by RSM and Mrs Dolly Gray and found that they had accommodation in PJ, with (shades of departed empires!) an amah.

Jim was to meet the Assistant Commandant, Captain Harry Burnard, who had been RSM at Ipoh, but it was the Commandant who figures large in Jim's remembrance. The Commandant was in the Black Watch and the 42nd Highlanders have produced their share of eccentric officers. The Commandant at Kinrara was one of them. A later Commandant was a keen gardener, but this one was a turkey raiser. The turkeys were housed in the cells of the singles block and SUS occupants often complained of sleep lost because of the nocturnal gobbling of turkeys. The birds were well fed on the hard tack from compo rations and they occupied a considerable part of the Commandant's time and thought.

The staff list, too, was not without its characters. S Sgt Bunyan, S Sgt Charlie Davis, S Sgt Moody, S Sgt Hutton, S Sgt Gordon and Peter Andrews.

Peter was not then a lieutenant colonel and adjutant but a keen young training sergeant. One night he was on watch, when his ability to move quickly in unusual circumstances was put to the test. In the middle of his watch, nature called. He had settled to his task, when he noticed an unusual sound, not associated with the plumbing, then saw that his cubicle was shared by a huge hissing snake. He showed the speed of decision that was later to make him a distinguished World Cup referee – though it is not normal on the world's stadia for the referee to move with his trousers around his ankles.

The SUS came from all services and many nationalities and the variety of national traits is the thing most often mentioned when the Old and Bold talk of Kinrara. The Australians usually came in aggressive and resenting discipline, but with the right kind of leadership became keen and hard workers. The New Zealanders were invariably pleasant and the Maori element was, according to Jim, a pleasure to instruct, their only weakness being on the soccer field, where every game became a game of rugby. The Chinese were reserved, very much their own man but the Indians were chatty and outgoing. Malays were easy living and easy to handle, whilst the Gurkhas were stick straight and regimental.

There was a Royal Navy presence on the training and administrative team, also a number of Malay NCOs. One of these was convinced that the camp was haunted by the ghost of a Japanese sergeant and he spent most night duties with his head under a blanket. He was exceptional and generally the Malays were good colleagues.

The mixture of service and nationality made training difficult – Jim remembers a squad of twenty, where only one was a British soldier. As only one squad trained at a time, new admissions joined the squad irrespective of the SUS's abilities and the stage that the squad had reached. Readers acquainted with the oddities of the Jack Tar Drill Manual can imagine the result when said Jack Tar joined a squad in its sixth week of training!

I have mentioned earlier in this book that the Naval powers that be often regarded life in a military penal institution as a soft option for erring Jack. This complaint was again to be made about Kinrara, a senior Naval officer pointing out that sailors in the Far Eastern theatre would often live in between deck temperatures of 120 degrees Farenheit and that, however tough Kinrara training might be, Jack would still regard it as a change of air station. The Commandant decided that training could not be made tougher for the naval element, but that they would receive sharper punishments if they stepped out of line.

Sport at Kinrara was sweaty and played at a slower pace. Jim Robinson recalls a sporting event of a somewhat different nature. It was reported that a crocodile was making a nuisance of itself at a local tin working and the MPSC members were asked to hunt it. The shikar set out, armed with rifles or cameras and refreshments, only to find that evening was not the time when the crocodile showed itself; that, in fact, early morning was its favourite time. Sgt Pat Bunyan resolved to hunt along at first light, but failed to make an early start and the crocodile was finally killed by a Chinese with an antiquated shot gun. This explains why no crocodile skin is displayed on the walls of the MCTC sergeants' mess.

The extreme humidity was wearing, particularly when

training was hard and for the families, so two weeks in the year were compulsorily spent in the change of air station in the Cameron Highlands. The cool of 5000 feet made it possible to enjoy a fire at night and the luxury of sleeping under blankets.

By the beginning of the sixties, with the emergency successfully ended, SUS admissions were falling. In 1961, the MCTC and the British Military Hospital were the only units in the Kuala Lumpur area. At one stage, the SUS strength was four, three of whom were sailors, and the writing was on the wall. Kinrara closed on the 7th of November 1962. It was to move down to Singapore, where it was to join 77 MPDB and to be renamed Combined Military Establishment, Singapore.

The journey, organised by Master at Arms Smith RN, took eight hours and had all the appearance of a gypsy migration, with a string of coaches, one ton vehicles and private cars. They were to move into the barracks that had contained a military prison since the 1870's.

At a cost of £45000 – big money in those days – Tanglin had been extensively modernised, the old labour sheds giving way to accommodation, which had been purpose designed. Formerly, coir mats had been woven. This Victorian labour was replaced by boot repairs, production of road signs and repairing packing cases.

The MPSC staff from Kinrara, although enjoying the facilities available in the barracks, and the nearness to the fleshpots of Singapore, found themselves in the minority: seventeen of them in a staff of 53.

The British presence in the Far East was fading and admissions continued to fall. A visit of the Adjutant General in 1968, led to a work study, which examined Tanglin and Stonecutters. I have the Work Study Report in front of me as I write. Something of a source document, it shows an average daily lock-up at Tanglin 23 SUS, 49% of whom are serving less than 28 days. Closure was inevitable.

The date for closure was fixed at the 30th June 1971. On the 26th May, the Inspector of Establishments FARELF, Lieutenant Colonel GA Gibb RMP, paid his last visit. The Journal recorded the occasion and showed a photograph of the MPSC flag being lowered for the last time; leaving only the flag of Singapore. Stonecutters was to represent the Corps in the Far East. In the same issue is the last Tanglin staff photograph, with Colonel Gibb sitting with the Commandant

Major J F Hart, the RSM WOI Moore, two young staff sergeants: Humphries and Goddard and an equally young DAPM, Major Jack Thomas. Did he realise at the time that he was to become the worldwide Inspector of Establishments?

34
Last of the Thirties

All the MPDBs in East Africa Command were numbered in the thirties. Most of them had died out at the end of the war and many would have been totally unknown to me had not ex RSM Vic Bint served in two of them during the war and is the sole survivor: No.32 in 1951.

The list is interesting, as not only the establishments have gone, but most of the countries in which they were, are now sailing under different colours and different names. They were:

31 (EA) MPDB Nairobi.
32 (EA) MPDB Mombasa.
33 (EA) MPDB Mandera, British Somaliland, now Somalia. This had also been established in Diredawa, Ehtiopia.
34 (EA) MPDB Mogadishu, Somalia.
35 (EA) MPDB Lusaka, Northern Rhodesia, now Zambia.
36 (EA) MPDB Mauritius.

Why Somaliland? Why Ethiopia? The campaigns in the desert had much publicity, but at the time they were being fought, a combined British, South African, Nigerian, Indian and French army was battling over some of the worst terrain in the world to throw the Italians out of Ethiopia and Eritrea, where they were threatening Kenya and the Sudan. It is a campaign well worth the study to anyone interested in military history.

Vic Bint, as a young sergeant, was posted in 1942 to Mauritius with two other MPSC members, WOII Stan Desny being in command. They were to find there a detention barracks that had figured in the Military Prison Reports of the 1890s, two ancient time-expired infantry sergeants who had spent many years in India and were waiting for the boat home, and one small black Mauritian SUS, serving 168 hours detention. I have mentioned elsewhere that the Gate Book they took over had been opened in 1919. . . . business was slack.

Things looked a little brighter when a battalion of the King's African Rifles was posted to the island. Then, they were locking up British, African and Mauritian soldiers, but they had the assistance of an African sergeant major and a detachment of askaris.

In 1945, Vic was posted to Lusaka, but was told enroute that the posting was altered to Mandera. In transit, he called in at No.34 in Mogadishu, in that part of Somaliland which had ceased to be called Italian Somaliland only a short time before. Here, the Commandant was a Lieutenant Lauri Kitwood and the sergeant major WOII Hargreaves of the Corps.

Mandera was reached after a 150 mile desert and scrub truck journey. It was forty miles from Berbera and had as its garrison the MPDB, a British Military Hospital and a battalion of infantry. The largest single group of whites in the area was a large Italian POW camp. The MPSC detachment numbered a WOII and four staff sergeants or sergeants. The DB was RE built and designed to be a civil prison after the war. Again, he had African assistance.

As I have already said, most of these establishments were to close immediately after the war finished, but one remained, was in fact to stay open until 1963. This was No.32, which was to have several names and three locations, all of them in Kenya.

Fort Jesus – not the most apt location for a MPDB – was four miles north of the port of Mombasa and near the sea, the kind of location now being sought by the jaded rich, who have tired of the Costa del Sol. A 1949 Journal report regrets that the staff are not able to play real games, but can compensate by swimming (if a shark-free beach is chosen) or sailing (but the sole sailing club has a long waiting list). Fishing is popular and the Indian shops of Mombasa, although not like shops at home, are cheap and interesting. The report then continues its bleat by complaining about the high humidity. Did the man really not like it or was he anxious to keep others away?

He must have been most relieved when No.32 moved in August 1951 to the friendly climate of the Rift Valley, to a former internment camp for enemy aliens near the small village of Gil Gil. Doubtless, he then complained about the masses of game in the area, or the dust in the dry season.

Perhaps the plate corrugated iron of the hut roofs displeased him. If so, he had not too long to worry, because the iron was replaced by tiles and the shaky wooden bridge over the storm ditch outside the mess (a hazard that must have caused many complaints and many nasty situations) was replaced by a concrete bridge.

He would certainly have had just cause to complain in the first half of the fifties, for Gil Gil was in Mau Mau country and the Journal report tells of a slowing down of social life, as people are reluctant to travel unnecessarily. The increase in troop numbers also led to an increase in customers.

The person who certainly would have had cause to complain would be his wife, if he were lucky enough to be able to get her out to Gil Gil: quarters were scarce and Gil Gil had only one small hotel. In the unlikely event that the family owned a car (and cars were not all that common in those days), then hubby could drive her the 75 dusty miles to Nairobi or the twenty five dusty miles in the other direction to Nakuru.

Major Sydney Harris went as Commandant to Gil Gil in 1955 and stayed for two years. He was appalled on his first parade to find that African soldiers admitted to the establishment for imprisonment arrived from their units with a pair of denims as their sole equipment, even their boots being withdrawn. He protested at this but his protest had little effect until the day of the Administrative Inspection, when he turned out in drunken tinker order to register his protest, Sydney having a natural feel for the dramatic. The point was made and equipment arrived with each imprisoned African.

His proudest achievement at Gil Gil was the establishing of a school for the children of the African staff and he recalls the morning crocodile to school, with the tallest children at the front and the smallest behind, invariably bare-bottomed but swinging their arms like little soldiers.

With the petering out of the Emergency, No.32 closed at Gil Gil in February 1957 and moved to Langarta, three miles outside Nairobi, where 618 SMPS RMP was to be their neighbour. The establishment had been reduced and there was no longer a Commandant, the Garrison Commander acting as Superintendant and the RSM having extra responsibilities as Superintending WO. Responsible for MPSC discipline and administration was a young DAPM, Major Jack Thomas, a name not unknown to the Corps, later to be Brigadier J F

Thomas, Provost Marshal, Inspector of Establishments and a frequent – very welcome – visitor to the last establishment he was required to inspect.

When Captain Maurice Saunders arrived at No.32 as RSM, he was amazed to find that, however long a SUS was to spend there, he would remain in Stage One, with minimal privileges for the full period of his sentence, a direct violation of the Rules and a situation hardly conducive to high morale. With the complete backing of the GOC, Maurice was able to have a new block added to the establishment, allowing for the accommodation of a Stage Two, which he promptly initiated. On the staff domestic front, he saw the old sergeants' mess transformed into a NAAFI and the mess moved to a smaller building, known as The Captains Table, where the rooms had a country club feeling, with panelled walls and an open fireplace. His wife Sheila was the prime mover in many of the projects to improve the lot of the wives.

June 1963 saw Kenya become independent and plans for a British base in Kenya fell through. MCTC Kenya went the way of so many other prime overseas postings. Colchester was rapidly becoming the only posting for the MPSC.

35
Odd Job in Aden

Aden was never anybody's favourite posting – the curried rear end of the world – and it was never a normal posting for the MPSC or their predecessors, not a fact that distressed them.

Their visit to this unholy part of the world between 1965 and 1967 is, to me one of the most interesting chapters in the history of the Corps. It is a departure from their normal role, but one which shows up well the qualities that make the outstanding Corps member and the qualities that Garsia originally stipulated.

The Corps had already, in Egypt, had a taste of the unpleasant task of securing Arab civilians in a state of insurrection. They had not particularly enjoyed the job then, but they had done it and done it well. They were again faced with it in Aden, when what amounted to civil war had made it impossible to rely on the local prison service – or, as you will see later, the local police force.

The government of the South Arabian Federation had broken down and there were two factions in the streets and the Federation, both of which were intent on ruling when Britain withdrew from its commitment to support the amirates. FLOSY: the Front for the Liberation of South Yemen, Egyptian backed at this time, and the NLF: the National Liberation Front. They were fighting each other and the British Army was in the middle. In 1965, the Aden Emergency Regulations were passed and an attempt was made to take the trouble-makers off the streets by detaining them.

Al Mansoura Prison, two years old and the property of the civil government, was to be the place of detention. It was nine miles from Aden, along a road which was an alley of small arms, mortar and rocket fire and was situated near Sheik Othman, a hotbed of trouble. The prison, according to Colonel Jim Robinson would have been a push-over for any SUS keen on escape, but he feels that the detainees preferred the heroic martyrdom of incarceration in a prison where they could not be shot at, to any nasty risky escaping.

The first MPSC group flew out in October 1965: Captain Fred Cross, WOI Ken Richards, WOsII Dodd and Len Harvey.

The prison, they found, consisted of three blocks, each of four buildings forming a square around a central compound. The two factions: the NLF and FLOSY had, of course, to be kept separate, but they soon realised that this did not prevent the flinging of Arab abuse – and more solid missiles – across the dividing fence.

The small MPSC contingent had assistant "warders" found from the NCOs of local regiments, who were all unfamiliar with security duties, usually recently promoted and often quite useless in an emergency. They carried loaded pistols at this early stage, much to the horror of the MPSC, who visualised the scene when some detainee managed to snatch a firearm or – possibly worse – when some young warder, driven to desperation by Arab abuse, suddenly drew his pistol and fired into the thick of them! Pistols were later withdrawn.

In addition to the security group for inside the prison, there was a guard company, under its company commander and their services were often called for, particularly during the worst of the riots. Several regiments supplied this guard, but Jim Robinson speaks particularly highly of the Welsh Guards and the Parachute Regiment. Towards the end of the British presence in Aden, the guard company was supplemented with armoured cars, the commander of one of them being killed by snipers.

The MPSC draft found living conditions to be appalling and not helped by frequent fire being brought to bear on the huts. And not only small arms fire: Christmas 1965 saw an attack by rocket launcher against the operations hut walls. As one correspondent wrote to the journal "There is now air conditioning in most rooms but some still have their windows". The mess was a temporary affair, but the detachment had a TV, though it used English language transmissions for only one hour per day. The correspondent humourist quoted above tells us that some members did not mind this and watched the pictures even when they were in Arabic.

On the culinary front, it was sand with everything, particularly when lunch coincided with the arrival of a helicopter.

There were problems, too, with water, mainly due to the habit of some of the terrorists sniping periodically at the water tank, resulting in regular visits from the water bowser.

The MPSC staff won a total of three Commander in Chief's Commendations during the time they were in Aden, the first one going to RSM Ken Richards, and I quote it here:

"In recognition of his enthusiasm, high standard and willingness to undertake responsibilities far and above his rank and service, WOI Kenneth Richards of the Military Provost Staff Corps has been awarded the Commendation of the Commander in Chief, Middle East."

"He has worked long hours under great pressure in a most depressing atmosphere" the citation records, "and yet has maintained a high standard that has won him the respect of all who came into contact with him."

The next Corps group was led by RSM John Stacey and comprised Jim Robinson, then a WOII, Captain Bill Humphries, then a staff sergeant and Staff Sergeant Slessor. They flew over in March 1966 and the handover coincided with the Moslem Festival of Id and visiting day, always something of a traumatic experience.

Jim Robinson, who had a smattering of Arabic from his Egyptian days, took on the visitors and outside duties with Len Harvey controlling inside the compounds. Jim soon found himself nicknamed Kassem and was reminded pointedly by the detainees that the original bearer of the name: Brigadier Abdul Karim Kassem had been assassinated. North Welshman don't panic as easily as that.

The prison came under the control of the High Commission and one has the distinct impression that the commission was composed of theoreticians: long on liberalism and short on action. The direct head of the establishment was a Governor, in the early days an RAF officer, probably a first class catering officer but with little talent for the difficult and nasty job with which he had been lumbered. He was succeeded by two professionals for whom my correspondent have nothing but praise: a Mr Russell, who had previously served with the Tanganykan prison service and knew what the job was all about; and Mr Guy Pearson.

The detainees were a mixed bag. Inevitably, many were students but there were also teachers and other professionals, even a magistrate. One, known to all as No 56, was a professional agitator and a constant source of trouble, very volatile and permanently looking for a reason to be offended. Did he really bite Len Harvey? The dog it was. . . .

Trouble was always under the surface, often came to the top. With the hot weather, the inmates refused to move into their blocks and insisted on sleeping in the compounds. The Governor requested permission of the High Commission to be allowed to move them forcibly but this was refused. Constant requests over the next three days were turned down and by this time, the detainees felt that they were in control of the situation. On the fourth day, permission to move them by force was finally granted.

The Welsh Guards were guard company and they marched into the compound, armed, and surrounded the detainees. A doctor had been alerted and was standing by for any emergency. Starting with the most troublesome block, the MPSC and attached NCOs then started to carry in the protestors. There was a hail of missiles, anything throwable being thrown. Bill Humphries, who was to be the only casualty of the day, was struck by a tin of fruit and knocked unconscious, but after the main troublemakers had been locked away, the other blocks created no problems.

The next day started with the detainees wrecking their rooms, breaking the furniture and tearing the tiles from the roofs. The Aden Armed Police were asked to assist, but only the European inspector was prepared to help. CS gas was used successfully and things quietened.

The damage had only just been repaired when the detainees decided that cleaning the prison area should be the responsibility of the soldiers and not themselves. Not even the High Commission would have entertained this idea, so the compounds soon became heaps of stinking rubbish, fly covered and all set to inspire an epidemic. At this stage, a member of the International Red Cross made one of his periodic visits. He gave a thorough rifting to the ringleaders of this most recent protest but managed to get nowhere. Finally, the Pioneers sent in troops with spray guns to attempt to neutralise the nauseous heaps. They were met with the usual barrage of missiles and abuse and it is hardly surprising that the contents of some of the spray guns found their way through the block windows.

This was the last major upset during the tour by John

Stacey's group, but not, of course, the end to the constant minor aggravation. The Chubb locks, for example were filled with sand and became impossible to open – until it was pointed out that this could result in detainee dying in agony with no way to get him to medical aid. Jim Robinson had a tray of rice hurled over him. They would object to anything and everything, even at one point refusing the services of a doctor.

Visiting days were a major headache, a brawl and screech of Arabs, male and female, all yelling the number and name of the person to be visited. Searches had to be thorough: detainees were allowed food and toiletries, but a constant watch had to be kept for radios and tools. Qif, the Arabian marijuana, was also an attractive item to be smuggled in, to be taken with coca cola. Every visiting day was a time for false accusations of the staff, using Arab high-decibel delivery.

John Stacey was also commended by the C in C.

"The Commander-in-Chief, Middle East Command, Admiral, Sir Michael Le Fanu, has approved the award of his Commendation to Warrant Officer I J W G Stacey, Military Provost Staff Corps."

"WOI Stacey has for the last six months been in charge of the warders at the Detention Centre at Al Mansoura. During this time he has efficiently and cheerfully dealt with the many problems of running a detention centre in conditions of austerity, dust storms and great heat. He has set and maintained a very difficult and depressing conditions.

He has worked long hours and under great pressure. During disturbances by the detainees in the Centre he displayed great calmness, tolerance and understanding and was directly responsible for the speedy restoration of law and order.

"WOI Stacey's conduct and example," the citation concludes, "has won him the commendation of the Commandant and the respect, not only of those who have worked under him but also of the detainees. His devotion to duty and outstanding leadership merits reward."

The next MPSC detachment in Aden consisted of Capt QM WA Bishop, WOI E Sweeney, WOII A Stewart, WOII O Taylor, S Sgt N Franklin, S Sgt H Parry, Sgt D Simpson and Sgt E Smith.

Bill Bishop spent October 1966 to April 1967 as Deputy

Governor of Al Mansoura and, before I deal with the fraught days after the climactic Crater Massacres, I think that his commendation should appear. Readers will recall that Bill had already been commended for his part in the putting down of the Shepton Mallet mutiny.

"Capt Bishop was deputy governor of Al Mansoura Detention Centre from October 1966-April 1967. Throughout this period he lived and worked in the Detention Centre without a break. The civilian Governor only visited the prison in the morning and during the rest of the day Capt Bishop had to handle the various and tricky problems of the Detention Centre which ranged from detainees complaints, problems with the warder staff and disturbances among the detainees.

There were two major riots in the Centre during his tour. On each occasion, with complete disregard for his own safety, he personally led the troops into the dissident blocks of detainees and played an important part in re-established law and order.

The Detention Centre has been frequently attacked with small fire arms fire from outside, and, rocket launchers and energa grenades. The only approach to the centre is along a particularly dangerous road which has been mined several times, and military vehicles are frequently the target for grenade and small arms attack. One of the prison warders was killed and several wounded while moving to and from the prison. Capt Bishop had to use this road frequently to make visits in the course of his duty.

He mastered the difficult technique of putting up with provocation by detainees and at times insults and personal abuse without letting these get him down or colour his attitude towards them. Capt Bishop through his loyalty, high sense of duty, unfailing cheerfulness and his ability to stand firm, was an inspiration to all the staff of the Detention Centre."

The last tense days in the prison were under the command of RSM Barber and it is his report that supplied me with my material.

Towards the end, the sniping, mortaring and rocket attacks intensified and the Crater Massacres had hardened attitudes on both sides. The detainees knew that the British were soon to leave and that now was their time to build up their reputations as fearless freedom fighters, ready for the time soon to come, when positions of power would go to the man with the strongest propaganda pull. . . . providing of course, that his party was the successful one.

In April 1967, a FLOSY member attacked the medical officer and was put into the punishment block. The FLOSY block spokesman gathered three of his bully boys, asked for an interview with the Civil Governor, then attacked him in his office. Fortunately, Bill Bishop was present and Barber had had the fore-thought to have Staff Sergeant Ken Burgess and an attached NCO on standby carrying handcuffs. The thugs were overpowered and hauled off to the punishment block. The spokesman, however, was earmarked for a key position if FLOSY got into power, so the Civilian Governor had to order his release. When Barber marched him back to the FLOSY block, he met a barrage of tins and tiles, then was hit over the head with a dustbin lid. The attached NCO's on duty in the block stood by as helpless spectators.

The FLOSY block started to riot, breaking up their rooms and starting a fire using bedding and oil from their cooking stoves. Bill Bishop arrived. He ordered the guard company to surround the compound, had the fire fighting group douse the bedding, then organised two assault groups from the MPSC, the attached warders and the guard company, all armed with batons and shields. They waded in.

There was the usual barrage of missiles, joined this time by brylcream bottles filled with paraffin and ignited. Several of the soldiers were hit, some quite badly and a sense of humour failure occured. Five tear gas grenades were followed by the baton parties and the ringleaders were quickly isolated and rushed to the punishment block. The High Commission were reluctant to punish them until Mr Guy Pearson threatened resignation.

This was to be the last major riot, but assault and abuse continued. Guy Pearson was three times the subject of assassination attempts, through car bombs or direct fire. In one of the attempts, Ken Burgess was driving but escaped with sand blast and a shaking.

During this tour, Pete Matthews was in charge of visitors and, with the increased numbers detained, visiting day became even more of a nightmare. On one visiting day, he was outside the gate, when a small arms fire fight started up between the factions and all around the screaming mass of visitors. He made for the gate, to find that the young attached

NCO had already closed it, thus gaining himself later very red ears and a choice new vocabulary.

At about this time, a new ingredient was introduced to the NLF – FLOSY alphabet soup within the prison. This was a group of PORPH (I don't know what the letters stand for!).

PORPH insisted on being separated from the other two groups, but this was refused by the High Commission. It emerged that PORPH was an Egyptian trained assassination group, sent in to help FLOSY by eliminating the NLF leadership. When separate accommodation was refused, the PORPH spokesman threatened the Governor with assassination and found that he had indeed achieved his wish for seclusion when he was marched to the punishment cells. There was, of course, a resultant uproar and Barber was hit by a flying tin of Dundee cake. The intelligent anticipation of the experienced Warrant Officer had ensured that a baton party was waiting in cover and more members of PORPH had their request for seclusion granted to them.

Barber, by this time, must have had an oddly shaped skull, but another dent in the cranium was due before he could leave Al Mansoura. The only time when FLOSY and the NLF were allowed together was at mosque on the Moslem Sabbath, with a truce usually reigning on this day of peace. One Sabbath information was received that the 140 strong NLF were to attack the 40 strong FLOSY immediately after prayers – Islam is a militant religion. Barber cancelled prayers for that day and was promptly hammered as a result.

As closure came nearer, threats and attacks increased, the potentially most serious one being against Captain Harry Boulter and CSM Pete Matthews. A mixture of harpic and water thrown in an attempt to blind, then both were beaten around the head with wooden staves, Harry so seriously that a considerable number of stitches were needed.

But it had come to an end. The MPSC left Mansoura during the early hours of 24 September 1967. . . . with few regrets. I ask myself if any other army could have handled the vile situation with the restraint shown at Al Mansoura? I also ask if any other army would have left written on Al Mansoura's main gate:

"No milk, no papers. Gone away".

36
Aden – Another Odd Job

The late Eric Milton wrote this account of his part in the Aden business, I have published it exactly as he wrote it for two reasons. Firstly, it is an excellent account. Secondly, I would like to think of it as a tribute to a man whose name has appeared often in these pages.

Eric joined the Royal Fusiliers in 1936 and served with them in India and the Middle East, then from Normandy to Berlin with the Queen's Regiment.

He transferred to the MPSC in 1945 and served in Brussels, Brunswick, Bielefeld, Shepton Mallet, Aden and Northern Ireland.

He was one of the first Quartermasters to be commissioned into the MPSC and he served until 1972.

It is my regret that I had no opportunity to talk to him before his death in 1984: his story would have been the story of this Corps over the past forty years and his experiences would have enriched this book.

The Detainee Holding Centre – Aden

The Detainee Holding Centre was formed at 1800hrs on April 15, 1967. We, the MPSC element consisting of WO2 Harvey, Sgt Cooper, Sgt Swan and myself, arrived in Aden fifteen minutes before the formation. This was to be a Joint Service Unit with two locations, the larger being at the RAF Corrective Training Centre, and a smaller building at Fort Morbut. This was known as the Interrogation Centre, and only used for the chosen few.

The role of the unit was simple, to ensure the security of suspected terrorists whilst they were being investigated. These suspects had been arrested by the Security Forces and the Special Branch of the Aden Police. In short, we were the "middle men" between the Security Forces and the Detention Centre at Al Mansoura.

Though we were administratively under the command of

HQ, MELF, our overall commander was a most distinguished policeman J. V. Prendagast, Esq, CBE, GM, who was Director of Intelligence and Head of Special Branch. I had met Mr Prendagast previously in Hong Kong, and was able to dispell any doubts about being commanded by a civilian. We formed part of "B" Group of the Aden Intelligence Centre, and instructions from the Director were passed to us by Major M Heath Intelligence Corps, who had the most impressive title of Centre Controller. I was most impressed with our welcome to this agency, and it was obvious that the unit could help to relieve pressure on the overworked Intelligence Officers. At the least we, not they, would be the targets for allegations of brutality and inhuman treatment which suspects had been making each day.

At this point it is necessary to know the procedure adopted when a suspect was arrested. He was brought along to us and medically inspected, then statements, etc were checked, and if there was no case, he was released immediately. However, the slightest suspicion was followed up and if necessary, the High Commissioner signed an order under the Emergency Regulations, which gave us the authority to hold the person for seven days, this could be extended for a further twenty one days. At the end of this period he was either committed to the Detention Centre at Al Mansoura or released.

From the latter it will be seen that time was not on the side of the officers concerned, and it is here that we were able to help. The ability to spot a trouble maker or ring leader amongst the suspects was our greatest asset. Though a nice friendly atmosphere existed amongst the ratings and NCOs off duty, on duty it was one of ruthless military discipline the whole time, no relaxing of this directive was ever contemplated by the most junior of the staff. Sgt Cooper was at Fort Morbut and Sgt Swann at Steamer Point, whilst WO2 Harvey looked after the day to day commitments of the ratings and NCOs. Most of the staff had no idea of what the word security meant to us, the MPSC, and it is to their credit that they learnt fast. Unfortunately, we changed round at different periods, the Royal Navy ratings did four months, Royal Airforce NCOs three months and the Army six months. This did cause a morale problem for a short time, after the other two Services had relieved their personnel. We worked in three shifts, and invariably the night shift was the busiest, the

Special Branch preferred the hours of darkness to arrest "targets". I had the opportunity to go out on a few of these operations, the skill and speed at which they were conducted was amazing. When Aden nationalists called a strike, we geared up to take our maximum figure, it was not unusual to have suspects and known terrorists delivered by the bus load, and on one occasion we even had the bus. I can recall one character being brought to us complete with twelve goats! It took a long time to find his friend and dispose of them.

From May onwards, the two nationalist fronts stepped up their activities. Murder of rivals, attacks on Security Forces and cold blooded assassinations were common occurrences; it was a sordid business. We had to hold the alleged perpetrators of these incidents; I use the word "alleged" deliberately, because none faced trial and this fact had to determine their treatment. Law had broken down, due to the intimidation of witnesses. We had to remain impersonal to these offences, and it is a fact that only one complaint of ill-treatment was made against us, this was found to be groundless. We also knew that during a "cordon and search" operation, quite a number of innocent people were arrested; these had to be protected from the hardened nationalists whilst in our charge. Naturally, the innocent were released quickly, but intimidation was always our biggest concern.

Duties at Fort Morbut were tedious, and at times boring. The daily programme was governed by the Centre Controller and we had no say in it. Most of the work there was highly classified however, and at times we were briefed on our charges, and this did help to make us realise that security of the suspects was not only desireable, but highly essential. No one, except an authorised "white face" was allowed in the Fort, and on one occasion, prior to a visit by the C in C MELF, I saw a Commander RN and a senior Major polishing their office floor, rather than run a security risk of importing doubtful labour for the job. We ourselves carried out the work needed to improve security; no one would determine if this was a High Commission responsibility or MPBW, so we got on with the job; this was one of the problems of a unit that was half service and half civilian.

The conduct of the detainees was, on the whole, good, we had the odd character who didn't want to conform, but after a spell with us they came round to our way of thinking. Food was good and they were medically inspected each day. They were visited by the International Red Cross representative, who ensured that they were being treated well. In most cases they complained daily about something; this was part of the nationalist campaign, and as the complaints followed the same pattern, I am certain it was included in their training programme; however these were only pinpricks and of nuisance value only. Unfortunately we had a moving population, and every complaint had to be investigated by a police officer; complaints ranged from brutality on arrest, down to a loss of a pin!

August was our busiest month and we stepped up the transfer of detainees to the Detention Centre. Then, quite abruptly, the number of suspects arrested began to drop until it was negligible. This was due to two reasons: (a) the political situation had developed whereby the two rival nationalist parties deemed it necessary to shoot each other and (b) any terrorist who attacked the security forces was in dire peril of being killed himself. Apart from this, most of the directing force of the two organisations were in the Detention Centre. Nevertheless we had to watch our own personal security very carefully and after one Saturday of ruthless murder, the Security Commander was forced to issue orders that confined everyone to their living and working area.

It was during September that things began to move. We had only one suspect to look after, and the Detention Centre had started to release detainees in batches of twenty. On the 18th, Mr Guy Pearson informed me that he was going to take over our Steamer Point building and house some 50 detainees from Al Mansoura. I agreed that we would cover for the Detention Centre whilst the transfer was being affected. At the same time I learnt that our RN Ratings and RAF NCOs were being returned to UK within seven days.

Security in the Steamer Point area was increased, on the morning of September 21, 48 detainees were transferred. It was an amazing sight, and every precaution to prevent an incident was taken. Each armoured vehicle carrying eight detainees was heavily escorted, the Press, who had been giving coverage to the detainee question were not around for this operation and we breathed a sigh of relief that they were absent. However the detainees were, for a change, well behaved and obeyed every instruction without question.

The guessing game then commenced on the likely date of the final transfer. This date was tied in with the plan to evacuate Sheik Othman and as such was in the top secret class. Captain Boulter was directly affected and he has supplied the following information.

September 23
0600 hrs   Ten detainees locked
1810 hrs   "O" Group by 1 Lancs Regt to plan move of attached staff to 518 Coy RPC.
2359 hrs   Remainder of staff to Steamer Point

September 24
0240 hrs   Ten detainees released
0257 hrs   South Arabian Army Officers take over buildings
0300 hrs   Capt Boulter and troops move out (it was at this stage some wit wrote on the main gate: "No milk or papers, gone away").

The following day we handed over security duties to the Detention Centre staff and commenced disbanding. A high priority for air passage was given, and on October 1st I was able to report that the DHC had disbanded and that the staff had left Aden. I emplaned on the 2nd.

PART SEVEN

Colchester

37
As it was

In the palmy old days when hitchhiking was not yet an invitation to rape and murder, my daughter Susan was using her thumb to come home from University. Somewhere at the other side of Chelmsford, a hundred tons of Volvo drew in. The driver had a dart players belly and earrings but seemed all right apart from that. "Colly, eh? Glasshouse, init?"

He wobbled at his own joke.

She said that she supposed that there was some glasshouses, but roses seemed to be the main thing.

He snorted and wobbled again. "Nah, Glasshouse Army nick, get me?"

Conversationally, she mentioned that I worked there and he blew out his cheeks, releasing a fine spit onto the fascia. "Works there? Bastards them in the nick".

She says that she agreed to be sociable and because she felt that there was an element of truth in the statement. "You were inside were you?" She has inherited her father's fine feelings and tact. "Me? nah. Known fact though, init? Colly Glasshouse. Bastards".

Colly! What do the Colcestrians feel about it? Here they are, with a nice town, Roman origins, castle and all that a great part of the rest of the British population knows about it is that the Army has a Military Corrective Training Centre there. No, that's wrong too: the whole process of reform is ignored and Colly is the Glasshouse.

It never was a Glasshouse. The irony is that Colchester, one of the biggest English garrisons, was one of the last to have a Military prison at all and that military prison had the shortest life of any of them.

There was a provost prison in Colchester, when Berechurch Hall Camp was still a wet meadow in the grounds of Berechurch Hall. It was in the South East corner of the Hyderabad Barracks and is clearly marked on the Colchester Town Library map. It would be like all of its kind: a place for the garrison's delinquents, run by some old sergeant finishing his time in the easy atmosphere of shaven heads and shot drill. It was the kind of place to which Garsia objected and resolved to eliminate as places unsuitable for reform.

He managed to eliminate it in 1897, when Army Order 123 of that year appointed it, together with York, a military prison. He knew that military prisons could be regulated and were open to his reforming zeal.

At first, the new military prison was under the control of a Head Warder and the subordinates were attached NCO's from the garrison, but soon five career warders (later replaced, of course, by MPSC) were in situation. The prison could house 47 prisoners in single cells.

The new status meant that the prisoners would come under the new rules and would benefit from the improved conditions introduced by Garsia. Oakum picking and stone breaking replaced shot drill. Drill and physical training were on the programme. There were difficulties, as the shot yard was too restricted for proper drill and the only PT possible was static exercises with dumb bells.

Readers acquainted with the geography of military Colchester will consider that church parade for the prison would be a simple matter of crossing the road to the garrison church, that fine wooden building, originally designed as a hospital to be transported to the Crimea but rejected by Florence Nightingale and erected as a temporary Garrison Church in 1856.

It was not so simple. Church parade for the Garrison was then something of an occasion with a duty band and Colcestrians gathered to see the fine sight of red and blue, flashing brass. Imagine introducing into this scene, a group grey shoddy-clad and wearing prison caps over scrubby-cut hair: not exactly keeping the Army in the public eye! Inside the church, they were crowded into the vestry and the report of 1898 complains that their closeness in there leads to the danger of communication. Church services are held in the prison after 1900.

1900 was to see another movement along Garsia's road to reform. On the 10th of April, a Governor, a retired major, is appointed. From this point on, the inside of the prison is seen through eyes that have also seen unsentenced soldiers.

The 1901 report on the new military prison is evidence of

a great deal of activity to convert the old restricted provost premises into a military prison of the type that could perform its new functions. The outer wall is raised and pushed westwards. Sixteen new cells are "in build", as are the gymnasium and laundry. Oakum picking has almost dropped from the routine and "woodchopping boxes" have been built. These were like stalls in a stable, designed to prevent communication as the Garrison's kindling was prepared. Prisoners are employed on bed and pillow making and the repair of tents and horse blankets. One enterprising young man has tried to exploit the chaos of the Re-build (a state not unknown to us in the year I write!) and has escaped through a gap in the wall, only to be recaptured three hours later.

Numbers sentenced are down in 1901 and 1902, due to the absence of much of the Garrison at the South African War. One warder, also, has been recalled from the reserve. There are militia inmates in these two years.

The Governor complains in his report that the smartest and most alert man in the prison is one due for compulsory discharge – a complaint not peculiar to the early years of the century. The soldier has married without permission and it is his wife, the Governor is convinced, who is behind the man's desire to leave. Times change, do they?

By 1908, the Detention Barracks, as it is now called, has 63 cells, but there are several days in the year when only six soldiers under sentence are confined.

All MPSC staff are qualified by this time, either at the Small Arms School in Hythe or the School of Physical Training in Aldershot. The gymnasium is in full use and there is an armoury.

1910 is a good year for SUS: the new King George V has granted a Royal Pardon. All soldiers sentenced for 56 days or fewer are instantly released. The rest are given a remission of half their sentence.

My last report is for 1913, when SUS are studying drill, PT, trench building, bridge building, signalling and the work of scouts and outposts. They were soon to apply their knowledge.

I have little to offer you from the time of the First World War. The Governor, Lieutenant Colonel Umfreville was, you will recall, to become the Inspector of Detention Barracks and Military Prisons with the British Expeditionary Force and was to finish the war as a Major General, but of the DB itself, I have been able to learn very little.

One thing that I have from this period, I find interesting and something of a puzzle. In my search for material, I put in a request to the magazine "Stand To", which concerns itself with the First World War and the letter I reproduce below came as a result of this request. The old gentleman who wrote it was 92 in 1986, yet every word of the letter was legible. What worries me is his reference to Meanee Barracks a quite positive reference and not to be put down to the forgetfulness of old age. I can only assume that extra DB accommodation was taken in Meanee Barracks, but my fellow researcher, Staff Sergeant Vic Leppard, found no Army Order designating Meanee as extra accommodation. Watch this space in the second edition. . . .

I make no apology for reproducing the letter in full, for I feel that it catches something of the atmosphere of the period:

Dear Major Boyes,

Seeing your letter in "Stand to" brought back to me memories of the early days of World War I. I was mobilized with my Battery the Shropshire RHA TF on 5th August 1914. I was promoted full Bombardier on that day, shortly afterwards with the rest of the Welsh Border Mounted Brigade we moved to the East Coast. My uncle was in Beccles.

In one of our sub sections we had 2 brothers one the sergeant and the other a gunner. During the stables the sergeant gave an order which his brother disobeyed and used bad language, just then the Orderly Officer appeared and ordered the sergeant to put his brother on a charge: result a sentence of one month at the Glass House MEANEE BARRACKS COLCHESTER. To my surprise (my name begins with A) I was ordered, with an escort of one man (we were both armed with the short carbine rifle) to take him to the detention barracks Colchester and what a place to go to for 3 recent civilians.

On before handing over my charge we were ordered to double round the parade ground at least 3 times by a stern sergeant. I began to think we were all criminals.

A month later I was ordered to proceed to Colchester on my own and bring the prisoner back. On leaving the barracks I took him to the nearest restaurant and stood him a good feed.

To my surprise I got the job of taking prisoners to Colchester for at least another year and they were by no means all from my own unit but I also stood all of them a good feed and thought no more about it.

However my father was in a Shrewsbury pub one day when he was asked if he was any relation to Bombardier Allwood, yes he said I am his father, The landlady then told him to tell me that when I cared to call there there would always be a free meal and free drink for me as I had been so good to her nephew. I hope you can read this I can't as my eyesight is bad.

Yours sincerely
Arthur Allwood (92)

The end of the War, you will recall, saw the rapid closure of the temporary DBs. The Geddes Axe ensured that some of the permanent DBs would also close. Army Order 167/24 closed the Colchester DB on 31st of March 1924.

In 1937, with Aldershot as the only MPDB for the United Kingdom, the Blue Book of Rules records only Branch Detention Rooms for the Colchester Garrison. I list them here, with the number of certified detention rooms shown in brackets:-
Meanee Barracks (4)
Hyderbad Barracks (1) I wonder what use was made of the old prison cells?
Sobraon Barracks (4)
Cavalry Barracks (2)
Goojerat (sic) Barracks (4)
Le Cateau Barracks (3) Reed Hall Hutments (4)

The last named, now a set of spider huts given over to a play school and training classrooms, was to become No.19 Detention Barracks during the Second World War. In 1946, Major Bob Firmstone was to be Commandant. Tex Rickard, another of the Corps now a part of its history, was also there. Bob Firmstone remembers it as holding 200 SUS and saw in it the beginning of a more enlightened attitude to military punishment. He had two education instructors permanently attached, teaching during the day and running woodwork and leatherwork during the evenings. There was a radio in all rooms and a training cinema. A favourite punishment was to forbid the showing of a cartoon film.

On completion of his probationers course at Fort Darland, ex WOI Avery was posted to Reed Hall in 1947, when the RSM was WOI Munday. He had barely settled in, when he was sent up the road to the recently evacuated POW camp at Berechurch Hall and told to prepare the Gate Book for the movement of SUS to the new site of 19 MCE. They were to be joined by No.14, which was to evacuate Fort Darland.

Major BO "Jimmy" James was in the party from Darland and recalls the organised chaos of trucking 1500 SUS. He also remembers the discomforts of the unlined Nissen that was to be the sergeants' Mess, standing where Corps HQ now stands and the freezing dash to the open ablutions located where the piggery now is.

Army Orders 151/47 had empowered the occupation of the new accommodation, with two distinct MCEs, one of the A Type and one of the B Type. This was the culmination of a series of conferences at the Directorate of Personal Services during 1946, when the future of penal institutions in the United Kingdom was defined. The War Office letter laying down the future is important enough to be reproduced here in full.

Sir,
1. I am commanded by the Army Council to inform you that they have had under consideration the future policy regarding the Military Penal Establishments.
2. They have decided that the Army at home will finally require a small Military Prison, which it is intended should be run on similar lines to a civil prison. This would be used for men convicted of serious military offences, who could not be rehabilitated as soldiers.
3. Soldiers convicted of civil offences or those sentenced to Penal Servitude or two years imprisonment for any offence, would continue to serve their sentences in civil prison as at present.
4. Military Detention Barracks will cease to exist as such but less serious offenders will be committed to Disciplinary Training Centres, where they will carry out rehabilitation as soldiers. Rehabilitation will be carried out in progressive stages, commencing with a month's strict disciplinary training on normal detention barrack lines and ending with a period of almost normal barrack life.
5. With regard to the Military Prison, this would be a military commitment initially, but since its occupants would not normally be returning to the army, the council consider that the question should be reviewed later, with a view to the possibility of the prison being taken over by the civil authorities on an agency basis. This would in fact be a reversion to the procedure existing before 1904, where the Inspector General of Military Prisons was established in the Home office.
6. The Army Council would be grateful if the arrangements for

committal to civil prisons, referred to in para 3 above, could be confirmed and would be glad to know the re-action of the Home Office to the proposals made in para 5 above.

I am sir,
Your obedient servant,
The Under Secretary of State.
The Home Office,
WHITEHALL.

The Home Office very quickly scotched the suggestions of paragraph 5!

The end of 1947 saw 1600 SUS in the hutments, which one of my correspondents nicely described as "like elephants sitting in rows" . . . The MPSC had found their permanent home.

38
Camp 186

Camp 186? The Old and Bold will be shaking their grizzled heads. 186, they'll say, no such number!

As I write, Camp 186 is coming down about me in a clank of corrugated iron and a fog of asbestos dust. The few remaining Nissens are dwarfed by the new buildings, no longer promises of paper drawings.

Camp 186 was, of course, Berechurch Hall Camp in its original use as a POW camp. It was built by them and they lived in it, some of them, for three years. I think it deserves a chapter in this book.

Amazingly, some of the young men who built it and lived in it still come back, older and sleeker than in those austere days. Sometimes they bring their families and, until the year of 1987, could take them to a particular hut in the lines and say "This is where I spent three years of my youth".

I was fortunate enough in being able to contact one of them, through Sydney Harris. I was even more fortunate, because Herr Nikolaus Plaetz, now retired and living in Bremen, visited me shortly after my writing to him and treated me to a tour of the Camp 186, each turn round a block bringing up new memories for him. I could help him along sometimes, because Major Joe Harding, former A Wing commander had passed me an account written by an Old German colleague, Herr Edmund Effenberger MBE, who had also spent a part of his youth here. In the City Library, I had found original copies of "Quadrat", a monthly POW magazine produced here and I am hoping we shall be able to include some of the woodcuts from this periodical in this book.

I had another informant, but more of him later.

The night of 19/20 September 1944 saw the first 1500 tired, bedraggled POWs march onto the wet meadow near Berechurch Hall. The weather was dingy and probably suited their mood, but there must have been some amongst them, who were glad that the war was over for them. They were searched for the umpteenth time and relieved of any pen or watch that had survived previous searches. This time, to their surprise, they were given receipts!

As we still know only too well, the water table of the meadow is such that it rapidly degenerates and soon they found that they were in a sea of mud. In the light of day it became obvious that the tents sat in four barbed wire compounds, these were lettered A to D. There was soon to be a sifting process, when each POW would be allocated to one or the other of the compounds, depending on his political colouring: "A" compound was for the non-Nazis and ranged through to "D" for the SS. A smaller compound stood where C Block was in the hutted camp now being demolished. It was a holding place for war criminals waiting to be shipped to Nuremberg for trial. Another, very small, camp on the piggery site was for a small number of officers.

New drafts arrived daily and the camp held 6000 men at the end of October 1944. They were mainly German but there were also some Austrians.

Rations were adequate, but ruined by being cooked outside until material arrived for the building of the Nissens. The kitchen they built then was still in use until the rebuild.

When the Essex cold moved in, tent life became rugged. The POWs built little stoves from food cans, but their use in the tents were strictly forbidden and a complicated system of signals had to be worked out to warn of impending inspections.

The first huts went up before Christmas. For Christmas itself, a tree was set up near the parade ground and decorated with stars cut from the precious food cans. The Protestant Chaplain, Pastor Kuhlendahl, took a choir round the huts and the theatre group staged a play and a variety performance.

By the end of January 1945, three huts were ready and drainage was being dug (the same drainage that is now seeing the light of day forty two years later!). The camp tracks were cinders and it was the job of one man from each hut, when they were finally built, to search through the cinders for burnable coal.

Herr Plaetz was Chief Interpreter, having taken over the job from Professor Fritz Bartsch of Kiel University. He and the labour supervisor occupied the hut that was later to become D Wing's dining room, then the trainasium. The theatre and the school were near the Commandant's oak tree.

The camp hospital was on the site of the old sergeants' mess. It started as a single black tent, with a pair of tailor's scissors the only instrument available. By November, it had taken the shape well known to generations of MPSC sergeants and the hurricane lamps of the tents had been replaced by electricity. There was steam heating, lino on the floors, books and games (many supplied by the International YMCA, of whom Herr Plaetz speaks with gratitude). By 1946, 49000 cases had been treated.

The Commandant, Lieutenant Colonel Squibb MC, is mentioned by all my informants with respect, as a fair man, who made every effort to ease the conditions of captivity. His office and all the administration was housed in Berechurch Hall itself, which was to burn down in the early Fifties. He, together with the Mayor of Colchester, even arranged art and craft exhibitions of POW work, some of which was quite excellent. From scraps and whatever material they could scrounge, paintings, wood carvings, even musical instruments were produced. Apart from the masterly wood cuts in "Quadrat", we still have one much valued example in the shape of the brickdust and toothpaste painting, still hanging in the sergeants mess. This was restored and framed by Brigadier Mike Matthews during his time as Provost Marshal, then presented to the mess. Major Sydney Harris made great efforts to trace the artist, Herr Otto Sieb, with the intention of inviting him to a future Corps Weekend. Unfortunately, Herr Sieb died shortly after contact had been made.

Dress for the POWs was their own uniform or dyed BD, with patches of another colour sewn to the back and sleeves. Patches were removed in 1946.

1946 saw a general improvement in conditions, the most important being permission to work on neighbouring farms. Herr Plaetz worked for Colonel Raynor DSO MC Whitehouse Farm, Fingringhoe (and still occasionally visits there.) Colonel Raynor had himself been a Turkish POW in the First World War. The work team consisted of Herr Plaetz, representative of a British oil company in Germany; a bank manager; an architect and a professor of horticulture. Their assistants in field and orchard were land girls. When fruit picking, they were allowed to eat as much as they wished and the frequent visits to the orchard edge as a result of this caused much amusement for the land girls. Using scrounged material, the architect built a store for Colonel Raynor that was long known locally as the German House.

Herr Plaetz remembers a time when the gang was manure spreading. Colonel Raynor handed them out his old cast-off uniforms to preserve their everyday gear, so a distinguished German work gang was to be seen plying muck forks in officer's barathea.

Beer money came from making and sale of wooden toys, the most popular being working models of pecking hens and hinged wooden dachshunds. These were demonstrated at the roadside on the way to work with the spiel "Have you interest for pecking hens and Wackel Dackels?". In those austerity days they sold well. The POWs also produced toys for the poor children of Colchester and for charity (1100 items in December 1947!)

All my informants mention one phenomenon: their amazement at the kindness offered to them when they were finally allowed out unescorted. They expected hatred and found very little of it. I shall have more to say about this later.

Much work was done by churchmen in this healing of wounds and Herr Plaetz remembers with admiration one of the prime movers in this reconcilliation. This was the Congregational minister, the Reverend William Morton Bardwell, who had been educated at a German University and spoke excellent German. He was to become the liaison between town and camp and even produced a magazine for ex POWs who had returned to Germany.

I have mentioned already another informant. Through my colleague, Mr Terry Quinlan, I learned that the camp had had a special function as a seminary for future Roman Catholic priests and I was determined to learn more about this. With the great help of Father Bernard O'Brien, parish priest of St James the Less in Colchester, I was able to contact one of the former theology students, Dr Hieronymus Dittrich, now a Canon in Paderborn. I expected from him a short letter of reminiscence but received instead a photocopy of twenty manuscript sides describing those days in great detail. It is thanks to him that I am able to say something of this unique use of Camp 186. I had the pleasure of meeting him in person during 1987.

The seminary was to be part of C Compound, with two study huts and four living huts. Ultimately, there were to be 120 priests trained there.

Beginnings were basic: no books and no stationery. In time, private individuals and religious organisations were to fill the needs, but in the early days, it was a reversion to the old Middle Ages pattern of learning by the spoken word. Notes were made on books made from cement bags being emptied during the building of the camp.

The day was much like the day in a civilian seminary with the added irritation of frequent head checks, which could drag on for hours. Mattresses in the living quarters were straw sacks and the furniture was any kind of scrounged box or crate and an issue table. Heating was supplied by a central stove – probably those same stoves which were to leave the huts only in 1986! As was normal in all military rooms in those austerity days, the stove was only allowed to burn in the evenings. Dr. Dittrich, in common with the old soldiers reading this book, remembers with pleasure some evenings spent around the stove, talking and singing.

Wednesday afternoon – surprise, surprise – was for recreational training! Another familiar feature: Friday mornings was Commandant's inspection. There is, I am sure, a quaver in his pen as he remembers lining up kit and searching for dust. The feeling is not unknown. . . .

Both Dr Dittrich and Herr Plaetz remember the theatrical group in the camp, organised by two professional actors and producing quite ambitious pieces. The seminary students also produced a play, directed by the camp priest, Chaplain Grones.

Christmas 1946 was the first occasion when POWs were allowed into English houses and Dr Dittrich retains that time as a very precious memory. Dr. Dittrich, wrote to Father O'Brien and mentioned this same subject recalling, amongst others, the Colchester families of the Perrys, the Henleys, the O'Sheas, the Petticans, Firmins, Fulchers and the O'Connors, all of whom had offered warmth and hospitality.

The high point for all the student priests – and for many more of the POWs – was to come in September 1946, when Cardinal Frings of Cologne, accompanied by our own Cardinal William Godfrey came directly from Germany to the camp. He was the first visitor from home. He spoke to all POWs on the square, pulling no punches and painting a true picture of life in Germany at that time.

After return to Germany, the young priests who trained here formed a society called the Colchestrianer, which still holds occasional reunions. Some of its members were to return to Britain in 1986, to attend the memorial service to an Englishman, the right Reverend Francis Davis, a lecturer at a theological college near Birmingham, who, despite the apalling conditions of wartime and post war travel, had often come to camp 186 to minister to the young students. His and the name of Father Charles Johnson of Colchester are held by them in high respect.

In time, all of them went home, many to distinguished careers. The camp was to empty, to be filled by the transfers for Fort Darland and Reed Hall. As I have said, some of the early occupiers still return, but now they will no longer be able to say "This is where I lived for three years". Perhaps sometime a plaque will be set so that the camp's early life will live not only in the minds of the Colchestrianer and the Herr Plaetzes of the world.

39
The Gold Fish Bowl and Other Matters

When young Corporal Robinson, all hackle and back-flash, reported to his Company Office in Wrexham in 1952, he was told to pack his kit for a course in Colchester. He had never heard of Colchester and had never heard of the MPSC, who were running the course. Older soldiers amongst his colleagues laughed.

It was a long way with a kit bag from the Mersea Road end of Berechurch Hall Road and he was relieved when he turned off and came to a small wooden hut, obviously some kind of guardroom. A grey haired old sergeant, blue and red titles and peaked cap, grunted something about sending babies on courses, then grudgingly pointed the way to the cluster of Nissen huts that formed the Depot and Training Wing MPSC. He drew bedding and a set of sergeant's stripes, which he proudly tacked on to his battledress as he sat near the small coke stove in the centre. The toilets, he found, were a route march away.

There were eight others on the course, which was run by Staff Sergeants Ernie Taylor and Chippy Reynolds, with a fierce and precise ex Guardsman, Staff Sergeant Preston, to teach the drill. There were others in the Depot, old sweats mainly, hanging around waiting for postings.

Lieutenant Colonel Taffy Lloyd was commander of the wing and he would ask Jim weekly what his age was and seemed not to believe the answer.

It is time that I said something about Taffy Lloyd, whose name has already appeared often in these pages. Taffy died in 1970 and I regret that I was never able to talk to him, because he spanned a huge period in the history of the Corps. He joined from the Welch Regiment in 1919 and did the limited pre-war tour of Aldershot, Cairo, Jamaica, amongst others, returning to Aldershot as RSM. He received an emergency commission when war broke out and was Assistant Commandant at Sowerby Bridge when it first opened. The rest of the war and the immediate post-war was a succession of Commandant jobs, with him in the right place at the right time during the troubles at Northallerton and Shepton Mallet. He was a hard man and a firm disciplinarian but he was also the man behind many of the reforms that were to humanise the military penal scene.

Back to Jim. He enjoyed the course and he passed it. He had no real idea of joining the MPSC: his yound mind was set on the glamour of irregular forces and romantic places overseas. Then he realised that three stripes were a distinct advantage and that the MPSC could offer a chance of an overseas posting more quickly than most. He decided to give it a try.

The organisation in Berechurch Hall Camp at the time was to last throughout the Fifties and a time afterwards. There were two MCEs, as I said in the last chapter. The A type MCE was for recidivists and had no stage system and was divided into two companies, the wasters "the gangsters in uniform" were mainly members of B Company. The B type MCE was staged, with Stage II in the D Coy to which Jim was posted.

Customers at Colchester in 1952 were the Kray twins. They had been drafted into the Royal Fusiliers, entered the Tower of London depot in their neat blue suits and smashed the jaw of a corporal who spoke to them in the fashion of corporals of that period. They then went home. Mr J Pearson's account of the Kray Twins "The Profession of Violence" published by Granada and well worth reading, has this to say about the twins in Colchester:

"The month they spent together after this in Colchester military detention barracks marked the turning point of their military career. Until then, with an optimism that does them credit, the Fusiliers had clung to the belief that the twins were redeemable private soldier material. Now it was plain they would never be, and this month at Colchester was to bring them face to face with some of the toughest delinquents in the army and strengthened their resolve to get out of the army the hard way. It was now too that they began forming rather more precise ideas about their own future when they were discharged, Reggie said: "I can't remember discussing armed robbery seriously with someone for the first time at Colchester. You see, by then, Ron and I had decided that when we came out we wanted the good life and that there was only one way to get it."

Before I return to Jim, a little more about the Krays. Inevitably, they were in trouble again and next time, to quote Mr Pearson:

"Private Reginald Kray and Private Ronald Kray were to be found guilty and confined to nine months' imprisonment at the army prison at Shepton Mallet and then ignominiously dismissed the service.

So the battle was over and the twins had won – after a fashion. The following nine months passed easily enough. They had no need to fight the army any more. The routine at Shepton Mallet proved no great hardship. Their parents and their brother Charlie visited regularly and although they were confined to their cells at night, much of the day passed in physical training and team games so that both could get back into peak physical condition. Morgan who was with them found the food uneatable. The twins didn't seem to notice.

By now they had both decided on their future. They knew their strength and they had learned a lot. After their release they would go all out to find that elusive something they had always wanted.

During these final months in prison they discussed their future life a lot and completed a further stage in the education thanks to which they hoped to reach it. For here at "the Mallet" was a selection of the most promising and up-and-coming young criminals in the country. Previously the twins' criminal acquaintanceship had been confined to London. Anyone who was not a Londoner was dismissed as a "foreigner" or a "swede".

But at Shepton Mallet this narrow-mindedness was rapidly dispelled. Here were young gangsters from the Gorbals and the docklands of Cardiff, thugs from Liverpool, hooligans from Belfast. Military prison was a useful meeting ground and they soon found how much they had in common – so much indeed that in the years to come, the Krays were to show a keen awareness of the nationwide possibilities of organised crime. Friendships made now were kept in good repair for many years to come, and the twins had an uncanny flair for never forgetting a face."

Tex Rickards remembers them in the Mallet as "big

muscular evil sods, but vain and handsome, who had to be separated onto different landings."

Jim was not dealing with the evil of B Coy, but life in D Coy for the young sergeant was not all beer and skittles. I use his words – they must ring many bells amongst the Old and Bold and will probably give the more recently joined a fit of the horrors.

"I started on morning shift and my first job was to supervise the "goldfish bowl", a favourite task for the newcomers. This involved standing near a raised manhole that had expanded mesh over it instead of a lid. The SUS came running out of their rooms for a wash and shave. Two men from each room would carry the latrine bucket which was inevitably filled to the brim – with 10 men to a room this wasn't surprising – carry it to the goldfish bowl and slop it in. They would then have to use a stiff broom to mash all the solids through the mesh, finally rinsing out the bucket. This was not a good job for anyone with a queasy stomach, or if you had had a rough night beforehand.

The SUS used to suffer on this too! The two men carrying the bucket had to move fast and you can imagine that some of the contents used to slop over and down their trouser legs, they couldn't dawdle or they would have no time to shave etc.

After a while I was detailed to take over the Main Gate as relief NCO, I took over from a man called S/Sgt Alec Pelling. The gate lodge was a little hut with just enough room for a bed, a desk and chair. It has a wooden floor and a small iron stove which was permanently alight from September onwards. Pelling and S/Sgt Charlie Duthie used to do this job almost permanently. At one time the two NCOs worked their own shift system, one which meant them staying in the gate lodge for almost 24 hours at a time.

Another favourite job for newcomers was to patrol the back wire. Often you would be forgotten and only when you realised how quiet the lines were, did you guess that the shift had gone for breakfast. You would then go off on your own. There was no sympathy for you if you were too late for your meal.

Patrols and nightwatch at this time meant pegging a clock. You would carry this tell-tale clock with you and at various points around your beat would be brass pegs fitted to the wall. As you passed them you would insert the key into the clock where it would register on a disc. This disc would later be removed from the clock and checked by the CSM. You were in serious trouble if you had missed any of the pegs. NCOs would try all ways to fiddle them so that they would not need to carry them around and of course have no need to peg them. They might have spare keys to open the clock – you could make one out of a brass button stick. They would have spare pegs or they would drop the clock, sometimes into a bucket of water, then you could say it was the rain. I too, was shown how to fiddle the clock, especially the spinner which cut the disc inside at the time it was opened, but with the skilful use of a nail file it was easy to do.

All sorts of tricks would be tried, so many in fact that it was almost unbelieveable. The new RSM we had, decided he would do something and he did. He warned everyone that if the clock disc was damaged or torn in anyway, that NCO would have to go in front of the Commandant. That is what happened and it stopped almost all of the clock fiddling."

Training organisation was rudimentary and several accounts tell of a young sergeant being told only after breakfast that he had a training commitment and finding that he was supposed to teach unspecified subjects to a squad which could number 80 SUS. Drill was on the square: an expanse of hard packed rubble and cinder with a tendency to turn into a lake in wet weather.

Life was a permanent battle to contain and control the often quite evil men caught in the National Service mesh. There were times when as many as thirty men would be in close confinement in the Singles Block at one time. On one such occasion, Sergeant Robson, who was by no means a softie, found that the SUS cleaner had freed the Singles, who beat him about the head with his own truncheon (an instrument carried on singles duty in those days), then kicked him when he went down. One of the SUS was so rattled by the huge pool of blood around Robson, that he shot out of the block, locked the door and went over the wire. He was caught when he tried to steal a car. What happened to Robson? After a week in hospital, he was given sick leave to heal the stitches, then returned to camp to collect his severe reprimand for laxity on duty. I said elsewhere that rooti gongs do not grow on trees for the MPSC.

Escapes were common – more than twenty escapes were recorded in 1951 alone and questions were asked in Parliament. The local – sometimes also the national Press had a flight of valuable space filling articles for every escape. Two of the escapers in 1951 broke into a clothing factory in Coggeshall, stealing clothing valued at £20.6.2d. They were caught when a policeman noticed their Army boots sticking out from under their newly obtained overcoats. A young Pioneer was caught by the same slip, after he had broken into a house in Layer de la Haye and stolen clothing. One of the "runners" in April 51 would have not been caught out by the same mistake: he escaped barefoot.

Jim Robinson remembers an escape later in the Fifties. By then, he was working in the Q Stores, when the escape siren was sounded. Jim was grabbed by the RSM, WOI Tommy Nash and the pair of them, with Eric Milton and the Second in command, Major Dick Collett, set out to search in the 2 i/c's car. The runner was soon spotted – he was wearing a red PT vest – and three of the staff gave chase.

After two hundred or so yards, Jim found himself ahead of the field, but with the quarry in sight. He crossed Oliver's Lane, then caught up with him after another quarter of a mile, where the lad turned, swinging a pick helve. Jim saw how big he was and the helve was swinging in a fairly unambiguous way. One blow connected, but the helve swung out of the lad's hand and Jim could get in closer, but both were so tired by this time that they were both punching feather light, by this time help arrived and he was bundled with difficulty into a police car. After being marched into the Commandant, he said to Jim "To think amother Welshman caught me. . . . they'll never believe me back home!" He was not to see home for some considerable time afterwards.

The Colcestrians were beginning to worry at the number of loosely running SUS about the area and Mr (later Lord) Alport, who was then MP for Colchester sought the reassurance of Mr Fitzroy Maclean, who was the Permanent under Secretary of State for War, that all possible was being done to protect his constituents from escaping soldiers. Mr Fitzroy Maclean assured him that staff strengths were being increased and new security lights fitted, but that anyway, there were no thugs held in Colchester, as these were all sent to Shepton Mallet. Like the Krays. . . . ?

Escape over the wire was not the only way that some of the SUS sought as a way out of their predicament and the Corps museum has a full display of items swallowed, some of them quite unbelievable. At the side of one item in the cutting book is written what must be a record swallow of all times. Can you really believe that a man can swallow three bed springs and a bent-up fork? Admittedly it was only a table fork, not a garden or field variety.

Tobacco was heavily restricted and a scarcity product, the ration being two cigarettes a day with the formalities of smoking them severely controlled. Again, a display in the museum shows the ingenuity employed in attempting to get tobacco from outside. Everything smokable was smoked and lights were obtained by the most inventive devices.

Time spent in detention did not count towards time served and many of the protestors, as we have seen elsewhere, ran far over the two years they were protesting about. One quoted in the Daily Express of 17th December 1953 I will use as an example. Private JH had joined the Army in November 1951 and by 1953 had not even completed his six weeks basic training. On his court martial, it is stated that he destroyed his clothing and equipment valued at £22.2.2d, whilst serving eighteen months detention. He was sentenced to a further twenty one months and his pay stopped until he had paid for his kit. JH had burned his kit, then reported to a member of staff that he was not prepared to continue soldiering. The court martial was his fourth and he had left Borstal to join the Army. It was the second case heard by the court martial on that day and the other charge was almost identical, though this time the soldier was sentenced to imprisonment and a psychiatrist was recommended. It was another Army, wasn't it?

The customers were not all batty or evil. In an Army where National Service was "wagging the dog" and where discipline to a great extent was built – inside the MCE and outside – on a fierce military law still hanging over from the old days, obviously many of the young and naive and foolish – and the many illiterates, whom we tend now to forget, were set to fall foul. I challenge any reader who was a young soldier in those days to say with certainty that he never came close to the gates of Colchester.

Sometimes – often – good or bad, the SUS turned up

trumps, particularly when faced with an emergency. Ray Ganner remembers the cheerful way the SUS reacted to the vile job of clearing up after myxamatosis. No complaints, no escapes, simply doing a job.

In 1953 it was the same, when high winds and high tides in combination caused the worst North Sea floods for centuries. The sea wall at Fingringhoe broke and one hundred SUS and staff worked ankle deep in mud, howling winds around them to fill sodden sandbags to fill the gap. They earned their rum and their double rations. I will write later about the firemen's strike and the emergency cover provided by the SUS. All these things happened with little mention in the Press – escapes and horror stories sell papers – lads grafting sell very few.

The Press like a story about Colchester Nick, whether DB MCE or MCTC, provided they can add a frisson of horror to it and can take out the old Glasshouse word, dust it up and use it again. One story that Ray Ganner remembers, however, has no attached horror, but there is a touch of the bizarre and the story has Heart, another acceptable commodity. A SUS was admitted after several previous visits and claimed that he was going absent so often because his mates made a joke of his over long and oddly shaped nose, the Press saw Heart in it and published the story, leading to a benefactor offering to pay for plastic surgery on the nose when the soldier's sentence was over. The soldier never returned, so one can assume that the operation was so successful as to change the lad's life or to so change the nose as to make him unrecognisable on his next visit here.

Visiting days for the SUS in the Fifties, when cars were scarce and the visitors had marathon journeys by train and bus, followed by a long trudge up to the gate lodge, were much sadder affairs. But Inspector D Pyatt, ex MPSC recalls non-drab visitors, arriving in Bentleys or Jaguars, mink coated and heavily jewelled, usually blonde, coming to visit their friends, who had done well when they were on the trot but who had finally been caught.

This chapter really spans the Fifties and it was in 1950 itself that MPSC were offered for the first time a chance to be commissioned into their own Corps. We have already met many Corps personalities, who were commissioned during and after the war, but always into other Corps or Regiments, usually into the one from which they had originally transferred. Many, like Taffy Lloyd, Wally Watson and Bob Firmstone, were to use their expertise as Commandants and Assistant Commandants. In 1946, a conference at the Directorate of Personal Services decided that there was a need for Quartermasters in the MPSC and three WOIs of the Corps were offered emergency Quartermaster commissions. Captains Jimmy James; Lovegrove and Fazackerley. Jimmy James and Lovegrove were later given Short Service Commissions in the KSLI, but Fazackerley left the Army in 1948. In this new, 1950, move, Bob Firmstone (who had been commissioned in the KSLI since 1942), Jimmy James and Osborne were to become the first Regular QMs.

The Old and Bold will remember the huffing and puffing of 1952/3, when the Powers decided that a uniform more suitable than battledress should be introduced for ceremonial and formal occasions. They will remember also that the final answer was Number One dress, a form of pre-war patrols designed, like the camel, by a committee. This was to be the dress for the MPSC detachment marching in the Coronation Parade for Queen Elizabeth II. I have a picture of the detachment before me as I write, posed after the event with the then Commandant, Lieutenant Colonel Hose and the RSM, WOI A Bishop.

Detachment members wear white pistol belts and holsters, with a white cross belt. Their badges are the Old cipher of King George VI, but a photograph taken in the same year and kindly sent to me by Mr AA Johnston, a military book seller from Langport, shows the staff of Colchester wearing the George VI cipher with a small Queen Elizabeth cipher superimposed – scarcity value, here, we would think and we would dearly like one for the Museum.

Training, you will recall from Jim's account, was a very hit and miss affair in the early days of the Fifties. This was to be changed by the personality of a Commandant, whom we last met in Egypt: Lieutenant Colonel J Macdonald of the KOSB. He arrived in Colchester in 1955, strolled the camp for two weeks, then exploded into action, completely reorganising the training set up; weeding out the staff and putting the MCTC into working order. He was to stay until 1958, leaving an establishment prepared for the Sixties and the decades to follow.

40
Horror Stories

We still get horror stories – as I have said, they appear to be useful Press space fillers. Our last was headed "GLASSHOUSE SLAVE SHOCK" a story, which at any rate gave some amusement to the SUS. The Observer saw a rather inept way of plaiting it in to another – totally unrelated – popular story of the time, but soon dropped it after an informed letter from someone who knew what the place was about and when the realised that there was little or no mileage in it. It was one of the string of horror stories, stretching all the way through the cuttings book. The classic was the Pyjama Game, which is worth a chapter to itself.

Reg Degavino sent me a rather different kind of work in the genre. When Lord Whitelaw, then plain Willy Whitelaw to the press, was examining the pros and cons of "the short, sharp shock", the Evening Echo, published in Basildon, ran a competition with £10 prizes for "the best letter from an old sweat about his time in a military prison". The heads in the press, (not in the Naval sense), were "WHAT DOES GO ON BEHIND THIS FENCE" with an attached picture of the Unit's signboard, and "NIGHTMARES OF THE GLASSHOUSE".

The first letter was from a National Serviceman of 1950:

"During the summer of 1950 as a National Serviceman – a junior NCO – I was silly enough to get myself a district court martial.

As a result, I was awarded six months at Colchester military Corrective Training Centre. My pal got the same. Until the day we left for Cochester, we were allowed the freedom of the camp. We were, in effect, still trusted NCOs.

On arrival at the gates our escorts and the pair of us were screamed at, verbally abused and ordered to go away as we were improperly dressed.

Our escorts' faces turned white with fear, so you can

imagine how we felt peering through the December fog at the iron gates.

Once inside we were hustled into the gatehouse and read the riot act, and told that one third of our sentence could be remitted, but any errors on our part and we would serve the full time.

We had to strip and take a cold shower. I think it was December 13!

We were marched at the double for 400 yards to another wired-off compound just like those in the German films.

I was terrified as the riot act was read to us once more while our heads were shaved.

The compound was about 300 yards long with the semi-circular asbestos huts on both sides, rolls and strands of barbed wire everywhere to about ten feet high.

The fear of God ran through me as I realised that human beings were being kept there.

The door of the hut was unlocked and I was ordered in by a red-necked screw, who was just waiting to get at me.

There was no glass in the windows, only wire mesh, for obvious reasons. The stories the inmates told me would have scared James Bond because if you did manage to escape would start again.

Our beds to be laid out to a specific order – full kit, everything square, bootlaces rolled, not one thing out of place.

Outside for parade now! Run, run, run; line up; stand still for roll call; answer when your name is called!

A big fat screw looked at me and said: "What's my name, lad?" "Don't know, staff?" I replied, to which he answered: "Go sick, lad."

This means seeing the medical officer to find out if you are fit to go on punishment diet PD 2 – bread and water.

I received three sessions of two days bread and water and two days' remission lost on each count.

One session was for having a few whiskers under my chin.

PD 1 consisted of porridge for breakfast, lunch was mashed watery dried potatoes, meat and cabbage; tea was a cheeseball one inch in diameter and a two inch cube of bread.

On my first three days I refused to eat the filth. On the fourth day I ate crumbs from the table.

One day we were running past the cookhouse about 30 of us and I saw the swill bins outside. As I passed the bins I saw an L shaped crust half submerged in custard and slops. I grabbed it, roughly wiped it and ate it. This memory will be with me for ever.

It was 100 per cent impossible to get through there without loss of remission.

I was ordered to sit in an empty hut, given an old cement bucket and a half a brick and told to wear a hole in it. I started to pound the bottom of the upside down bucket. My great coat was covered in brick dust and I had a highly polished bucket.

Another time in the hut I had to shift a large heap of sand to the far end and sweep the corner. Having done this, I had to shift it to corner number three and then a fourth time.

I thank God that I haven't had to go near the place since."

The next has the sub-heading "**Cruel, Hard and Outdated**"

I was sentenced by court-martial at Winchester to be reduced to the ranks and six months' detention at Colchester.

The food was awful, not enough and not properly cooked. Plus you get one cigarette a day.

The hardest thing there is the training, it's not so bad for the young ones but when you are in your late 30's it kills you.

May I say it's not a place to go to – it's cruel, hard and out-dated.

It didn't hurt me physically but it broke my heart.

Yes, it's rough on the late 30s, but nobody asked him to come!

Next a youngster. Without cant, I would say that he sums up the feelings of most of our customers and I feel strongly that some of the deterrent value is to be lost, when the SUS of the future turns into the avenue and sees a group of buildings superior, possibly, to his own barracks, rather than the squat threatening shapes of the Old Nissens.

Comradeship in Godforsaken hole

At the tender age of 19 I was sentenced by court-martial to serve 84 days at this training centre for absenteeism.

My first impression on arrival was of a German stalag. I understand all commands were obeyed at the double – in my particular wing – and this included going to and from the cookhouse.

During my entire three years' enlistment I never found

such a high quality of comradeship as I did in this Godforsaken hole.

On reflection, although it was never anything like a picnic, I don't think I came away bearing any grudge or hard feelings.

If Mr. Whitelaw's get-tough centres for young offenders are to be a success I don't think he should take his guidelines from Colchester.

After all – even though we were offenders – we were soldiers and most of us proud of it. The pride we had in ourselves and our regiments helped us overcome the discipline and hardships we underwent at Colchester.

Age has dulled the memory of the next prize winner, but the yearning for tobacco sticks in his mind.

Two puffs at your cigarette

I did 56 days there in 1949 and I can tell you it was no holiday camp.

I had a kit check and shower in less than 20 minutes then we were doubled round to the cookhouse for a meal.

My God, a meal! It comprised watery soup and four slices of bread. If you were a bit slow at eating, the staff sergeant would make you light up your cigarette. If he decided to say cigarettes out you might only have had two puffs from it and they would come round with a bowl of water for you to put it out.

If you got caught with a cigarette end in your pocket you would lose three days' remission on your sentence.

These are just a few things that went on in that hell hole – a typical timetable for private soldiers or prisoners as we were called:

5.30 Reveille 6am Cold shower 6.30 am PT with additions 7 am Breakfast 7.30am Kit check 8.00am Parade 8.30am Route march varies 10–15 miles a day 11.30am Shower (cold) 12 noon PT 12.30pm Dinner.

These are just a few of the things that went on in my day as a prisoner in Colchester.

I leave you with the last of the prize winners. I still haven't quite worked out what it's about!

There was just nothing to say

As a peacetime soldier in the beginning of the 30's I heard stories about the glasshouse, North Camp, Aldershot. Some of them scared me.

Second stage men – 14 days' good conduct you're in it.

I wondered what it meant. March round to the end of the detention block. Two ranks open order. Front rank about turn. Ten paces forward march. About turn. You are now on second stage as a reward for good conduct. You can talk but not to the men either side of you, but the men opposite. You cannot talk about the glasshouse, food, your regiment, the crime that got you here, or women!

Get on with it, don't abuse your privileges. It took the permitted ten minutes to think what to say. Then it was too late. Now I could say lots more.

Well, what is he saying?

41
The Pyjama Game.

The sub heading to this should be "How to give the Press a treat" and the cuttings should be required reading for the future aspiring Army PROs. The Pyjama Game was to be the longest lasting Glasshouse and Torture story supplied by the Army since Northallerton and Aldershot. It ran, even in the cuttings held here, for something like six feet of column inches – and that does not include cartoons, artists' impressions and photographs of Members of Parliament!

As soon as soldiers were ordered to bring their own kit into detention, they started to cut it up or burn it, not all soldiers, of course, but the nutty minority. The choice was then to allow them to run around naked or to put them into suits they were not able to destroy. Thus was born the canvas suit, known according to some imaginative hack as "Pyjamas". The Pyjama Game as a headline was, I suppose a logical progression.

The suit – I will call it this from now on – was subject to stringent rules in its application. It was to be of sailcloth; not to weigh more than twelve pounds and authorisation for its use and its strict control, were in the hands of the Commandant.

Doubtless, during National Service, it was much in use – I have no figures. What I have is a Daily Express report for 1956 under the (somewhat ambiguous!) heading "War Minister told "Screws were used to fasten him into a suit!' ". Mr. Victor Yates MP for Ladywood, Birmingham had told the Commons that one of his constitutents, a member of the Plymouth Brethren, had refused to wear uniform during his post NS camp and had been forced at Colchester to wear a canvas suit. This story died after one run.

But the 1967 story died hard.

The National Council for Civil Liberties published a demand for the abolition of canvas suits "a military detention device which makes it difficult to swallow and to lie on the back". Their informant was a Mr MC Gee, who had served 84 days in Colchester in 1962.

Mr. MC Gee had also informed them that wearers were put on bread and water and placed in a damp unheated cell.

It had all the components for a crusade.

Mr. Ben Whittaker, Labour MP for Hampstead raised it first in the Commons, then the Press picked it up. It was, to quote reporters "the stuff of the Middle Ages" and "belonging to the Chamber of Horrors". Army discipline, it appeared was "stuck in the Crimea Age". The People, under a two inch headline "Agony of the Army Torture Jacket", subheaded "shocking new evidence", revealed the evidence of two ex Service readers, one of whom had had his shoulders left raw and bleeding and had gone to pieces under the ordeal. The other who, incidentally like Mr. MC Gee, had never worn the suit, had spoken to one prisoner who had not been allowed to go to the toilet and had to do it in the suit. At the end of three days, he was hosed down and given a fresh suit.

The Sunday Times produced an artist's impression, based 'on the details supplied by a fromer detainee,' who appears to have had an artist's imagination.

The Observer condemned outright.

What did the Army do about it? Not much. First reaction from some PRO who had obviously lunched well was that he doubted if the suits existed – he had never seen one, at any rate. Another made the flip remark that the alternative to the suit was a SUS running around in his underwear. Another had the common sense to consult and quoted the I&D Rules, which laid some of the phantoms. Nobody thought of saying let's let in the Press. When the Press finally were allowed in, almost three weeks after the hooha started, the story was killed stone dead.

Mr Gerald Reynolds, Minister of Defence (Administration) was helicoptered down to see for himself on the 1st of May and the interview he subsequently gave was good for several more column inches. He gave reporters the first factual account of the suit, then invited MPs and the Press to visit the MCTC on the 10th of May, including Mr. Ben Whittaker, who had first asked the question and who had stated that he wanted to try on the suit for himself.

Mr (now Sir) Anthony Buck, MP for Colchester and for many years one of the MCTC's most dedicated Board of

Independent Visitors, had already practised a magnificent piece of Empeemanship and had paid a private visit to the MCTC on the day before the minister's visit. He, of course, immediately volunteered to be one of the visitors on the 10th.

The visitors were given carte blanche, seeing the suit, seeing the whole camp and talking to SUS, amazed that they did not cower away from the expected blow, that they actually grinned. They complained, of course, about the food. . . . Mr. Marcus Lipton, veteran MP for Brixton admitted that he was impressed. Mr. Ron Ledger, Labour MP for Romford, said that he was also impressed. One of the complainants, he said, was a constituent of his but had never complained about his treatment to him personally. One of the reporters tried on the suit and found it uncomfortable, but Mr. Ben Whittaker, decided against trying it on. All agreed that the suit was not Saville Row and that the design should be changed. All also deplored the fact that Press photographers had not been allowed on the visit. Well, the Rules are the Rules, but I think I see their point.

The storm was almost over. Mr. Reynolds announced next day that the suit would be withdrawn and a new one designed. This was done, and somewhere over in C Block must be sitting an example of the sateen replacement, steadily gathering dust, possibly mouldering in the damp unheated cells.

There's a lesson in it for all of us, but I'm not sure what it is.

42

Not a Horror Story

I have said elsewhere how much I regret that so few SUS of former days came forward to describe the military penal experience from the consumer's point of view. One of the few, Mr Colin Ward, whom we met in Ronaldshay, lent me two items which could justifiably be described as horror stories: a short story appearing in that excellent old publication, "Penguin New Writing" No. 31 of 1947, which was written by a "Lieut Z" – then a tract, published in 1937 in a series called "A Monograph a Month". This last was entitled "I Joined the Army" and was written by Private YXZ, possibly a relation of Lieut Z! This was a harrowing account of a young soldier's life in the Tank Corps and contains a detention barrack scene.

For something more objective, I would like here to reprint an article appearing in the now defunct John Bull and written at the time in the mid Fifties, when the Glasshouse season was open for the Press. I think that it is fair picture of what life must have been like for the SUS of the period and I would welcome Old and Bold opinions on it.

My Stretch in an Army Glasshouse

On the afternoon of Monday, September 23, 1950, the troop-carrier into which I had been crammed with about a score more prisoners and escorts lurched to a halt outside Colchester Military Corrective Training Establishment – "the glasshouse". It was an ex POW camp: about three hundred asbestos huts entirely surrounded by barbed wire. Inside the main enclosure were four separate compounds, containing four companies into which the camp was divided.

We tumbled out of the truck and walked haphazardly up the short drive to the gate lodge, a small wooden hut beside the wire netting gate. A sergeant in the peaked cap and bright blue and red flashes of the Military Provost Staff Corps let us in. "Get into two lines," he ordered. "Escorts on the left."

The gate swung to behind us. "Right, first man – number, rank and name. How long have you got?" He passed down the line. One man called him sergeant. "In here you call everybody below warrant officer "Staff", WOs and above, "Sir". That understood?"

Quick March: Double March.

He set us marching to the reception office, a large corrugated-iron Nissen hut about twenty yards away. Halfway across, another sergeant took up the sharp "Left right, left right" in double quick time, and marched us inside. Down each side, a series of oblong bays had been marked out. Each prisoner was assigned to a bay, ordered to strip to gym shoes and overcoat and "chase" to the building opposite for a shower. When we returned, our kit was checked and searched. Everything not on the official list and especially prohibited articles such as tobacco, food, drink and valuables – had to be stored away until our release. We were, however, allowed to keep three photographs.

One by one we were called to a table where a Staff checked our documents. With several other prisoners I was then quick-marched to "B" compound.

In the company office, our kit was checked yet again. We were each given five blankets, a mattress, a pillow, two sheets, a pillow case, two mugs (one for shaving, the other for drinking), two tin plates, sticks to make a "laundry box", and cardboard for squaring our kit. Under a load of kit I was doubled marched to my room. I dumped the kit on the vacant bed and was marched out for tea. After that I was locked up with the others for the night.

I sat on my barrack box and looked miserably round my new home, a small asbestos Nissen hut with windows at both ends. Down one side of the centre gangway were six beds, down the other, four, with a trestle table and two forms in between. In the centre was a stove which almost smothered the night's ration of three-quarters of a scuttle of coke. At one end was a recess in which a latrine bucket stood. When our food was doctored, as occasionally it was, the stench was appalling.

What depressed me most was the spotless blanco and gleaming brasses of the kit laid out on the beds. I arranged mine as best I could, but without cleaning materials this wasn't good. No one was inclined to help me – I found that every man was for himself. Suddenly, in desperation, I threw the whole lot on the floor.

"Would you mind getting on with your kit?" said a voice from the window. "I'll pay special attention to yours on inspection tomorrow." It was a Staff prowling in the dark, the first intimation I had of the methods used to watch prisoners.

At eight thirty there was a rattle on the window. The nearest man opened it. "Stand by your beds," snapped a voice, and the staff, who was going off duty, counted us. "As you were," and the window slammed to. A few minutes later, there was another rattle, this time for the Staff coming on duty to count us. Satisfied, he gave the order "beds down". Immediately every man stripped his kit off his bed and wrapped it carefully in newspaper: blanco lasted longer that way. Then everyone slipped into bed, the warmest and most comfortable place in the camp. With a hospital bedstead, good mattress clean sheets and five blankets apiece, it was comfortable by any standards. Though "Lights out" was at nine, one of the four lights, the security light, was left on all night.

Reveille came at six with a loud banging on the door. Stripped to the waist, we lined up outside with the rest of the company. There was a blast on the whistle and 180 men scrambled to the wash-house, where all had to wash and shave at forty-eight basins in a little over ten minutes. I took one look at the icy water and fled. Old-timers sneaked a wash in their room from a mug of water heated on the stove the night before.

By a quarter to seven we were back in our lines with mugs and cutlery. To a succession of whistles, we formed two ranks and marched through the company gates (where we were checked) to the dining room in the main compound.

Six weeks on weapons and drill

By nine o'clock everything was ship-shape. Except for a short break in the morning when we drew cleaning materials and had a pep talk from the company commander, we were given military training tests for the rest of the day. We were then allotted to one of the thirteen training squads, according to our skill. Starting in squad 4, I spent the next six weeks on weapons and drill.

At twelve thirty we were recounted and taken to dinner,

marched back to our own lines while the Staff changed shifts, checked yet again and marched back to the main compound to spend the rest of the day training. Tea was from four thirty until five, and after that we were locked up until next morning. Though we were supposed to clean our kit until eight, I soon found that I could safely sit on my kitbox, mechanically polishing a boot while I read a book between my feet.

The days followed monotonously. Very soon my kit was immaculate like the rest. I scrounged pieces of asbestos to square my bed, but the most absurd piece of "bull" I have ever seen was the laundry box made of three contrasting layers of underwear, stiffened at the front with sticks specially sewn in and wrapped round with a towel squared with cardboard. It took an hour to make.

In the room itself, the table had to be scrubbed white, the drinking-water bucket polished (and for that reason never used), the scrubbing bucket cleaned with bathbrick, and the handle of the sweeping brush scraped with a razor blade. Though it was not compulsory, we blacked the stove with boot polish to create a good impression, and sometimes blancoed the slab khaki. On special occasions, blanco was also applied to the crosspieces of the door.

The search for cardboard to stiffen our kit became a mania. One day the whistles blew. We were lined up outside out huts and carefully counted. The barbed wire dividing us from the main compound had been propped up by sticks, making a hole big enough to crawl through. "I shan't punish the person who did it," said the sergeant major, "but I'd like to know who it was."

A man stepped forward. "It was me, Sir. There was some cardboard I needed for squaring my kit at the other side of the wire."

"That's a relief," said the sergeant major. "I thought someone had escaped."

Move that made life easier

After six weeks I was told I was eligible for promotion to Stage Two, where discipline was less strict. This was what every Stage One man longed for. In a six months' sentence, two months would be remitted for good conduct and the rest divided more or less equally between the three stages if a prisoner managed to "keep his nose clean". Two days before the up-grading I and seven others were moved into a vacant hut which we had to make spotless. The same applied to our kit and turn out.

Things were definitely easier in Stage Two. While much of the discipline was normally the same, offences tended to be overlooked. From six forty-five each evening until eight thirty we had the run of the company area, the use of the games room (draughts, cards and chess, but no gambling), and a good library. There was no military training, but we did such jobs as carting coal to married quarters, scrubbing out cookhouses and cleaning sergeants' messes.

It was now that the lack of nourishment in the food began to tell. Though full immediately after a meal, we would feel hungry and tired by mid-morning. But now, at least, there were occasional opportunities for getting food on the side. Four men were taken each day to work in the Stage Three Kitchen. Sometimes soldiers' wives would give us a cup of tea and a bun when we delivered coal. One day I got quite merry on spirits left over from a sergeants' mess party.

Through a run of bad luck I found myself on three charges in one week in Stage Two. The first was "Losing by neglect a pair of shoes" which were stolen from my bed. I had to pay for them. On both the other charges I was technically guilty. For one I got two extra parades, an hour's non-stop drill on Saturday afternoons. On prison food it was killing. For the other I got three days' extra fatigues.

Other punishments in the glasshouses included solitary confinement (rare), loss of remission, down-grading and punishment diet. The last, which could be awarded for only three days at a time, consisted of eight ounces of bread for breakfast. Potatoes and porridge for dinner and eight ounces of bread for tea.

Charge made to fit case

Punishments which were, rightly or wrongly, regarded as unfair caused more discontent than anything else. Both NCOs and officers were certainly astute even when a man proved his innocence on a technical point, so long as they were satisfied he was guilty in fact, they found another charge to fit the case.

Six weeks later, after another "bull" parade, I was transferred to Stage Three, where one lived like a normal serviceman in a unit. True, we were confined to the main compound, but we went out working each day and were not locked up at nights. We had normal Army food and were even allowed an afternoon out once a fortnight.

I hope I have written enough to show that the place was anything but paradise. Though there were certain comforts, especially in Stage Three, most of one's sentence was served in Stages One and Two where, for most of the time, life was utterly miserable. Besides the indignity of being locked up and watched, there were the physical discomforts of continuous hunger and craving for tobacco.

The glasshouse certainly served its purpose as a deterrent, for our sole aim was to get out and stay out. The military training and the long periods set aside for cleaning kit, while soul-destroying achieved the purpose of making most us into smarter soldiers than we were on entry.

In a wider sense, the glasshouse failed. The lesson it in fact taught was that the real crime is being found out. It taught men to be crafty and cunning and not only men, for there were boys of sixteen there. A few it permanently embittered.

43
The Customer: Some Curiosities of the Period.

This is not a chapter, merely an entertainment. In reports for some years in the Seventies, a section was headed "Tales from the Wings". I feel that it would be a pity if the tales were simply to gather dust in the archives, so here is a selected few.

One heading was "Absentee of the year. In 1976: We would have liked to have given our nomination to the Gunner who says that he lived with a striptease dancer for two years in Sweden. However, in the absence of any verification of this story, our award goes instead to the Private soldier who left his unit in Germany and obtained free transport back to the UK by representing himself as a stranded tourist to one of HM Consulates.

The consolation prize, though, must surely go to the absent Guardsman who while employed as a scaffolder fell from the roof on which he was working into a Police Station yard to be promptly arrested.

In 1977: Absentee of the year. We would like to have given the prize this year to the absentee who claimed he worked in a Recruiting Office whilst on the run. In absence of any confirmation, however, the award goes instead to the Life Guard who made sufficient money while absent to actually welcome his period in detention for "tax relief" purposes.

The consolation prize though must surely be awarded to the SUS who while an absentee, in some way became a Policeman. He gave himself up as a matter of conscience after arresting another absentee.

The Escaper of the year – 1976: Our nomination goes to the young airman who went "over the wire" one evening. Having spent four hours wandering in the dark, he became thoroughly disorientated and found himself unwittingly, sometime after midnight, at a cross roads not four hundred

289

yards from the main gate. He thumbed a lift from the first car to pass without realising that the driver was none other than his own wing RSM. A rugby player, perhaps not surprisingly he plays in the second row.

Celebrity of the year 1977: Our nomination this year goes to the sailor who actually appeared in the TV series about HMS Ark Royal – in the cells. He was closely followed in our opinion by an airman whose previous civil offence was that of being found in a public place looking for his mother in law with a bread knife in his hand.

In 1980, under the heading "Humour":

a. Two troopers who borrowed their Brigadier's car to go on leave.

b. Three troopers who went to the local pub in a Chieftain tank.

c. Two troopers who counterfeited 10 and 50 pence coins and made over £2000. (They were admitted for AWOL)

d. The trooper who, whilst AWOL, joined the French Foreign Legion and returned having deserted from that organisation. Since then we have entertained many more of the Etrangers.

e. Two Gunners who planned and executed the theft of the valuable contents of a Stadt Art Exhibition faultlessly, just to prove it possible. They subsequently returned the contents anonymously.

A former Officer I/C Beagles, who was also Welfare Officer and a man with a honed sense of the absurd but who shall remain nameless, engaged in the collection of occupations pursued by SUS when absent from the service. I enclose a short list of the more exotic, omitting those not suitable for family reading: Casino bouncer; professional golfer; Danish factory hand; fruit picking in Israel; Disco dancer; chef in French restaurant; Scissors salesman; House building in Canada; Boxing sparring partner; burglar alarm salesman; Tangiers tourist guide; Ice cream seller; St Tropez Shepherd (?); Circus hand; Greek hotel waiter; Pop group road manager; Oyster fisherman; Grape picker, France and Germany; Scent mixer; Waffle cook, South Carolina; Unviersity degree course; Steeple jack, Australia; Nurse in Switzerland.

44
Fetch Astiz!

None of this is my work: I consider the report far too good for me to doctor. It appeared originally in the Corps Journal and was written by Lt Col P Andrews, MBE, WO2 (RQMS) C Garrity, S Sgt L Greenwood, S Sgt P Carew and Sgt D Langdon, who, of course, saw the operation at first hand.

Not a normal job for the Corps, but one could argue that burying diseased rabbits or guarding Arab terrorists are equally unusual. Flexibility is all!

"The operation started on the 21st May 1982 when the five of us were briefed by the 2 i/c as to our commitment which was, as you all now know, the escorting of Lt Cmdr A Astiz from Ascension Island to the UK.

By 1200hrs. 23rd May we were all sitting in the departure lounge at Brize Norton and by 1630hrs, were taking off in a VC 10 on our first leg to Dakar.

It was by coincidence that on this leg of our journey the aircraft was captained by Chris Garrity's brother, Sqn Ldr Mike Garrity. As can be imagined we were all treated like VIPs and the cabin service was excellent.

Having landed at Dakar about 0010 hrs, we were allowed off the aircraft for approx one hour, this was where Les Greenwood successfully went big game hunting, his size 11½ to 12 boot crushing a large 2" ant. When finally all the cheering had stopped Les admitted he had been scared at the time.

After a further three hours we found ourselves at Ascension. We were not met, nor did anyone seem to want to know us. However, we eventually found transport and trundled off into the night, in the company of some RAF personnel. They told us that Ascension was not big. Well, it may not be, but there is one hell of a lot of road and it goes round and round, crosses uphill and dare I say it, down "dale".

Many of the buildings we passed appeared to be fitted out with washing machines and tumble dryers and even, would you believe, a drive-in cinema. It was near these buildings that the vehicle stopped. Everybody went to jump off (all thinking this can't be bad) – our first mistake! We were told only RAF out! As you might have guessed this was going to be RAF accommodation, not ours.

We eventually arrived (so we were told later) at English Bay. I could agree with the English bit, but where the bay came from – well, I leave it up to your imagination bearing in mind that this island was used by the Americans to test their "Luna Buggy". Anyway to continue, we had arrived. We were met and the senior office was asked for – we despatched, guess who? our Peter into the darkness. Eventually he returned a bit dazed and told us that we could sleep in any of the accommodation ahead of us. Great we thought. We walked ahead then we stumbled on our quarters, x numbers of 160 pounders! (At least we didn't have to put them up.)

We piled in, and to our amazement found camp beds. After selecting our spaces and being at this stage very tired we went to bed. The silence was only broken by the big ZZZZs of our Les, and the yell and cry of help as our leader's bed collapsed around him. Well, he should have tested it first!

The next morning after breakfast we went to see the CBF to receive further orders, and were told that we were to be taken aboard the MV British Avon (25,000 ton "BP" oil tanker) where, after satisfying ourselves about the security aboard, we would receive Lt Cmdr Astiz.

We were then waiting for transport to the ship when a naval helicopter winchman turned up with life jackets and proceeded to give us crash drill should we crash over water. It was at this stage, being bright, intelligent individuals, that we realised just how we were going to get to this ship, "down a rope". All except one of us, who will remain anonymous, had not done this before. However, the winchman was overheard to say,"now sir, you must set an example to your men", and with that a big boot sent him into space.

We all landed safely on the ship by 1000hrs. 24th May and were welcomed aboard by the Master, Capt. Guy, who then had us shown to our cabins and to the cabin to which our guest was to stay in. However, on being shown to our cabins we were passed in the passageway of our living quarters by a person with multi-coloured hair who looked distinctly queer to us all, this turned out to be "Daisy", one of the ship's stewards, now to be known as "she".

What a person! She looked after us all (don't let your imaginations run riot), and was an extremely clever, quick and intelligent person, a ship's character who was not only respected by the crew but held in high esteem by the ship's Master.

Conversation overheard between Daisy and S Sgt Les Greenwood: Les. "Daisy, can you get me a cloth I can use as a sweat rag?"

Daisy. "Yes, no problem".

Two hours later.

Les. "Daisy, you got this cloth yet?"

Daisy. "You'll have to (censored) wait, I'm a fairy not a magician".

We were then asked how secure we would like our guest's cabin made. Our instructions were given to the engineering department who were extremely good and fitted every item we asked for. What would be worth mentioning is the fact that all the devices, bars, etc. were made from "scratch" by this department, painted and fitted within a day, nothing was too much trouble and they should be congratulated on their performance. Lt Cmdr Astiz was transferred from the MV Dunbarton Castle to us at 0700hrs. 25th May, when he was winched down by helicopter and then escorted to his cabin.

Cmdr Astiz along with his kit, was then searched and made secure, during which time our ship had set sail for the UK.

Our passage took approx 10 days during which time our "guest" had to be exercised for 1 hour per day, fed, visited and generally looked after. He was a very intelligent individual who had a good command of the English language and world affairs and spoke quite freely about himself and his country. He told us in no uncertain terms that he would escape at the first opportunity, even if it meant going overboard near land. He was also a very moody person who one day would be cheerful and talk readily to you and yet the next day would be very quiet and cunning. He had to be watched continually with the utmost vigilance and could not be trusted one inch.

The passage was very tiring as we were all doing alternate 6 hour shifts. This was unavoidable due to manning levels throughout, though I cannot at this stage elaborate any more on this. Added to this was the general tiredness one might expect not being used to ship life and not to mention the continual "rolling" and "corkscrewing" effect. A couple of us were also sick during the early stages though only for 24 hours. Although at times you lost your sense of balance, it was a most strange experience.

The trip was made easier by the whole ship's crew and special mention must go to the catering side ably led by Dave "Grocer" Abdy who produced some of the most amazing dishes. The whole crew's attitude towards us was wonderful and they could not have been more helpful.

The passage ended in Southampton Docks in the early hours of the morning of 4th June, when we were met by a naval cutter who took us ashore. There we met the RMP escort who was to take us to the RMPTC at Chichester.

It must be said that at this point the transfer from the British Avon to the cutter did not go smoothly (as one might have guessed). The idea was good – the practice well – we were supposed to have been lowered down the ship's side in the lifeboat to the level of the naval cutter. Then we were to jump from one to the other. We were lowered into the water and as the cutter approached (at this time we knew what a nut must feel like in a pair of nut crackers), its radar scanner fouled the stern end of the tanker. There was a crash and bits flew off. It then caught the stern end of our lifeboat and pushed us underneath the tanker side. At this stage the Captain of the naval vessel decided to "stand off" and try again, this made us feel just a little happier, but as we were waiting Major Pete Andrews reckoned he could hear running water. (What a joke we all thought, sitting in a lifeboat in the middle of the sea). Then he said, "my feet are getting wet". S Sgt Dave Langdon then made a further startling discovery – we were sinking! The lifeboats, which incidentally were checked only the day before, did not have any bungs in. Well, what do you do? Silence for about half a second then a yell to the first mate – "Get us up".

When we were raised it must have been like a colander with water pouring out. We could not find the bungs, so the next time down they held us just above water level. The cutter came in for the second time, contact was made and we successfully transferred.

As I mentioned previously, we were conveyed by the RMP to their Training Centre where we were met by the Commandant Lt Col "Jumbo" Wood, RMP. For those who are not familiar with the RMPTC it has a building attached to its guardroom called the "Keep". This building was part of the old barracks which was originally built to hold prisoners of war many years ago. As you might realise it was indeed very secure in its structure. It had been converted with modern day technology to be a 100% secure area with sleeping and living accommodation for those responsible for its running. One or two minor adjustments to the security had to be done for our satisfaction and this was undertaken by the RMP and completed within a few hours.

Lt Comdr. Astiz was held in the keep for approx one week and during this time it was an MPSC responsibility for his security. We were given additional support from the RMP which made the task a lot easier. We were completely self-contained during this week and even had our meals brought in. Everything we asked for was supplied and everybody got together to make it as comfortable as possible.

Due to the nature of our brief MPSC NCOs could not socialize during their off duty periods and in fact the O i/c could not leave the building at all. The press were not around for a few hours, but eventually found out that Lt Cmdr Astiz had arrived and gathered around the guardroom area. We did not at any time have contact with the press although a public relations officer was always present.

Lt Cmdr Astiz was interviewed by the authorities during this week and though he behaved himself would still have made a break if given the opportunity. Later it was decided by the powers that be that the Commander was to be repatriated and it was also decided that he had to be escorted to Rio by our leader. (What a holiday!).

The first arrangements to move him fell through as the airline concerned did not want the responsibility, but the second time it went well, when he was airlifted to Heathrow by helicopter to join his flight.

The remainder of the detachment had to stay operational for the time it took for him to reach Rio, this was just in case he was returned by the authorities. However, this did not happen and we returned to the MCTC after it's successful completion on Friday 11th June.

There is a lot more to this operation that unfortunately cannot be told, mainly because of security. The description and the layout of the keep, the manning problem, all would have been interesting to those who are generally interested in what we were doing. To those who might at a later date be called upon to repeat this kind of commitment, we have made a very comprehensive colour video so that you may learn from our experience and from our mistakes.

45
Minute Memories

As I think I said elsewhere, Army history has been a passion with me for many years. In those years, I have read a great number of regimental histories, but I can't remember a single one that drew on the minutes of the Warrant Officers' and Sergeants' Mess for source material. As an outsider, I do so now with considerable hesitation – I feel almost like someone who visits a house and pokes his nose into the cupboards. But, let's face it, the old truism trotted out by senior visiting officers is true: the sergeants' mess is the heart of all the regiments, all corps and this is certainly true of a Corps, where all members are, or were, members as much of the mess as of the Corps.

I hesitate, then, but I have still received considerable enjoyment from reading the mess minutes stored in the archives. They date back, unfortunately, only to 1954 but for me they were a Memory Lane trip. All right, I was not serving in this mess and every mess is different, but there are common factors and I found that what I was reading was not just the bare bones of innumerable nights where decisions were made as thirsts built up. I suddenly realised that I was reading the social history of Britain, as well as the recent history of the Corps.

Many of the names mentioned are the names of people, who have contacted me with information for this book, but I have also been delighted to see the progress of young Sergeant Andrews and that eternal Messing member Sergeant Humphries, then to see young Sergeants Carroll and Harris and Goddard finally sitting in the seat of power.

To preserve the inner sanctum, I ceased my researches at January 1980: yesterday is already history, but even a snooper such as myself knows that a line has to be drawn!

One thing to strike me, a thing that I remember from no sergeants' mess to which I belonged, was the open-handedness for charity, a wide spectrum of charities, ranging from the

Sunshine Homes for Blind Children, through a multiplicity of others. I counted off a total of twenty two widely different charities, some supported more than once. The causes are sometimes a reflection of the history of the time: money is sent to Skopje, the town in Yugoslavia hit by the earthquake in 1963; the 1968 Olympic Fund is supported and the Longhay Lifeboat Fund in 1969. Not a charity, but you sent a telegram to the Lord Mayor of Manchester to offer condolences after the air crash of 1958.

Dancing is popular, but how many of the younger end will have been to a flannel dance? And dress for the dances twice becomes the subject of a Commandant's comment on the minutes. In March 1964, with WO I Maurice Saunders in the chair, the proposal (CSM Munro, seconded by RQMS Mace) is that a St. Patrick's Dance be held, the dress to be informal, the cost to be £50. "No!" says the Commandant, "I do not like informal dances in either mess. If you are going to spend these monies, then I feel that members can take the trouble of getting properly dressed!" Earlier, in December 1960, the mess under RSM Tommy Nash, had discussed the idea of white mess jackets as an alternative to blues and I remembered the satisfaction we felt when blues had been issued in 1954, then the disillusion when we found how uncomfortable they were and how the National Service element enjoyed our discomfort, preferring the boiler suit joys of ill fitting battledress. . . .

Costing? Well, you have seen that St. Patrick's was to cost £50 in 1964. In 1957, the Christmas festivities, organised by WOI Eric Milton, WOII Ken Day and WOII Ernie Taylor, were to cost £200, including presents for the ten orphan children invited. Corps weekend in 1954 made a profit of £9.5s-. It was moved by CSM Bill Flecknoe, seconded by CSM Lew Butler, that this sum, augmented by £10.15s. from the General Fund, be sent to the Sunshine Home. Incursions of this kind into the General Fund were illegal, so the Sunshine Home gets the £9.5s. only. An interesting item in June 1954, when RSM Vic Bint is in the chair, is a purchase of ten dozen half pint glasses at £3.16. We remark the cheapness of the glasses and express our surprise at the need for so many half pint glasses in a sergeants' mess of that period!! Were they for the use of National Service Schoolies? Orange juice, with the sandwiches kept carefully under the bar, so that some, at any rate, would be left for the Night Watch?

I had forgotten completely about mess outings to breweries, which were such a feature of former mess life. Do they still happen? There are four enthusiastically moved in the minutes and I suspect that some of the breweries no longer exist, eaten by the big boys. In April 1957, such an outing was proposed by Sgt Simpson, seconded by WOII Taylor. It was, of course, to be a stag outing and the mess would pay ten guineas for the coach. The brewery named was Taylor Walker's. I suspect the outing was successful, but there were some repercussions when the party came home, for, at the May meeting, Sgt Pat Bunyan moves and S/Sgt Les Osborne seconds, that a families outing to Great Yarmouth take place on Whit Monday. What happened to Whitsuntide? Yes, there were visits to breweries, but the motion for a visit to conduct a whisky tasting in Southend takes me outside my own mess experience. I was pleased to see, in a minute of January 1972, that the other traditional link with the breweries is maintained, when Newcastle Brewery offers £100 towards the refurbishing of the mess!

The improvement of the mess plays a great part in the minutes: rightly so, when one thinks of the excellent accommodation created from what in effect was a series of long half-cylinders of corrugated iron. The main effort is made between 1977 and 1980 and Mr. Terry Quinlan is thanked for his efforts.

The equipment of the mess is also something of an essay in social history. Two fruit machines appear in 1955. In 1956, a motion is made for the purchase of a radiogram, to cost £30, but this is not carried. An attempt in the same year to finance two tennis courts for members use only is also not carried. A tape recorder is bought in 1963, at a cost not to exceed £60. This is replaced through the years, but the first use of the word "disco" is in 1971, when £150 is allowed for a disco evening.

Television first figures in November 1955, when WOII Johnny Gough proposes that a new set be bought, able to receive ITV. The existing set has then a property value of £45, but the set owned in 1964 (was this the ITV tuned set of the previous minute?) has a value on the property book of 10 shillings. RQMS Mace moves that it be written off and he is seconded by S/Sgt Franklin, but the Commandant rules that it will be auctioned with a reserve price of 10 shillings. We were all more careful with money in those days!

The billiard table had a long and complicated – sometimes heated – history and I found finally that I could not really say whether it was owned by the mess or by the NAAFI. Perhaps some ex-member knows! What I certainly know is that the attempt to introduce a juke box into the ante-room in September 1970 aroused the Commandant to comment "No! This is quite below the requirements of a sergeants' mess . . . or should be!"

Outside the mess a bucolic atmosphere prevails. A pergola is built, but a patio is denied. Chickens are purchased in 1957 at a cost of £50, then a further £50 is spent on hens at point of lay. A member objects at the amount of livestock now owned by the mess but makes little progress against the smallholders. Livestock figures again in September 1964, when forty week-old cockerels are bought for fattening together with one hundred pullets. There is a drama here, for the next minute asks for seventy eight cockerels, killed by foxes, to be written off.

In July 1971, at a meeting chaired by RSM Larry Wright and with 107(!) members present, WOII Don Probyn, seconded by S/Sgt John Hannay, move that a clay pigeon shoot be held, the first mention of this now popular mess pastime. One clay and one cartridge are to cost 6p. The Commandant Lieutenant Colonel Denniston comments that a clay pigeon shoot in the mess area is NOT ON. Alternative areas may be considered, but that he will pass them as safe or otherwise. There is no further mention of clay pigeon shooting until May 1972, when the new Commandant, Lieutenant Colonel Gabb gives permission for a shoot, but stipulates that no drinking takes place by any shot until the shoot is completed!

Requests for private use of the mess must conjure up memories for many. WOII Ken Burgess thanks for the use of the ballroom for his daughter's wedding in 1969, as does ex RSM Sammy Moore in 1974, a year obviously popular for weddings, as SSgt Ron Hudson and CPO Don Streatfield both ask permission to use the facilities in that year. In 1975, S/Sgt Hood celebrates his wedding anniversary, then there appears to be a gap in celebrations until 1977, when S/Sgt

Giles asks to use the ballroom. WOII John Haymes asks for its use in 1978. WOII Wallace does not ask to use the mess, but he receives a wedding present in 1979. In the same year, WOI Peter Goddard, with Yorkshire generosity, requests the use of the mess but invites members to the disco after the ceremony, at no cost to them. S/Sgt Maudling marries and all members are invited. In the same year, S/Sgt Bain arranges his private function: it would appear to have been a vintage year!

I could go on, snooping, attempting to unravel the stories behind the bare statements of minutes and finding it a fascinating vehicle for my own memory. Before I leave the subject, I would like to ask one of the Old and Bold what happened to the 51 tins of Pickerings' blanco at 10d each in 1956? Did the one guinea MPSC scarves finally sell for five shillings?

46

The Sixties and After.

In 1963, the last National Serviceman crossed off the last date on the calendar he kept in his locker like a good luck charm. The Regular Army sighed with relief and the Old and Bold of the period shouted exultantly for a return to the Old and real soldiering Army.

There was no return to the Old Army. The Old Army had been an imperial army. . . . and an imperial army needs an empire. All that remained to Britain was the untidy stubby end of an empire.

The Army was forced to rethink itself. Not only was there no Army, but there was also a totally changed Britain and it was from this Britain that the Army's recruits would be drawn.

If the Army had to change, so also did its penal institutions. If the penal institutions change, then so must the kind of person who works in the institution. What was right for "the gangster in uniform" would not be right for a new professional army.

Sydney Harris came to Colchester in 1960 to the Depot and Training Wing. He was a man of wide experience, never in the Corps, but serving with the Corps for a large slice of his service – and a considerable time after his service. He knew what the Corps needed.

Before his arrival, selection for the Corps was a very hit and miss affair. It produced many excellent men, by chance, rather than by design. Sydney knew from experience that it had also produced its share of rubbish. A large Corps might have been able to carry rubbish: for a small Corps it would be fatal.

Selection, then, was to be his first priority, so he devised a system, constructed like a series of sieves, each with a smaller mesh. If a NCO applied for the Corps and his CO approved the application, his documents were sent to Sydney with his application form. He could be rejected on the strength of his documents alone. If they were satisfactory, he was interviewed. If he passed the interview – and it was no rubber stamp – he would be required to attend a probationers' course, then satisfactorily complete a practical probationary period. Only then could he wear the badge.

To show the system at work, I will take an extreme year: that of 1971. In 1971, eighty nine NCOs applied to join the Corps. Forty four were rejected on perusal of documents. Fourteen failed the interview. Nine withdrew their applications. . . . twenty two joined the Corps.

What kind of an organisation would the probationer of the sixties be joining? One thing had stayed over from the old system and that was the division of A and B Companies, with A as first offenders and B as previous old customers, ex Borstal or prison cases, escapees and any who had been fined more than £15 in a civil court. The division was maintained until 1971.

If the probationer joined after 1965, he would find that a new Wing was being established. In that year, Shepton Mallet had closed and soldiers under sentence who were to be discharged were to become members of D Wing. It was lodged in recently refurbished derelict huts. Other derelict nissens were patched up at the same time to become Education Wing.

The first year of D Wing was experimental, very much a matter of trial and error. It was agreed that the domestic chores of the camp would mainly fall on them, thus relieving the other wings for training. They would also do foot drill and PT, but there would be no earnings scheme and no equivalent to Stage III.

During the year, trade courses were introduced and they were given the opportunity to attend half day courses for fourteen days in motor maintenance, carpentry or brickwork. Painting and decorating was to be added in 1969 and after two years, it was decided that all courses would extend to four weeks. In the Seventies, it was further arranged that a long sentenced soldier could do more than one course, some even managing to fit in all four.

To run the courses, obviously, skilled trade instructors were needed at first MPSC then civilians. One of the earliest recruited is still with us: Mr Terry Quinlan. This is I feel an appropriate time to point out that the presence of skilled instructors in the unit affects far more than the SUS they teach. Without their skills, the sergeants' mess main room in the hutted camp would still have been a barn; the piggery would have been financially unviable to rebuild. They have enhanced the reputation of the unit outside its walls by a multiplicity of works on behalf of schools, churches and charities. The garrison would also be poorer without them.

I mentioned the piggery. The unit has run a piggery and a market garden for years but it was only with the introduction of D Wing that both were able to expand and become places of positive vocational skill instruction. Many SUS have learned new skills on the estates and some have found a career as a result of those skills. Produce also supplies the unit's only source of extra funds.

From its introduction in 1965, a succession of Commandants and Wing Commanders, Welfare Officers and padres have fought to improve the conditions of D Wing, attempting to ease the difficult transit into a civil life. They have been supported by the Probation Service and SSAFA. On the education side, short rehabilitation courses are run to ease the passage, but earlier arrangements, which allowed a SUS to apply for a Government Training Course and offered the opportunity to speak to a Job Centre Officer fell victim to the financial restraint of the eighties.

Of course, concern was not only for D Wing. In 1964, volley ball pitches had been constructed in the company lines – a small thing, you will say, but the aim was not only exercise, but to extend the time when the soldier was not locked up. In the same year, Lieutenant Colonel Parker, who was then Commandant, ruled that A Wing would be allowed to retain in their rooms at night razors, table knives, pokers, floor bumpers. Even boots! B Wing and D Wing were required still to hand in such lethal ware. . . . "in that he did willfully strike Pte Snooks with a floor bumper", sounds unlikely but possible.

In 1965, Stage II gained permission to watch selected TV programmes. They were allowed to stay unlocked at night. By 1969, A and B Wing Stage III were allowed three shillings per day, but the Special Stagers: the D Wing equivalent of Stage II, now established, were allowed nothing. The Commandant Lt Col Denniston, hammers this discrimination in report after report until the powers weaken. In 1971, Lt Col Gabb requests that D Wingers be paid for tasks performed in the same way that civil prisoners are paid. This dies a death.

Golonel Gabb uses a good phrase in his report of 1972: "lowering the temperature". He has started to replace the ugly, threatening rolls of dannert wire with chain link fence. In the same report, 50% of cases brought before him are concerned with illicit smoking: cabbage leaves, tea leaves, grass – not pot! A new system is introduced, allowing Stage I an issue of 14 cigarettes or 10 ounces of sweets; Stage II 21 cigarettes or 14 ounces of sweets. In 1973, pay ranging from 10p to 28p per day is allowed.

One of the reforms that is to let air into the unit is introduced in 1977, when local notables, including an MP from each leading party, become the Board of Independent Visitors. Since that year they have visited at least twice a year with no fixed programme and with encouragement to roam freely. After all the silly hush-hush of the Pyjama Game episode, which is dealt with elsewhere, the visit of open-minded people from the big world outside has become a normal event.

1977 was to see the MCTC in the public eye in another way. I have said elsewhere that the Press and TV only look for the Glasshouse Horror kind of story but one they could not avoid was the Fire Service Strike.

The staff worked in Harwich, Nottingham and Bassingbourne, each group leading a team of D Wing SUS and manning the antiquated "Green Goddesses" of the Old National Fire Service. They were required from December 1977 until January 1978. At Harwich were Staff Sergeant John Embling, Sergeants Brian Nunn, Dennis Wray and Barry Gower. They lived in the Shaftesbury Centre and their efforts were so appreciated that they were visited for Christmas Dinner by the Mayor and Mayoress of Harwich, Mr and Mrs Fred Good. A typical and very generous gesture made by the SUS was to distribute sweets to the children in Harwich High Street on Christmas Eve. The sweets had been bought from their meagre pay.

The Harwich detachment handled only house fires and so on, but Nottingham had a fire in the bus station and also a lift fire. Leading from the front in Nottingham were ex RSM Cliff Gingell and ex Staff Sergeants Brett and Dennis Carr. Capt Mike Russell, then RQMS, had a liaison task, based on

Bassingbourne, but covering Hertfordshire, Bedfordshire and Leicestershire.

The end of the emergency saw many D Wingers applying to join the Fire Service!

A concern of the Medical Officer and the Welfare Officer throughout the whole period is the problem of drugs and alcohol. Both monitored admissions quite closely and there were exhaustive reports, well worth the reading but too long for this small book. Many of the offences were alcohol-related and the problem was particularly severe in BAOR. One twenty two year old made the claim that he averaged 20 rum and cokes per night!

The drugs scene was also very pronounced in BAOR and many SUS claimed that obtaining even the most sophisticated dope was easy in Germany, the foreign workers and GIs being the most common source. Most drug offenders who finished in MCTC had picked up the habit before joining and one admitted that he started smoking opium when still at school. Wellington would have understood the rum built-in hazard of the British soldier. Dope, I think would not have pleased him.

"We are keeping the old man alive." Jim Robinson said this to me one day, when, as Quartermaster, he took time off from his hobby of fuel economy (when the only warm place was the Quartermaster's office), to look again at the tumble-down relics of POW Camp 186.

I was standing in a pool of water, that had used its normal point of ingress above my desk. He looked at my unwebbed feet and added, "Mind, it's got all the old man's complaints, particularly the waterworks." The camp in fact was already decaying when the Sixties started. By the end of the Seventies the waterproofing contractors were hesitating to tender, as they could no longer guarantee that their work would-literally-hold water. I suspect that they were also worried that employees would disappear through the flimsy roofs or be lost in the cracks in the floor. Progressively – if that is the term – huts were being dismantled: 51 in 1973 alone. In the same year, the sergeants' mess was again waterproofed but 75 other huts needed treatment and the maintenance bill ran to £87,865 for the year. Much self-help was expertly applied by all the trade instructors and other, but it is all a part of the old lady and the sea syndrome. The snows of 1982 put a knife into the "old man" and gave it a twist.

A rat catcher is engaged. . . .

This all sounds as if it belongs to the "I went through hell" school of military reminiscence so popular in the MCTC Officers' Mess. . . . but there seemed to be light on the horizon, everyone was sure that there was: the camp was down for rebuilding. It becomes a serial story.

Dates were forecast, as were costs – they had been already forecast in the years before this chapter, but now they sounded real and convincing. The Rebuild will be started in 1967. Great! 1967 passes. Try September 1970 (adding the month gave an air of seriousness). The bombshell of 1970: the Rebuild, if it happens at all, will not be at Berechurch Hall. Where then? The staff who have wives working and kids at school, a few with mortgages, begin to worry. Nothing firm in 1971, so they still worry, then there is talk of a start in 1975, with a completion – a completion – in 1977, at a cost of £1.6 million. . . . Another price for 1973: £3 million. It becomes £7 million in 1979.

Suddenly – if I may use the term – foundations are laid in 1983. On the 6th of July, 1984, the Colonel Commandant, Sir Norman Arthur, performs the topping-out ceremony and the silver trowel – solid, material proof that a Rebuild is possible, becomes a feature of officers' mess decoration. Jim Robinson looks smug, as if he had laid the egg himself. Hiccups, roof hiccups, floor hiccups, but the SUS move into the new accommodation in 1986 – into accommodation superior probably to their own regimental barracks. As I write brick buildings are encircling me and the "grey elephants in rows" are disappearing. All the elephants have sadly peeling hides.

Bill Flecknoe in his account tells of a sergeant who was late on shift, because his bicycle had hit a brick in Roman Way: he brought the brick as proof to show his sergeant major! I think a severe reprimand in this case was distinctly unfair, though not untypical. You are now wondering why I brought the story up at all. It illustrates a bone of contention, running for many years through the Corps' history. If a married NCO is living out and far enough out not to be able to hear the alarm siren or bell, then the slog of pursuit falls upon the people that can hear it. . . . and they feel bitter.

In 1964, the problem appears to be solved and the answer appears to be Lethe Grove. Lethe Grove, in the trade phraseology of the estate agent (and I am sure that ex WOI Chris Garrity will correct me if I am wrong) was a choicely sited estate development, purpose built to cater for the staff of MCTC. All mod cons, including alarm bell in each quarter, and cycle path to camp, avoiding the dangers of Berechurch Hall Road. I often wonder what the civilians who recently bought them cheap, make of the alarm bell in the hall!

Sorry, I've banged on rather about bricks and mortar, when all old soldiers know that buildings are important but not the most important part of the job. People are the important part, particularly of our job.

Something else is important too and that is a clear understanding of what the job is all about. After the Maunsell Committee of 1974, what we are and what we do is clearly stated and bears repetition. The punitive function, says the statement, is fulfilled by the SUS losing his liberty, his pay and association with his friends. His training is to be exacting and constructive. He will be improved only by a staff able to understand him, lead him and show him an example. That's it in a nutshell, and the highly selected staff of the Sixties and after were well up to the challenge. In the way of personal qualification, they were able to measure up to any equivalent sized group in the Army and proved it again and again on the range and in a wide spectrum of sports fields. I hope to add an appendix to this book, summarising the performance of the men of this unit over the past years. Their reputation was not only gladiatorial; their know-how was sought again and again by units needing to train their soldiers in military skills.

The skills acquired for the job showed the staff to be flexible and this flexibility was used to great effect in a variety of situations throughout the period. I have dealt elsewhere with the nasty job of Al Mansoura, which was done by the Corps members in a totally admirable fashion. They were next called to show what they could do in Northern Ireland, the first MPSC group reporting there in August 1971 and the last group leaving in April 1980.

The commitment was to four main establishments: Long Kesh, Crumlin Road, McGilligan Camp and the ship, the Maidstone. The MPSC officer's role, performed by amongst others, Major Jimmy James, Captain Owen Taylor, Major

John Carroll and Captain Larry Bielby-Wright, was to act as liaison officer and security advisor between Army HQ and the civilian security council. The tour for all was four or six months, often under rather nasty conditions.

The task at Long Kesh involved, amongst other duties, the control of visitors through the tally lodge and Staff Sergeant George Ward, punter and Thespian (and the only serving WO or NCO to submit an account!) remembers an occasion when a visiting priest was cleared through the lodge and a clerical-clad figure was booked out two hours later. The bound and gagged priest was found in his brother's cell and the brother ran free until the opposition shot him down some months later. Jimmy James remembers a similar incident involving police officers' uniforms, which led to the introduction of an ID card with photograph for all prison personnel.

The task had been done well and led to congratulatory telegrams from the GOC Northern Ireland to the then Commandant, Lt Col Leon Paul, who had been a regular visitor to the outpost of his empire. The two Provost Marshals at the time: Brigadier Mike Matthews and Brigadier Jack Thomas (whom we last met as a young RMP officer in Kenya) had both been welcome visitors to the detachments.

In the year that Northern Ireland ceased to be a MPSC commitment, another crisis evolved: the Prison Officers' dispute.

Operation Paddock was launched.

The MPSC were required to use their expertise in two of her Majesty's Prisons: Frankland, a prison still under construction, near (appropriately) Pity Me, in County Durham, and Rollestone, a disused Army camp on Salisbury Plain.

Captain Bill Humphries arrived with forty MPSC members at Frankland on 29th October 1980. The task was to open and man four living units and to control a segregation unit. As the prison was incomplete, sappers were hard at work when they arrived, welding locks and bolts onto cell doors. Bill found that he was to be assisted by an infantry battalion: the Gordon Highlanders, and attached RMP.

When customers arrived, the MPSC were to find them very different from the SUS back in Colchester. There were old Old Lags and young Old Lags, the odd tearaway, the completely institutionalised creep, all shapes and sizes and conditions of evil doers. It may have been classical crawling to the screw, but most insisted that they felt happier with the Army, than with the Prison Service.

After first reconnaissance of Frankland, Major (now Lt. Col) Peter Andrews was required to fly to Rollestone, where he was to work with a civilian prison governor. Here the task of the MPSC was to control the main gate, and to supervise the segregation, visits, admissions and discharges . . . in a camp not built as a penal institution. The arrangement was to be that 48 prisoners would be admitted daily, but a fire in Bournemouth Police Cells led to the first intake numbering ninety. Within eight working days, 353 prisoners had been admitted, with the maximum capacity set at 360. Occupying such numbers with minimal trade and sporting facilities was to be a major problem. Another problem was that the young RMP members attached, although very keen and willing to learn, had obviously no previous knowledge of the techniques required in the situation. One thing is certain: not one of them had prison officer ambitions by the end of the operation! George Ward, inevitably supplied staff entertainment.

Troops could be withdrawn when the operation ended, much to their relief. Much also to the relief of the skeleton staff who had slogged on, double shifting, back in Colchester! The SUS performed well during the emergency – as they do in every emergency. The Old and Bold, recalling past battles with the yobboes and slobbos of the time past, will be growling and spitting at this. . . . different army, init?

A much valued memento of the operation is the original cartoon, signed by Giles, which hangs on the MCTC Officers' Mess wall.

The Falkland War was to provide the next example of flexibility, but I took the easy way on this and let the expedition tell its own story: they know what we are allowed to know about it all – militarily and socially – so why gild the lily?

As I have said so often, Colchester is now the only station for the MPSC. Having said that, there are ways out for the fortunate chosen. I refer to the six extra-regimental posts filled by the Corps in Germany and Gibraltar, where the chosen may blossom forth in fresh duty – free soil. And blossom they do! The last two warrant officers in Gibraltar WOII Denis

Codd and WOII Bob McLoughlin each returned to home base with a British Empire Medal.

An extra-regimental "one off" was typically scored by Major Graham Harris, with his posting as Garrison Adjutant to Belize. He was to return to Colchester with an MBE.

We have recently received from the RMP Depot, Chichester, a copy book written by one L/Cpl Burden H in 1935 on the occasion of his attending a course in Provost Duties at the Military Detention Barracks, Aldershot. It is intrinsically interesting, but also interesting because this same role: the teaching of the unit provost staff, has returned to the MCTC and is again a MPSC responsibility. One of the early students, a young lance corporal in a famous cavalry regiment, visited me during the course to remind me of his palmy days on my map reading course when he last visited the MCTC: as a SUS! There's a saying about poachers and gamekeepers. . . .

As you will have seen in this book, preparation and planning for the establishment of Field Punishments Centres was only done in a British "muddle through" fashion at the start of both major wars, resulting in serious blunders. For a time, Sydney Harris was able to run courses for a Reserve unit: 21 Field Punishment Centre, but this fell foul of one of the spate of Army Reserve reorganisations and was disbanded.

In 1985, under Lieutenant Colonel Andrew Parsons OBE, the then Commandant, the FPC problem was again aired. He used his well-known powers of military manipulation and arranged for Lieutenant Colonel Jim Robinson and Major Bill Humphries to participate in the large scale NATO exercise, Operation Lionheart, with a view to examining the problems of FPCs and Military Prisons in a modern context. Corps expertise was also sought in the organisation of POW cages. As I write this chapter, Major Graham Harris is rewriting FPC regulations – the task, readers may remember of Wally Watson at a time when the Second World War had already started.

The future? Well, we already have – almost – a new Centre. We even have a new name: The Joint Services Corrective Training Centre, last in the line of MPs, MPDBs, MCEs and MCTCs. We still have customers, though not so many and not so evil as many in this book. Whatever comes up, I am certain that the MPSC will rise to the occasion. I am also certain that, should Lieutenant Colonel Michael Clare Garsia ever join one of the frequent tours of visitors to the Centre, he will look around and nod his approval. There are worse tributes to a unit.

The last word, but not my last word, which belongs traditionally to the female sex. Mrs Joyce Thompson wrote these lines some years ago for the Journal and I think they say it all.

The Song of the Screw

So you want to join the Army, son; you want to serve the queen.
To wear a khaki uniform, be tall and smart and keen,
To "come and do a man's job" like they tell you in the ads.
To drive a tank and fire a gun, with all the other lads.
Then see the sights in foreign parts, the dusky, sexy girl.
Who wiggles everything she's got and makes your eyebrows curl.
She's full of Eastern promise sure, but I've got news for you,
A Western Sergeant Major has a job for you to do.

To learn to be a squaddie in the good old Army way,
You'll bash the square for hours on end, then march for miles next day.
Go over the assault course, climb the ropes and wade the bog,
Then march again and think, "This shouldn't happen to a dog".
But not to worry lad, because one day when you get back,
You'll find it's all okay because they've made you a Lance Jack.
You'll proudly wear your single stripe and pass your EPCs,
Then volunteer for some place where you'll make the Mess with ease.

And now you're here at Colchester as M.P.S.C. staff
You've got your third stripe on your arm, and all the world's a laugh.
As long as you remember every hour to punch the clock,
Inspect the wires and count the SUS and check each blasted lock.
Because if you slip up just once, do something slightly wrong,
It's underneath the Oak, a dig and goodbye Rootie gong.
It's hanging on that oak tree with the legions of the lost

Of those who went before, and erred, then had to pay the cost.

But that's the way it goes, of course, you may lose on the swings
Then find upon the roundabouts you suddenly have wings.
The canvas suit that's sometimes used to hold a naked SUS
has suddenly become the centre of a stupid fuss.
With questions asked in Parliament and headlines in the Press
And M.P.s coming down to view the prisoners in distress!
The fuss soon settles down, of course, but one and all can say
The "Nick" like very little dog, has had its little day.

So soldier on for pension, do your 22 and cob, You'll soon be free in Civvy Street to do a different job.
No DCI's or ECO's or RD ones and twos,
Be nice to get a pub perhaps, sell sandwiches and booze.
Take in Bed and Breakfast guests, the wife will always cope,
Or else a village store with ham and cheese and sweets and soap.
But deep inside you know the truth, you've heard it all before,
Because old soldiers never die, they join SECURICOR.

Joan Thompson (Mrs.)

47
The Very Last Word
by Lt Col T J R (Tim) Illingworth OBE

Of all the most extraordinary tasks for an Officer in The Services, to be Commandant of the MCTC must surely rank to the fore. To be chosen defies all wizardry and MS compution! The writer was informed on a glorious day in East Africa by what he thought was a jesting Chief Clerk. "It's here in a signal. . . . he said your next posting – straight to the nick!" Wrong man thought the writer, and wrote for confirmation to the then Provost Marshal who happened to have been an old friend. "Indeed" was the reply, "chosen by PM"! So off I went to Colchester.

My image and reflections before arrival were to the days as a Subaltern in my Regiment in 1952 travelling to Harwich for the boat to BAOR to catch those Red, Blue and Green Military trains. As we rattled through Colchester on the Hook of Holland Express from Liverpool Street – (steam driven), I had seen some very large gentlemen escorting other Servicemen and handcuffed to them. I imagined prison life, and remembered stories of the Glass House in Aldershot and the rigours of Shepton Mallet.

My predecessor I had known before: he had distinguished himself both as a Staff Officer looking after the Territorial Army in Northern Ireland and as an outstanding Commandant. He wrote to me in glowing terms about the MPSC – "The Corps", and what a marvellous unit I was to command. His introduction when I arrived was brief and to the point – "Never worry whatever goes wrong the Corps will look you!" Those words were to ring true throughout my term as Commandant, at no time was I left without sound advice and never without support.

The weather on my arrival day in November was wet and miserable, the rain rattled on the roofs of the Nissen huts and in any other custodial establishment we would have thought it might have provided a real dampener to the place – not a bit of it!

Everywhere we went there was enthusiasm. Enthusasim from the staff in knowing that they were helping, training and caring for the Servicemen under Sentence and achieving results, and enthusiasm from the servicemen themselves to make a better life in the future.

First impressions are rarely forgotten, mine here was that although men were held in custody they were actively improving, a vast contrast to the present civil prison environment where men are locked up for most of the day, sometimes 22 hours of that day and have no chance of actively showing improvement. The MCTC has much to offer these civilian establishments.

Within a few days I had met most of the staff and many of the servicemen under sentence. Those in "A" Wing commanded by Lieutenant Colonel Larry Orpen Smellie a renowned Army Shot and trainer "Par excallance" knew that they had to improve to get back into the Regiments. If they didn't the penalty was to be recommended for discharge. They therefore tried immensely hard, the physically and mentally weak became stronger and the strong became more balanced in their views of working together as a team and not being 'tough' individuals. Here in "A" Wing it was all military training at high speed, looking fit and being proficient in all the qualities of an Infantry Soldier.

The proof and success of this excellent regime was shown and is still shown that at least a third of "A" Wing Servicemen returned to their units became NCO's within a year to 18 months.

A Royal Anglian platoon commander visiting in the first few weeks of my tenure said "the best Secton Commanders I had in Ireland were from here."

The contrast in "D" Wing was noticeable. Here one never knew the results of active training because there was no military training and no Commanding Officer to refer ones' questions after the release of a Servicemen as to how he was progressing. Schemes were tried to obtain information but with no real success. The odd letter arrived, one to the Adjutant saying "You remember me, I was one of the three fellers that smashed up Colchester, the Odeon Cinema, Mr Marks the tailors, and all those bikes in the park. I've improved!

I'm now standing on guard outside the Gate of a French Foreign Legion Barracks as a sentry and I'm proud to have succeeded somewhere at last" and he meant it!

Escapes featured now and again but to no avail. All knew that there would be three Police forces after them not just one in the form of The RMP, Ministry of Defence Police and the Essex Police, and they would be caught and punished yet "again". The staff if anything felt let down in an escape because their confidence and understanding with the men had been broken: there was no question of "to hell with the fellow now he can stew"! they knew that they would have to take up the problem again once the Serviceman was arrested and get him right back on a straight course. One man managed to scale the wire using his bedside mat but once over he couldn't make a decision of what to do next so called the staff and asked to come back again! Others ran to the sea at Mersea and not to London in their confusion. This behaviour seemed to me to show that the environment had a hold on them which was developing a different attitude of advancement, and continual thoughts of escape were not in the forefront of a man's mind throughout any one day but mainly came on the spur of the moment.

And what of the Nissen Huts housing 8 men with their coke stoves, chimneys red hot to the ceiling in winter. They leaked both from the roofs and through the foundations in heavy rain the Quartermaster Jim Robinson had to have lines of buckets to the fore to cope with the deluge of flooded areas. There was comradeship in those huts, men had to help one another and work as a team, and here again the simple accommodation concept in civilian establishments fails as does the bunk bed tight future environment of small inadequate prison rooms. It was interesting to visit the Royal Naval Portsmouth Detention Quarters where simple cell accommodation is used for the short sentences of men returning to Her Majesty's Ships: these conditions might suit short periods of detention but as a punishment the environment of a single cell brings self pity and a backward drain to improvement.

The centre of any unit is the sergeants mess. One was lucky to have a fantastic sergeants mess looked after by no less than three RSM's with another two warrant officers in support. The atmosphere in the establishment was electrifying based on a sense of duty and excellence in knowing that their work was appreciated. Most of the members played some form of sport from golf to an inter service chess player. The hockey and cricket teams excelled in the Minor Unit Competitions. There were tennis players but above all the Tug-O-War team provided the greatest following and still does today. Largely due to the enthusiasm of Major Peter Andrews and some real stalwarts who spent endless hours ensuring that the Military Provost Staff Corps was noticed for its powers on the sporting field.

And what of Education and the farm and the gardens, and all the 17 departments to which a servicemen is assigned to work to improve particularly those in the Discharge Wing. The Bricks and Mortar course was run by Mr Tull. Most of the Farm as it stands today was built under his direction with design by Sgt Cavan and Sgt Sibbons. Mr Fred Kerry ran the Painting and Decorating course and Mr Terry Quinlan the Carpentry and Mr Keith Giles on MT. All were experts in their own right and provided confidence, understanding as well as enthusiasm to make a job look and be well done at the end of the day. Map reading and German were taught by Bob Boyes and numerative and communication skills by Leo Jolley. All the members of this education team were totally dedicated to the regime and gained immense satisfaction that the men in their charge responded.

On Sundays the church services were short and sweet, lasting about half an hour and taken by local padres. These periods had a lasting impression on most and indeed me since they showed the power of God to draw people together and enjoy their prayers and singing together. Padre Norman Smith described the little church as the Cathedral of Colchester and many a day the singing and prayers were loud enough to raise the roof. Padre John Murray also described this part of the environment as one of the greatest assets to the MCTC, allowing men to make their own contribution to "the man upstairs" in their own way but with others equally less or more fortunate standing next to them.

Any Commandant of the MCTC finds (suspect) lines of individual loneliness when he has few to help him in decision making if any. I had four different real confidents. They will know who they are but one of them I must mention: Captain Graham Harris now Major Harris, One could be allowed to describe his greatest asset as of being fair to the men and not necessarily to the unit from which he came in order to achieve confidence in the system. Always gregarious, sharp, totally ahead in his application of the Rules, and with a wily sense of humour. Far from fit physically he made up for it by eventually persuading the PT Staff that he would pass the BFT, and did with the help from all sides. I owe an enormous debt of gratitude to him and all the seconds in command and Orderly Room Staff who gave one total support and loyalty.

And then there was RHQ MPSC. Here Major Sydney Harris worked tirelessly as the link between the Corps and the Provost Marshal ensuring that the Annual Reunions were a great success and keeping the Commandant informed of recruiting demands and promotion prospects for all the staff. Sydney was a Queen's man having served with that Regiment, but you would never have known it since he appeared always to be the central focus of the MPSC itself and his work at RHQ particularly in the journal and its accounts, and the development of the printing Centre was outstanding and far beyond the call of duty.

There were two outstanding events which took place during my term of duty as Commandant: the first almost immediately on taking over was the Prison Officers strike of December 1980 to Apr/May 1981. MCTC had to provide the replacement staff. The Corps for this event had to be halved one half being posted to Frankland Prison in Durham a brand new establishment, and to Rollestone Camp on Salisbury Plains, the other half remaining in Colchester. Both "A" and "D" wing had to be combined which was not to the appropriate accommodation rules, although the training was almost maintained at a normal standard. The training and supervision of the civilian prisoners in the two prisons was a great challenge and most successfully achieved. The Staff earned a great reputation for their care and attention and in their efforts to try and achieve a more active programme in the open air in winter in the daily routine. The PT Staff were invaluable, a close liaison with Governors and HMP Staff was achieved and continues with frequent liaison visit between establishments today.

The second event was the escort and detention of Commander Alfredo Astiz from Ascension Island to Colchester in 1983 Major Peter Andrews commanded the escort being helicoptered to the ship on which the prisoner was held and bringing him to the Keep in Chichester – the home of the Royal Military Police. Here he was held and watched throughout his detention.

After 3¼ years as Commandant I left to be a Permanent President of Courts Martial. Many said "to put em in" – not "keep em in".

Looking back no man could have had a more enjoyable command. Many might feel that the Superior Command of Provost Marshal, Garrison Commander, Eastern District Commander would interfere in the small unit of roughly 200 servicemen and 130 Staff, after all no man can serve 2 masters let alone 3! One rarely experienced any feeling of overpower and one was left properly to make ones own decisions. One was totally invigorated by the environment and never felt locked into a passive existence which is surely a reflection of the value and excellence of the Military Provost Staff Corps. Woe betide any man who thinks that their expertise can be thrown away for the sake of economy, it would be a false move of immense folly, which could never be replaced.

Perhaps the confidence shown in a magnificent new rebuild which although it replaces almost half a century of tradition will combine the basis of the centre as the foundation of discipline in two if not three of our Armed Services.

List of Subscribers

Major R H Boyes
Lt. Col. R J Robinson
Brig B. Thomas CBE
SSgt G H Ward
SSgt G H Ward
SSgt G H Ward
Mr L Greenwood
Mr L Greenwood
Mr J A Nicholson
Mr H G Belsham
Captain M J Russell MPSC
Mr C Garrity
Mr K E Ford
Major E J Deeble
Mr T G Parker
Mr S Donaghue
Major J Hart
Mr A D Moody
Sgt M Harris
Mr J A Brown
Mr R Steers
Mr R Searle
Captain M Saunders
Mr D V Carr
SSgt A W Ullman
Mr L R Hayward
Mr W Fitzsimmons
Mrs A Milton
Mr W A Reeve
WO2 A Purves
Mr A Kirk
Mrs A Kirk
Mr B C Gower
Mr R K Ganner

Mrs C I Baker
Mr W Bain
Mr V C Bint
Major W Humphries MPSC
Sgt B Marshall
WO2 E Deighton
Mr R G Degavino
Mr H R Brivent-Barnes
Sgt J M Barr
SSgt R Cardwell
Mr H Corbett
WO1 (RSM) P Burton
Mr C H Rickards
Captain C B Dawes
Mr H J Spatchurst
Mr W P Ingram
Mr R Perry
Major (QM) G P Harris MBE MPSC
Major (QM) G P Harris MBE MPSC
Lt. Col. (QM) P Andrews MBE MPSC
Major (QM) J J Carroll MPSC
Mr B Phillips
Lt. G F Yates MPSC
Captain P Goddard MPSC
Mr B G Smith
WO2 A D Licence
Mr J Hanney
SSgt V Peters
SSgt F H Walker
Sgt I C Cruickshank
WO2 L Charlton
WO2 J D Bridgeman
WO2 J D Bridgeman
WO2 J D Bridgeman
WO2 J D Bridgeman
Lt. Col. S Fordham W.G.
Major D A Jackson R.A.
Sgt J R Howat
Sgt L W Pearce
SSgt S Gregory
Sgt G Richardson
Major D J Wickens RAEC

Sgt R Parfitt
Sgt P J Scales
SSgt A Farrell
Sgt J Blair
Sgt B D Lampard
Sgt P Cullough
Sgt S F Theal
Sgt J Brassington
Sgt B J Baker
Sgt R Hirst
Sgt S I Kempe
Mr F J Simpson
Mr R Boulter
Major H W Boulter
Mrs D Bailey
Miss J Smith
WO2 R Hey
Sgt D E Wilkinson BEM
Mr H Gray
Major S F Harris
Lt Col T J R Illingworth OBE R IRISH
Lt Col A P H Parsons OBE SG

Illustrations in order of Appearance

1. Barrack Square, Aldershot circa 1910. Garsia's reforms in operation.
2. Governor's office, Aldershot circa 1912. Major Henderson (?) in chair.
3. A workshop in Aldershot MP & DB.
4. One of a series of cartoons held by RHQ MPSC.
5. Governor and Civilian warders, Brixton Military Prison 1896.
6. MPSC staff on SS Immingham – one of the prison ships of World War I.
7. A typical cell at Aldershot 1939–45.
8. Colonel J McK Gordon MC, late Cameron Highlanders – Inspector General of Prisons, Italy and Austria.
9. Fort Darland 1939–45. A soldier under sentence presents his diet tin.
10. Fort Darland – a barrack cart (see 'Murderers of Poor Sammy Clayton').
11. Colchester 1945 – POW sick-bay (later to become MPSC Sergeants' Mess).
12. The Mallet.
13. Interior of a cell, mat making.